A Challenge
To The Reader:

Over 425 actual films are described in this book, but one is a complete hoax. Can you find it?

THE GOLDEN TURKEY AWARDS
Harry and Michael Medved

Nominees and Winners—
The Worst Achievements
in Hollywood History

BERKLEY BOOKS, NEW YORK

Photograph credits and acknowledgments: United Artists, Universal Pictures, American International Pictures, Columbia Pictures, Twentieth Century-Fox, RKO Radio Pictures, Republic Pictures, Allied Artists, Paramount Pictures, Warner Brothers, Astor Films, Metro-Goldwyn-Mayer, Embassy Pictures, Box Office Spectaculars, Distributors Corporation of America.
All photographs from the personal collection of Harry Medved. Photographs from *Robot Monster*, *Blackenstein*, *Cat Women of the Moon*, *Plan Nine from Outer Space* and photograph of Edward D. Wood, Jr., courtesy of Eric Hoffman.
Quote from interview on page 266 reprinted by permission of E. P. Dutton from *Kings of the B's* by Todd McCarthy and Charles Flynn, © 1975 by Todd McCarthy and Charles Flynn.

This Berkley book contains the complete
text of the original trade paperback edition.
It has been completely reset in a type face
designed for easy reading, and was printed
from new film.

THE GOLDEN TURKEY AWARDS

A Berkley Book / published by arrangement with
Perigee Books

PRINTING HISTORY
Perigee edition published 1980
Berkley edition / December 1981

ISBN: 0-425-05187-0

A BERKLEY BOOK ® TM 757,375
Berkley Books are published by Berkley Publishing Corporation,
200 Madison Avenue, New York, New York 10016.
PRINTED IN THE UNITED STATES OF AMERICA

Acknowledgments

Bad films, like all of life's trials, are hard to endure in solitude. This project, therefore, represents a genuine team effort involving many friends and colleagues in addition to the two authors.

Our valiant editor at Putnam's, Judy Linden, provided guidance, encouragement and expertise in helping this volume find its final form.

Three dedicated research assistants put in long hours at various institutions—in particular the library of the Academy of Motion Picture Arts and Sciences—to supply background information on the films in our book. These unsung heroes are:

Sol Genuth, the brilliant Bad Boy of Borough Park and hotdog King of the Venice ocean front,

Lawrence Calmus, Mad Dog Englishman and master builder,

and Mr. Kevin Allman of Riverside, California. Kevin wrote us several letters following publication of *The Fifty Worst Films of All Time* and we found ourselves so impressed by his wit and writing skills that we wanted to meet him. During the last weeks of work on this project he literally moved in with us and his participation in every phase of our endeavor proved absolutely invaluable.

Securing the more than one hundred photographs used in the book would not have been possible without the generous assistance of Eric Caidin and the other good people at the Hollywood Book and Poster Company.

Others who helped with suggestions, information and opinions included our two "middle" brothers, Jonathan and Ben Medved; Rabbi and Mrs. Daniel Lapin; David Altschuler; Jim Matthews; Michael Auerbach; Paul Clemens; Joel Gotler, Ray Stark; Bennett Yellin; Bruce Akiyama; Charlie Kaufman and Kalby; Betsy Newman; Betty Bandy; the Right Honorable H. J. Mandelberg; Steve Hyman; Kim Thornhill; Leonard Maltin; Ruth and Larry Herman; Art & Ink Inc.; Greg Tucker and Eric Hoffman.

Last, but hardly least, Nancy Medved (Michael's long-suffering wife) deserves formal recognition. She not only supervised the *Worst Films* Poll and tallied the thousands of responses, but also coordinated the acquisition of all photographs that appear here. Most of all, she cheerfully puts up with the ongoing madness of that raving brigade of bad film fanatics who use her home as their headquarters. For this—and so much more—appreciation can never be sufficiently expressed.

THE MEDVED BROTHERS

*For Our Parents,
David and Renate,
and for all our friends
in the Venice Community*

Contents

Introduction

The Academy Awards have become an American Institution—
like baseball opening day, Presidential nominating conventions, or the Rose Bowl Parade. Every year, millions wait
breathlessly for the presentation of a number of bald, gold
statuettes to the most glamorous people in the world. This well-
known ritual has taken on an almost religious solemnity, as
"The Envelopes" are passed and opened, the orchestra thrums
away with movie theme songs, and tears gush forth from the
grateful winners.

We propose a ceremony of a different sort: The Golden
Turkey Awards. For every successful and well-made film that
receives consideration by the Academy, there are literally
hundreds that never make the grade. Among them are some
of the most astonishing achievements in Hollywood history—
films so unbearably bad that it seems hard to believe they were
ever made. Isn't it time that these neglected gems received
their proper recognition?

To remedy the situation we have prepared specific awards
for specific achievements: The Worst Performance by an Animal, The Worst Performance by an Actor as Jesus Christ, The
Worst Lines of Romantic Dialogue in Movie History, and so
forth. We follow the prototype of the Oscar ceremony by listing
and discussing the nominees for each distinction before naming
the winner. The nominations are presented in simple alpha-

betical order, as required by a scrupulous sense of dignity and fair play.

We know that our choices will not please everyone—least of all the actors, producers, writers and directors who are honored in the pages that follow. We further recognize that the number of bad films is so enormous, and the competition for the very worst is so intense, that all decisions reached here are subject to considerable second-guessing. Nevertheless, we have researched the subject thoroughly—sitting through more than 2,000 wretched films in the last few years—and we believe that our nominees and award winners can stand the test of time.

In some ways, this book is a sequel to our previous effort, The Fifty Worst Films of All Time, published in 1978. We divided the responsibilities in preparing that project: Harry did the research and suffered through all the films under consideration; Michael did most of the writing. Before that book's release, Michael requested that his name be removed from the cover. A volume about bad movies seemed a mildly embarrassing project for someone with aspirations as a serious writer; besides, it offered an excellent means of making unnecessary enemies in the Hollywood world that had just begun using him as a screenwriter on feature films.

The public response to the first book, however, swept away such squeamishness. It proved that bad film fanatics comprise a flourishing American subculture, and that many movie-industry insiders are proudly counted among its members. The obsessions of this little known cult are easy to understand. We have made a fundamental observation about numerous social situations: it's more enjoyable for people to laugh together over absurdities and disasters than it is for them to praise the all-time movie greats. When fine films are discussed, most people will sit quietly, nodding in agreement or scratching their heads. When the subject turns to the immortal turkeys, however, nearly everyone has a strong opinion and will come forward to express it with eloquent enthusiasm.

Without question, this phenomenon reflects a curious twist in the public's response to motion pictures. We tend to see the people who make movies as demigods—larger-than-life figures who can do no wrong. Despite the demise of the star system, the suspicion persists that these Hollywood greats are better than the rest of us. It is therefore reassuring, as well as amusing, to discover that they can make horrible mistakes just as we do. It is deeply satisfying to watch, say, a Victor Mature embarrass himself on screen; a clown is always funniest if his pratfalls are unintentional. Watching one of the unbelievable baddies, knowing that almost anyone could have made a better film, asking himself how a piece of work so wretched could possibly have come about, the average citizen will resemble that "Dutch sailor" described by Scott Fitzgerald at the end of Gatsby, "compelled into an aesthetic contemplation he neither understood nor desired, face to face for the last time in history with something commensurate to his capacity for wonder."

We offer these thoughts not only to justify our endeavor but to explain the extraordinary volume of mail we have received from across the country and around the world, nominating various films for the distinction of the all-time worst. The results of this poll—with more than 3,000 ballots received—are reported in the concluding chapters of this book. We have also taken the will of the people into account in selecting the nominees in the various categories, trying to include most of those films with particularly strong grassroots support.

As a final service to our readers, we have prepared a Worst Films Compendium that indexes and annotates all of the awful movies that drew 15 ballots or more in our national survey. Perhaps this handy guide can serve to instruct the public when it's best not to wait up for The Late Show. As an ad for a bad movie once declared: "Remember, You Have Been Warned."

Finally, we include a "Suggestion Box" requesting your comments, complaints and ingenious ideas, for our own edification and for future reference. While Hollywood continues to grind out bad films, with promising new titles appearing all the time, the least we can do is to continue to appreciate them. It is hard to imagine a field with more infinite possibilities. In chronicling these achievements, we are reminded of the legendary fellow in Eastern Europe who climbed the walls of his town, day after day, staring off toward the horizon. He explained to his friends that he had to be there in order to await the arrival of the Messiah.

"But don't you get tired of it?" they wanted to know.

"Sure," he answered, "But it's steady work."

Venice, California
January, 1980

I wish the Bald Eagle had not been chosen as the Representative of our Country... The Turkey is a much more respectable Bird, and withal a true original Native of America.

—BENJAMIN FRANKLIN, 1784

Farrah and Raquel: cuddlemates in Myra Breckinridge.

The Most Embarrassing Movie Debut of All Time

ALL ACTORS and actresses have played certain roles that they would rather forget. Frequently, these skeletons-in-the-closet involve the early, difficult days of a struggling performer. The astonishing fact concerning the movie debuts described below is that the stars involved went on to piece together successful careers following putrid, unpromising beginnings.

And the Nominees Are...

Farrah Fawcett in *Myra Breckinridge* [1970]

Before she developed her wholesome, athletic image on *Charlie's Angels*, before she decorated the walls of millions of American homes as an ebullient poster girl, before she hooked up with the Six Million Dollar Man and added the "Majors" to her name, Farrah had an undercover assignment in this film—under-the-covers with Raquel Welch. Raquel, in the title role, is seeking some offbeat sexual stimulation, having exhausted the possibilities of sodomy, sex-change operations, sadomasochism, and artificial organs. Farrah, as an innocent, dumb-blonde sweetie pie named Mary-Ann, offers a new world to conquer. Farrah is uniquely suited to play a woman of limited intelligence, but the subtle sexual tension intended for her role is completely lost on her. She fits in perfectly with the general texture of this abysmal film and radiates all the intense sensuality of an inflatable sex doll. After going through all the normal preliminaries with Raquel, Farrah gets out of bed and refuses to consummate their affair. (Anita Bryant, take heart!) In subsequent movie work, Farrah's parts have been a good deal less humiliating, but her acting ability has remained reassuringly consistent.

Sally Kellerman (center) as a lesbian in Reform School Girl.

Sally Kellerman in *Reform School Girl* [1957]

We have constructed an elaborate fantasy about how Sally Kellerman wound up in this miserable part. Imagine her walking in to see a theatrical agent for the first time, shortly after her arrival in Hollywood. "What can I do for you, girlie?" he inquires. Full of nervous intensity, our breathless ingenue declaims: "I want to be a thespian!" The veteran agent listens to her words and furrows his brow, for he believes that a thespian is a female homosexual. (After all, it got Farrah Fawcett on her way, didn't it?) He proceeds immediately to follow Sally's presumed wishes by winning her a role as the black-leather school dyke in a wretched exploitation piece called *Reform*

School Girl. At least this is the way it *should* have happened—this set of imaginary circumstances might have actually consoled Ms. Kellerman. As it was, not even the presence of teen idol Ed "Kookie" Byrnes as star of the film could help her overcome feelings of disgust of her own screen debut. "I should get an *award* for having the courage to go on after I saw *that*," she recalls. "I didn't work again for three years." Well, Sally, your dream has come true: you are finally receiving an award—or at least a *nomination*—for your part in *Reform School Girl*. Congratulations, and enjoy it.

Paul Newman shields himself from hostile critics in his debut role as Basil the Defender in The Silver Chalice.

Paul Newman in *The Silver Chalice* [1955]

Here's some trivia for you Biblical scholars: who designed the ornamental chalice that holds the cup used by Jesus during the Last Supper? Give up? Actually, it was a Greek slave known as "Basil the Defender" who happened to look exactly like Paul Newman. Does it all come back to you now? If not, don't worry—it just means that you've missed *The Silver Chalice*— a $4.5 million epic disaster which billed itself as "The Mightiest Story of Truth and Temptation Ever Produced!" In addition to the young Newman, sporting a white miniskirt and v-neck tunic, the film features such luminaries as: Jack Palance, Natalie Wood, E. G. Marshall, Lorne Greene, and the irrepressible Virginia Mayo as a wily seductress who tries (unsuccessfully) to win Paul's attention. The most revealing name on the list of credits, however, is that of the screenwriter, one "Lesser Samuels." Perhaps if his big brother Greater Samuels had written the film, it would have been more of a success. At least it might have provided Paul Newman with a more suitable vehicle for his first screen appearance. Concerning the performance of the fledgling star, *The New Yorker* commented: "Paul Newman, a lad who resembles Marlon Brando, delivers his lines with the emotional fervor of a Putnam Division conductor announcing local stops." *The New York Times* described the newcomer as "rarely better than wooden." Like the other actors, Newman found himself consistently upstaged by the horrendous sets designed to represent ancient Jerusalem. These outlandish geometric shapes reminded *The New Yorker* of "a cross between an igloo community and one of Frank Lloyd Wright's more advanced designs," and helped deflect public and critical attention from Newman's dismal debut.

John Travolta in *The Devil's Rain* [1975]

Unfortunately, the millions of teeny-bopper girls that idolize Travolta's face won't be able to recognize much of him in this production; he is made-up beyond recognition. Sorry, girls. Those who get their kicks by listening to the sweet music of his voice are also out of luck. His only line, which occurs near the film's conclusion, is "Blasphemer! Get him, he is a blasphemer!" After a statement like that, what can you do for an encore? Well, the inventive Mr. Travolta melts into a pool of liquid before your very eyes. If all this sounds confusing, it's because it *is*. This tacky horror story about a devil-worshiping cult was shot entirely at Churubusco Studios in ol' Mexico, with such distinguished stars as Ernest Borgnine, Ida Lupino,

4

John Travolta (foreground) melts away in the warm waters of The Devil's Rain.

William Shatner and Eddie Albert. The ads made the most of these "big names" and hailed the film as "One of the Most Ambitious Projects Ever Undertaken—And Definitely the Most Different!" Tom Skerritt, a co-star, more accurately described *The Devil's Rain* as "A Picture to Throw Up By." Even Travolta's fellow Sweat Hogs, with their notoriously strong stomachs and hearty appetites, would find this material hard to digest.

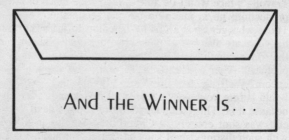

And the Winner Is...

... PAUL NEWMAN
IN *The Silver Chalice*

Paul Newman's school-boy earnestness as "Basil the Defender" has provoked laughter from a whole generation of viewers. Unlike the other nominees in this category, his screen debut involved more than an obscure bit part; he had the opportunity to humiliate himself in a full-blown starring role.

Mr. Newman, secure in his current reputation as one of Hollywood's most talented and versatile performers, can now afford to be philosophical about this long-ago disaster. "I used to put that picture down," he sighs, "but to have the honor of being in the worst picture of the fifties and surviving is no mean feat."

It has been even more of a feat—for the people of Tokyo and other locales—to survive the onslaught of deadly but laughable monsters who have paraded across the silver screen and qualified themselves as nominees for our next award...

The Most Ridiculous Monster in Screen History

And the Nominees Are...

The Alligator People [1959]

A mad doctor, fascinated by reptiles, transforms poor Richard Crane into a laughable creature vaguely resembling an alligator—the monster's costume only partially conceals the human identity of the wearer. The title of this film is misleading because Crane is the only "alligator person" to make an appearance in this Ultra Cheapie. Lon Chaney, Jr., plays the scientist's crazed assistant, and provokes a fight and a few feeble explosions in a vain attempt to keep our interest. Beverly Garland is the long-suffering spouse who loses a husband and gains a strong distaste for alligator shoes.

Attack of the Fifty-Foot Woman [1958]

A gigantic baldy from outer space falls in love with buxom
earthling Allison Hayes and enlarges her to suit his specifi-
cations. She magically becomes fifty feet tall and at least forty
feet broad at the chest. This killer bathing beauty then proceeds
to smash miniature dollhouses in search of her long lost mate
intoning "HARRY! I want my husband, HARRY!"

The Creeping Terror [1964]

The title monster is a long, deadly carpet with a group of college students underneath to move it along. The alternate title for this film, *The Crawling Monster*, is perfectly descriptive. The creature arrives from outer space in a strange craft resembling a customized van, with the mission of itemizing the chemical composition of human beings. To perform this sophisti-

cated analysis, the monster has to eat people, sending the results back to a computer onboard the van. There are actually twin creatures featured here, one of whom sleeps through the entire first half of the film along with the audience. The Killer Carpet invades a hootenanny, a fishing trip and a high school dance, where one perceptive teenager screams out in horror, "Oh my God what is it?" Director Art J. Nelson lost the soundtrack to his masterpiece and wisely hired a narrator to explain what is going on. *The Creeping Terror* is distinguished as one of the few films in history to be shot entirely in Lake Tahoe, Nevada.

From Hell It Came [1959]

"And to Hell it can go!" comments critic Ed Naha. This film concerns a South Sea islander who suffers an untimely death and is reincarnated in the trunk of a tree. The Walking Tree, with the dead man's face protruding from its bark, shuffles around the island, devouring natives and destroying villages. The wooden monster, who takes the name Tabonga, also develops lustful impulses and tries to rape a comely lass who resists his leafy advances. Finally, this uprooted horror is destroyed by a sharpshooter who takes careful aim at the hilt of a knife that has been lodged in its bark all along. Driven by this well-placed shot, the blade finally plunges deep into the wood pulp and puts everyone concerned with this film out of their misery.

Gamera, The Invincible [1962]

This Japanese saga tells the heart-warming story of a monster turtle, nearly 400 feet long. If that's not bizarre enough for you, Gamera flies through the air like a snapping space shuttle and breathes fire when aroused. Though this curious airborne reptile wreaks havoc on the fair city of Tokyo, one small child takes a liking to him. "Gamera doesn't mean to step on people," the Japanese boy explains. "He's just lonely. Even turtles get lonely sometimes." This sort of touching dialogue helped make the film so popular that the flying, fire-breathing turtle made a triumphal return in numerous sequels, including *Gamera Versus Monster X*, *The Return of the Giant Monsters*, and *Destroy all Planets*.

Robot Monster [1953]

As every schoolchild knows, the moon is inhabited by a race of killer robots who invade the earth periodically to drool over Grade Z starlets like Claudia Barret. The featured robot in this celebrated stinker is portrayed by an overweight actor in a gorilla suit, wearing a deep-sea diving helmet over his head. In fact, this same actor in the same costume also plays the king robot back on the moon, Great One, who directs from a distance the destruction of the human race. The key weapon in their assault is "the calcinator death ray," produced when the fearsome "Earth Ro-Man" waves his furry arms.

Teenagers from Outer Space [1959]

A juvenile scientist from another galaxy comes to earth on a crucial mission, but falls in love with the local teen queen. He is so sorely distracted by this bubble-gum romance, that he allows the ferocious monster who has accompanied him from outer space to escape the flying saucer. We are told that this creature—"a gigantic lobster"—threatens to destroy the world, but we never get a chance to see it. The producers of the film didn't have enough money to construct a huge lobster, so they try to get away with showing us the crustacean's ominous shadow, and nothing more.

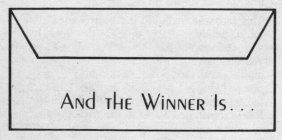

And the Winner Is. . .

... Robot Monster

For sheer stupidity, nothing can equal the concept of plump, hairy robots that look like giant apes. We were so inspired by this ridiculous movie that we interviewed Phil Tucker, who produced and directed it as a whiz-kid of age twenty-six. "I originally envisioned the monster as kind of a robot," he recalls. "I talked to several guys that I knew who had robot suits, but it was just out-of-the-way, money-wise. I thought, 'Okay, I know George Barrows.' George's occupation was gorilla-suit man. When they needed a gorilla in a picture they called George, because he owned his own suit and got like forty bucks a day. I thought, 'I know George will work for me for nothing. I'll get a diving helmet, put it on him, and it'll work!'"

Whether the scheme worked as the filmmaker intended is open to serious question, though Mr. Tucker (*See:* Life Achievement Award: The Worst Director of All Time) unquestionably deserves high marks for his resourcefulness and daring. Not even this audacious *auteur*, however, could have conceived a more outrageous misuse of the nation's leading vocalists than the producers who created the films in the category that follows...

The Worst Performance by a Popular Singer

FOR EVERY Barbra Streisand or Frank Sinatra who has made the successful transition from musical to dramatic entertainment, there are dozens of accomplished warblers and thrushes who have tried their hands at acting and failed miserably. The nominees in this category involved themselves in some particularly humiliating and hilarious disasters. It is easy to see why they remain known to the public as singers rather than as actors.

And the Nominees Are...

Tony Bennett as "Hymie Kelly" gives Elke Sommer sage advice in The Oscar.

Tony Bennett in *The Oscar* [1966]

The film opens on the night of the Academy Awards. Tony Bennett sits in the audience while his friend, actor Frankie Fane

(Stephen Boyd), is considered for the Oscar. As the veteran singer watches the proceedings intently, his voice suddenly comes onto the soundtrack. Since his lips remain still, we can only conclude that he is either a ventriloquist or a character in a bad movie experiencing a moment of meaningful introspection. Bennett's voice-over lines of narration, which set the tone for the entire film, are worth repeating:

> You finally made it, Frankie—Oscar night. And here you sit—on top of a glass mountain called success. You are one of the chosen five—and the whole town's holding its breath to see who'll win it. Been quite a climb, hasn't it, Frankie? Down at the bottom—scuffling for dimes at the "smokers"—all the way to the top. Ever think about it? I do, friend Frankie. I do.

Now, . . . can you guess what happens next? If you said "flashbacks" then you win a full scholarship to the Famous Screenwriter's School in Westport, Connecticut—you can write Hollywood clichés with the best of them, or at least with the hacks who perpetrated this odious mess. To show us that our narrator has a heart of gold, despite his association with the ruthless Stephen Boyd, the creators of the film give Mr. Bennett a solid ethnic background. The only problem is that they can't quite decide which ethnic group to use, and so compromise by anointing him with the preposterous name "Hymie Kelly." An Italian-American from San Francisco playing Hymie Kelly? Well, only in America—or only in Hollywood, at least.

In terms of his dramatic approach, Mr. Bennett manages to sink to the occasion. He delivers his lines like a grade schooler reading Shakespeare aloud for the first time; he is so totally amazed by the remarkable literacy of the script that he lingers over every other word. This results in a long series of meaningless pauses and a senseless overemphasis on words like "up" and "with." No wonder that *Cue* magazine commented: "Tony looks like a sad, abandoned bulldog." As far as genuine emotion is concerned, he left his heart in San Francisco.

Sonny Bono as a fearless, freedom-loving, anti-fascist Italian partisan in Escape to Athena.

Sonny Bono in *Escape to Athena* [1979]

Since breaking up with his erstwhile partner, Cher, Sonny Bono's career has suffered some painful bumps and grinds. ABC abruptly canceled his 1974 television show "The Sonny Comedy Hour" and his Vegas appearances drew disappointing crowds and notices. Since nothing else seemed to work, he felt ready for a shot at the silver screen. As his vehicle he chose *Escape to Athena*, a quickie World War II adventure that featured the likes of Elliott Gould, Telly Savalas, Claudia Car-

17

dinale and David Niven against most of the German Army. Since the producers discovered that Sonny's real name had been *Salvatore* Bono, they decided to cast him as an antifascist Italian who winds up with American and British heroes in a German prison camp on a Greek island. This must be what they mean by an "international spectacle." It is some measure of Mr. Bono's dramatic aspirations that he makes not even the slightest attempt to render an Italian accent—in fact, he speaks without inflection of any kind. He mumbles his lines in an insecure monotone like the shy child in the school Christmas pageant who can't wait to run from the stage. The makeup department succeeds in making him look disreputable, what with his long stringy hair and unshaven face, but as a ferocious guerilla fighter he fails completely. To put the matter bluntly, Mr. Bono comes across as what generations of American high school students have colorfully termed "a wimp." It is not surprising that the Los Angeles *Herald-Examiner* described *Escape to Athena* as "No *Dirty Dozen*—it's just a Seedy Seven."

Even before the film's release, reporters on the set expressed doubts about Bono's acting ability. He reassured them by explaining: "If you believe you can do something and you've got the talent, you can." This statement represents an admirable example of positive thinking. We only hope that Sonny Bono never applies its logic to the possible future belief that he can learn to fly.

Bob Dylan in *Pat Garrett and Billy the Kid* [1973]

The character Dylan plays in *Pat Garrett* is known as "Alias"—perhaps a subtle suggestion that the singer should have changed his name as soon as the reviews came out. This sloppy Western spurred *Newsweek* to comment: "Bob Dylan twitches at the mouth in a disastrous screen debut." Indeed, the violent tics that seize Dylan's face at inopportune moments in the film suggest a Chihuahua in heat. *Variety* seemed absolutely amazed at the range of Dylan's expressive powers, observing that "his acting is currently limited to an embarrassing assortment of tics, smirks, shrugs, winks and smiles." What more do they want? Obscene finger gestures?

Bob Dylan as "Alias" twitches his way through Pat Garrett and Billy the Kid.

In addition to his priceless contributions as an actor, Dylan wrote the title song for this Sam Peckinpah turkey. It's socko lyrics included lines such as: "They say that Pat Garrett has got your number/So sleep with one eye open when you slumber..."

In addition to Dylan, *Pat Garrett and Billy the Kid* featured his fellow singers Rita Coolidge and Kris Kristofferson. Perhaps these fun-loving balladeers found the blood-gore-and-excitement of this production a welcome change from the atmosphere of a quiet recording studio. The United Kingdom originally censored the film ("There'll always be an England"!) owing to its excessive violence, rather than the artistic gaffes within. At the end of the movie, the rambling story line deposits us unceremoniously outside a room in which Pat Garrett is waiting to kill Billy. The lawman hesitates, however, when he sees that Billy is making love to an Indian maiden. (Somewhere along the way this Kid grew up.) Pat, respecting the honor code of the Old West, cannot bring himself to shoot a man before he reaches a climax. The intelligent viewer, on the other hand, should feel no such compunctions and would be well advised to walk out long before the huffing-puffing conclusion of this tedious picture.

Neil Sedaka in *Playgirl Killer* [1969] (Alternate Title: *Decoy for Terror*)

Before making his spectacular comeback in the early seventies, the gifted singer-songwriter Neil Sedaka must have been desperate for work. How else can one explain his participation in this wretched melodrama, filmed entirely in scenic Montreal?

Sedaka plays a rock star named Bob, who is backed up by an energetic group called "J.B. and the Playboys." This Bob is supposed to be something of a local teen idol, but he wanders through much of the picture in a bathing suit that exposes his substantial belly and gives clear evidence of approaching middle age. Unfortunately, this does not prevent Sedaka from belting out several forgettable tunes, including "If You Don't Wanna, You Don't Hafta" and "Waterbug." This last number is presented during a swingin' party at poolside, as Sedaka croons:

See a bug walkin' on the ground
He moves in a straight line
But the waterbug must have flipped his tug...

The plot of the film features William Kirwin as "Bill," an eccentric artist who has devised an ingenious solution for the problem of models who can't sit still: he kills them. The plot thickens, or rather coagulates, when Bill is hired by Arlene, a curvaceous blonde, to help her clean house. He murders the seductive beauty and puts her in the meat locker where he stores his other models. Finally, Bill himself is killed during a power failure when one of his frozen honeys begins to thaw and her grip releases on a bow-and-arrow she has been holding. This arrow finds its way directly into Bill's throat in one of the least credible movie coincidences since Anthony Quinn's "unintentional" resemblance to Aristotle Onassis in *The Greek Tycoon*. (*See:* Biggest Ripoff in Hollywood History.)

Sedaka's role in all of these fun and games is never clearly defined. For the most part, he appears as the boyfriend of Arlene's lovable kid sister, Betty. In one emotion-packed scene he two-times his lover by seductively rubbing suntan oil into big sister's bare back. Caught in the act, he gets up to appease his offended Betty while calling back over his shoulder, "I didn't mean to leave you half-oiled, Arlene!"

Whereas Bob Dylan's versatile acting included a variety of facial distortions, Sedaka can manage only a goofy smile. This happy-go-lucky smirk, worn consistently throughout the movie, might help him compete in a Gomer Pyle look-alike contest but it hardly bodes well for his movie future. We can only be thankful that Sedaka has gotten his musical career back on track, and spared us further adventures on the silver screen.

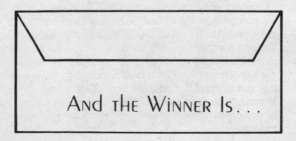

AND THE WINNER IS...

. . . TONY BENNETT IN *THE OSCAR*

Bono, Dylan and Sedaka at least retain some dim traces of their vivid personalities onscreen, but Tony Bennett, with his solemn pompous narration, is completely erased as a recognizable presence.

According to a Paramount press release, it was fate, rather than free will which forced the unsuspecting singer into the role of Hymie Kelly. Producer Charles Greene and director Russell Rouse had both been avid fans of Bennett's vocal work for years. Then one night they happened to tune in *The Andy Williams Show* while Tony made a guest appearance. Instantly they "were struck by an extraordinary warmth and sensitivity which came over the television screen." In the classic tradition of these stories, they whisked him to Hollywood for a screen test. As the studio hype duly reported: "The result is a role in *The Oscar*, which can easily make him a candidate for one."

Sorry, Tony. No Oscar. But how about a Golden Turkey? (As your consolation prize.)

Tony Bennett shares a moment of tenderness with co-star Jill St. John.

The Worst Title of All Time

And the Nominees Are...

I Dismember Mama [1974]

This film was advertised with the unforgettable lines: "A Frenzy of Blood! Haunting Desires Seething in His Mind Lead to a Night of Ghastly Atrocities!!!" Need we say more? Well, there is one additional point worth making: the title here is not only tasteless, it is misleading. Though psychotic killer Albert (Zooey Hall) demonstrates his carving technique on assorted nurses, housekeepers, department-store mannequins and ladies of the night, he never does get to work on his mother. The title tells us more about the psychological hangups of the filmmakers than it does about the action onscreen. This same producer gave the world the immortal "Please Don't Eat My Mother." (*See:* The Worst Vegetable Movie of All Time.)

Jesse James' buddy Cal Bolder is transformed into a monster by Frankenstein's granddaughter, Maria Frankenstein, in Jesse James Meets Frankenstein's Daughter.

The Incredibly Strange Creatures Who Stopped Living and Became Mixed-Up Zombies [1964]

A tour-de-force for Ray Dennis Steckler, who not only produced and directed this epic but starred in it under the pseudonym "Cash Flagg." The plot concerns a sinister gypsy fortune-teller who hypnotizes people on a carnival midway, then throws acid in their faces so they will be sufficiently disfigured to serve as caged monsters in his sideshow. The film attempted to launch a new national dance craze with its bewitching musical interlude "The Zombie Stomp" . . . not to be confused with the classic theme music from *The Horror of Party Beach*, which (Incredibly Strange!) bears the same title.

Jesse James Meets Frankenstein's Daughter [1965]

This is the work of celebrated director William ("One Shot") Beaudine, the same *auteur* whose sure hand guided *Bela Lugosi Meets a Brooklyn Gorilla* and *Billy the Kid Versus Dracula*. The action of the film actually involves Dr. Frankenstein's naughty *grand*-daughter, who lives in a laboratory in Mexico and attempts to capture the famed Western outlaw (John Lupton) and his fat sidekick to use them in her nefarious experiments.

Matango, The Fungus of Terror (Alternate Title: Attack of the Mushroom People) [1963]

This Japanese epic seems to have been inspired by the sequence in Walt Disney's *Fantasia* in which a number of sprightly mushrooms perform a dance to the strains of Tchaikovsky's *Nutcracker*. In this film, however, the murderous fungus attempts to give truffles and toadstools a bad name. The victims are portrayed by an all-star cast, including: Akira Kubo (star of *Destroy All Monsters* and *Son of Godzilla*); Hiroshi Koisumi (star of *Godzilla versus The Thing, Mothra* and *Ghidrah the Three-Headed Monster*). Yoshio Tsuchiya and Kumi Musuno are also featured.

Rat Fink a Boo Boo [1964]

Ray Dennis Steckler strikes again! This time the maker of "The Incredibly Strange Creature Who . . . [yawn] etc., etc.," wrote, photographed, produced and directed. Attempting to capitalize on the popularity of the *Batman and Robin* TV series, Steckler creates two superheroes of his own: Rat Pfink and Boo Boo. These two flat-footed meddlers use an array of dazzling technological innovations, all apparently purchased at Woolworth's, to combat a host of criminals and conspirators. Despite the strenuous efforts of romantic lead Vin Saxon, the film is stolen by an animal star who is billed as Kogar, the Swinging Ape.

Wine, Women and Horses [1937]

No, it's not a Western, it's a racetrack picture. When it was released *Variety* hailed it with the line: "Even the horses aren't much good in what they slapped together for Barton MacLane, Ann Sheridan and some lesser players." Lesser than Barton MacLane? Oh well. The tension in the plot is provided by MacLane's first wife (Peggy Bates), a righteous little lady from the sticks, who tries to prevent hubby from playing the ponies. Instead, our hero dumps his wet-blanket spouse, proving that it's always easier to find a new wife than to develop a new hobby.

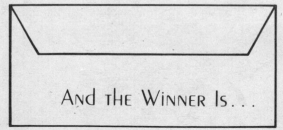

AND THE WINNER IS...

... *Rat Fink a Boo Boo*

Yes, fans, this was a tough choice with extremely stiff competition. Rat Fink gets the nod in this case, however, because it not only sounds inane, but the title tells you absolutely nothing about the subject of the film. Is it a go-go dance musical extravaganza? Japanese monster movie? Walt Disney true-life nature adventure? Romantic comedy? Concentration camp comedy? James Bond spinoff? None of the above? You have thirty seconds to complete this multiple-choice quiz. Please do not turn back to our previous description of the film, which might give away the answer.

The Most Brainless Brain Movie of All Time

And the Nominees Are...

Joanna Lee watches in horror as a kamikaze man-eating bedroom slipper attacks Ed Nelson's arm in The Brain-Eaters.

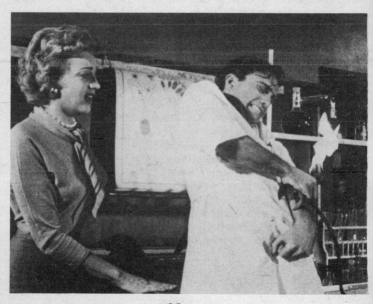

The Brain Eaters [1958]

Lovely title, eh? The basic concept of this film is even lovelier: small, wiggly creatures from outer space invade the earth and begin drilling holes in the heads of their victims to suck out their brains. This might actually be frightening except for the fact that the invaders bear a close resemblance to fluffy bedroom slippers. When reports of their antics reach Washington, D.C., the government is naturally concerned—after all, these man-eating slippers might be dangerous enough to give our shoe industry a permanent black eye. "Senator Powers" (Jack Hill) dispatches two of his best scientists to investigate the situation. One of them (the one with the breasts and the hairdo) is played by Joanna Lee, who won immortality of sorts by starring in that timeless stink-bomb *Plan 9 from Outer Space*. This time she is slurped-up by the fluffy fiends, leaving her partner-lover Dr. Ketterling (Ed Nelson, who also produced this movie) in a quandary. Fortunately, the good doctor has watched enough Grade Z sci-fi sagas to know what to do: he will destroy the monsters by electrocuting them with two high-voltage cables. That is precisely what happens, but our hero also manages to kill himself in the process. At least it's better than losing his head as the main ingredient in today's fresh helping of brain salad.

The Brain from Planet Arous [1957]

This Howco International production tells the heartwarming story of not one but two (count 'em—two!) floating brains from outer space. As should go without saying, one of them ("Gor") is an evil brain while the other ("Vol"—who speaks in the soothing yet authoritative tones of Werner Erhard) is a nice brain. Both of them, however, have two beady eyes set right in the midst of their jellylike gray matter, which make them look like Charles Addams' cartoon creations. Gor, the sinister member of this dynamic duo, takes over the body of nuclear physicist John Agar, properly assuming that an alien mind from the planet Arous will provide a notable improvement over Agar's home-grown equipment. With Gor occupying his cranium, this unhappy earthling develops a swelled head and begins laying insidious plans to blow up the world. "I've got the power to make an atom bomb look like a firecracker!" he chortles. Agar's girlfriend (Joyce Meadows) hardly approves of his new-found sense of humor. In the nick of time, Vol, the good brain, arrives on earth to thwart the schemes of his traditional rival in what amounts to the planet Arous's version of the annual Yale-Harvard game. Vol takes possession of a cheerful dog (well, it's not much worse as a vehicle than John Agar) and tells The Girlfriend and her father how to conquer his evil counterpart. Listening to Bowser's instructions, they wait until Gor takes a coffee break from his possession of Agar and manifests himself in his natural brain state. At that point, Ms. Meadows chases Gor around the laboratory with an ax, and eventually prepares a yummy-bloody mess worthy of The Brain Eaters. Vol returns happily to his home on Arous, leaving the puzzled earthlings to wonder, "Who was that masked brain?" Or, even more to the point, who was the studio "brain" at Howco International who thought up this inane project? For the record, the director was Nathan (*Attack of the Fifty-Foot Woman*) Hertz. Publicity for the film promised "Science's Most Astounding Story. . . . See the Most Diabolical Power of the Most Feared Man on Earth." The *Los Angeles Times* more accurately summarized this movie as "pure hash from the cutting-room floor."

The Brain That Wouldn't Die [1963]

This one is a love story—well, sort of. The main character is a mad doctor who specializes in transplants. The actor who plays this role is Herb Evers, but shortly after this film's release he decided to change his name (for obvious reasons) to Jason Evers. In any event, this fun-loving man of medicine makes a habit of robbing graves in order to facilitate his macabre experiments. During one romantic, moonlit romp to a local cemetery with his lovely fiancée (Virginia Leith), the two lovebirds suffer a severe auto accident. Herb/Jason is uninjured but his lady friend is decapitated. This is a great tragedy, because his engagement ring is now completely useless unless she agrees to wear it through her nose. Miraculously, the sappy surgeon manages to keep Virginia's head alive by hooking it

Herb Evers cuddles Virginia Leith's noggin which he hopes to transplant onto a stripper's body in The Brain That Wouldn't Die.

up to some sophisticated equipment in his laboratory. She pleads with him to let her die in peace, but our hero has a better idea: he will kidnap another young woman with a beautiful body and graft Virginia's brain onto this new piece of merchandise. After checking out a stripper and a few B-girls, he finds a perfectly proportioned model with an unfortunately disfigured face. She is so embarrassed by this handicap, that Herb assumes she will be pleased to have her defective head replaced by Virginia's more presentable noggin. Before this logical switcheroo can be accomplished, the detached brain in the lab begins acting up, apparently upset because its fiancée has ignored its pleas for death. Showing shamefully bad sportsmanship, the brain arranges to let loose the dreaded "thing in the closet"—a household monster that Herb has constructed from the leftovers from his operating table. This vivacious charmer proceeds to assault Virginia's brother, ripping his arm out of its socket in one horrendously gory scene, and then sets the laboratory on fire in order to destroy Herb, Virginia and, hopefully, the entire production crew. As the brain perishes in flames, it manages to giggle: "See! I told you to let me die . . . hee! hee! hee!" So ends this touching and persuasive plea for timely euthanasia.

They Saved Hitler's Brain (Alternate Titles: The Madmen of Mandoras and The Return of "Mr. H.") [1964]

Adolf Hitler was without question a terrifying personality. And so, reasoned the producers of this film, why not frighten people with a grim tale of Hitler's brain, rescued from his burning body, and kept alive all these years by some of the Führer's medically skilled and imaginative followers? That is the basic premise of this film, as even an executive in Howco International might have guessed after a few seconds' reflection on the title. The problem is that the filmmakers use this tasteless and idiotic premise to justify seventy-four minutes of an outrageously padded plot concerning: kidnappings, nerve gas, scientific conferences, a Latin American banana republic (don't all retired Nazis spend their sunset years in Latin America?), revolutions, a corrupt El Presidente, sleepy villagers who look

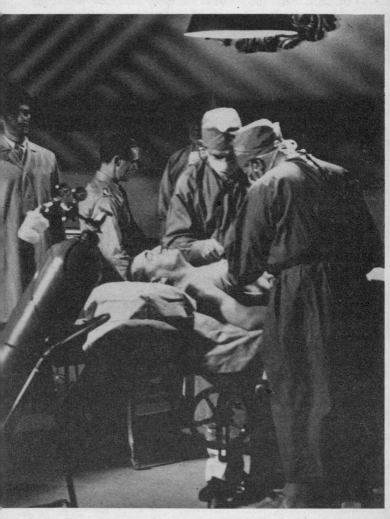

Nazi surgeons perform a top-secret operation to preserve the mind of their leader, "Mr. H.," in They Saved Hitler's Brain.

like they just wandered off the set of *Zorro*, a brilliant American professor with an antidote to the nerve gas, his beautiful daughter and son-in-law (love interest), murders, fires, explosions, conspiracies and counterplots. Unfortunately, this brief description makes the action of the film sound more interesting and coherent than it actually is. Through it all, the brain of "Mr. H." (as he is respectfully known) is represented by a gooey, waxed face poured into a pickle jar and hooked up to bubbling, crackling, hissing life-support systems. As the forces of goodness close in around this odd creature and his colleagues, the German diehards leave their bunker (again?) and make their way to the scenic beach of this island nation, Mandoras. There, where the surf gently laps against the silver sand, they find themselves surrounded and destroyed, thereby ending the threat of a sequel, *Beach Blanket Führer*. As the pressbook for the film describes this inspiring conclusion: "The story ends with the purifying, agonizing death by fire of the monster head." Most viewers will feel decidedly more agonized than purified.

And the Winner Is...

... They Saved Hitler's Brain

As it sloshes around inside its bullet-proof glass jar, the pickled head of "Mr. H." makes for the most ridiculous brain of all. The props department, however, doesn't deserve all the credit: actor Bill Freed, who provides the voice of the late, lamented German leader, certainly makes a major contribution. He shrieks away with tremendous enthusiasm in a bogus German accent that couldn't even pass muster in *Hogan's Heroes*. Occasionally, he tells his underlings to *"Mach schnell! Mach schnell!"* in their efforts to release the deadly "Nerve Gas G" that will destroy the world. When released, under its original title, *The Madmen of Mandoras*, this film received the warm critical reception it so richly deserved. *Variety* hailed it as "a melodramatic fiasco" and went on to observe that "the sting of this 'B' will poison any double feature program unlucky enough to inherit it."

This raises the entire question of bee movies. No, not "B" movies, but bee movies. You know, buzz-buzz, bumble-bumble, as in our next category...

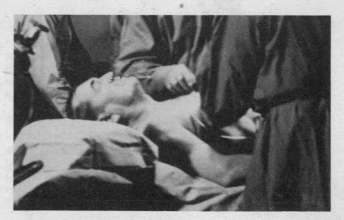

The Most Badly Bumbled Bee Movie of All Time

IN THE MIDST of Irwin Allen's celebrated stinkeroo The Swarm, *Michael Caine delivers a line that serves as an apt introduction to all the films nominated here. "I never dreamed it would turn out to be the bees," Caine declares. "They've always been our friends." Indeed. What is it about these industrious little honey-makers that has called forth the very worst from such a wide variety of filmmakers? Perhaps the Not-Ready-for-Prime-Time-Players, who dress up as "Killer Bees" and perform their terrifying skits on* Saturday Night Live, *are actually in tune with a deep, resonant chord in the collective unconscious.*

And the Nominees Are...

The Bees [1978]

This low-budget exploitation epic was rushed through production and released just in time to capitalize on some of the massive advertising surrounding *The Swarm*. The producers thereby proved that they could turn out a terrible movie about murderous bees for just a fraction of what it cost Irwin Allen to do so.

The plot begins as a ragged Brazilian peasant tiptoes with his son through the private hives of a leading U.S. entomologist (Claudio Brook). In their vain attempt to steal honey, they unintentionally release a swarm of experimental killer bees that proceed to make a snack of the howling boy. The next day the father returns bearing his child's corpse and wails, "Devil bees kill my son!" This upsets the neighbors to such an extent that they begin throwing stones at the American scientist. He retreats to his laboratory where more killer bees are let loose and he is stung to death while trying to save his beautiful wife (Angel Tompkins).

Quick cut back to the U.S. of A., where Angel Tompkins works with her eccentric Uncle Ziggy (John Carradine) to halt the onslaught of the insect invaders from Brazil. We learn that the bees have now devastated all of South America. We also learn that John Carradine couldn't simulate a German accent if his life depended on it—instead, the best he can do is insert the phrase "*Auf Wiedersehen!*" into every other sentence. Meanwhile, our brave Angel falls in love with another insect specialist (John Saxon) in what must be the shortest period of mourning since Hamlet's mother got together with Uncle Claudius. Saxon and Tompkins attempt to dissuade a top cosmetics firm from using that treasured royal jelly—frozen Brazilian bee sperm—in its perfume, but alas, corporate greed prevails, and the beastly buzzers are soon running wild in the streets of America. We see the brutal effects of mass hysteria—watching bees invading the brown-bagged lunch of a fat girl on a beach, bees attacking jet airliners, bees causing a horse and rider to tumble, bees bothering an old man with a gimp leg on a park bench, etc., etc. These "invasion scenes" are interspersed with reaction shots showing "ordinary Americans" covering their mouths with their hands in horror. Finally, the Brazilian bees—who have no respect for sacred American Institutions—invade the Pasadena Rose Parade where ex-President Gerald Ford makes an appearance. As the ominous black cloud disturbs the parade, Los Angeles sportscaster Eddie ("Fast Eddie") Alexander wittily observes, "I've never seen anything like this before. It looks like bees." Finally, Angel Tompkins and John Saxon persuade the U.S. government to hold a convention on methods for dealing with the bee problem. An army official asks Saxon, "You want us to conduct peace negotiations with bugs?" Yes, they do. To underscore the point, the bees invade the convention hall and Angel delivers the film's most memorable line: "You HAVE to listen! You have to listen to what the bees have to say!" As it turns out, these Brazilian insects aren't such bad fellows after all. Their entire rampage has been a form of civil disobedience to protest environmental pollution. The harried politicians are soon convinced that the little buggers mean business, and so promise to reach new levels of ecological consciousness. Thanks to the Brazilian killer bees, the world lives happily ever after. This only goes to prove the wisdom of what Uncle Ziggy has long before observed: "They—the bees—can think like man"—or at least like the man who wrote, produced and directed this movie. Among its other distinctions, *The Bees* marks the worst performance to date by Ms. Angel Tompkins—and that covers a lot of ground. Ms. Tompkins' other (dis)credits include: *The Teacher, Trip with Teacher, Little Cigars,* and *The Don Is Dead.*

The Deadly Bees [1962]

The pesky critters featured in this film have no desire to take over the world or devour major cities; they content themselves with discreet little murders in an English country setting

Suzanna Leigh plays an exhausted pop singer who visits a remote and tranquil island to recuperate after a nervous break-down. Much to her delight, she finds that many of the quaint and picturesque natives spend their spare time as beekeepers. Obviously, she has not invested enough time watching garbage cinema to realize that beehives represent a mortal danger to any young singer. Sure enough, a series of mysterious deaths sweeps the neighborhood as grumbling, bad-tempered bees attack a dog, an old lady, and even—horrors! our lovely heroine. In fear, she flees to the farm of a kindly beekeeper, portrayed by Frank Finlay. Actually, it is Finlay himself who is breeding and controlling the deadly bees. She should have been suspicious because of the absurd thickness of his makeup—it is clearly an attempt to protect himself while deal-ing with his nasty little protégés. Highlights of the film include innumerable close-up shots of beestingers entering human flesh—unfortunately, the human extras who participated in this bit of unselfish acting do not receive the credit they deserve. Fatal bee attacks in the film are invariably preceded by a low-pitched, ominous buzzing. Is it the approaching killer bees? Or is it the snoring of most of the audience? Reviews of this film compared it unfavorably to Alfred Hitchcock's *The Birds,* which was released at about the same time. It's too bad that the two films were never mated as the twin ends of a double bill, inviting the viewers to investigate *The Birds* and *The (Deadly) Bees.*

Note the chilling special effects as the voracious insects (all four of them) devour another victim in The Deadly Bees.

The Invasion of the Bee Girls [1973]

As every schoolchild knows, when Queen Bees make love, the males of the species sacrifice their lives along with their seed.

This racy premise provides the flimsy basis for *Invasion of the Bee Girls*, a film that proves that these versatile insects can contribute just as effectively to a softcore porn feature as they can to an absurd disaster epic. This time, the millions of swarming bees create a cocoon of sorts around formerly plain housewives and transform them into glamorous "bee girls." As the science-minded publicity for the film explains, these honey pots "have acquired the genetic characteristics of queen bees whose male partners die following sexual consummation." This exciting new technology has been developed at a government subsidized facility called Brandt Institute, not to be confused with Brand X Institute. Not surprisingly, most of the men associated with this super-secret research operation have recently died from massive coronary attacks which the county coroner cleverly diagnoses as related to sexual fatigue. A U.S. State Department investigator arrives on the scene, portrayed by none other than William Smith. This broad-shouldered actor is known to aficionados as the king of motorcycle movies, where he is generally listed as "Big Bill" Smith. In most of his greatest roles he plays the leader of the rival gang that takes on the Hells Angels. He follows the same pattern here, representing the U.S. government in its attempts to spoil the fun of those mischievous bees and their human/female counterparts. He eventually succeeds in his mission by the subtle masterstroke of firing his gun into the central control panel of the institute's laboratory. This creates an explosion and fire that are purest Buck Rogers, making the world once again safe for middle-aged masculinity.

The Swarm [1978]

Few films in Hollywood history have received more prerelease ballyhoo than *The Swarm*. Producer-Director Irwin Allen, the "Master of Disaster" who had previously given the world such hits as *The Poseidon Adventure* and *The Towering Inferno*, told an interviewer before the film's premiere: "I think *The Swarm* is going to be the most terrifying movie ever made." Warner Brothers apparently agreed with him—spending $6 million on advertising and running fourteen hundred prints of the film to make it the biggest release in the studio's history. With this sort of buildup, a number of scientists worried in public that the showing of the film might create mass hysteria about bees.

They need not have worried. Shortly after *The Swarm* made its debut, *The New York Times* described it as "the surprise comedy hit of the season." The plot describes a nasty group of African killer bees who, in the course of 24 hours, destroy a large part of the American Southwest. They attack picnickers and steal peanut-butter-and-jelly sandwiches, derail a train, down helicopters, and, to show the U.S. Air Force who really rules the skies, invade an underground missile silo and devour the personnel. Moving on to bigger and better things, they cause the explosion of a nuclear power plant (Ralph Nader, take note!) because the fail-safe system provided by the utility company had not been programmed for killer bees. This little episode kills 32,432 people in one town alone, as the bees charge forward for a climax, threatening (gulp!) the entire city of Houston. At the last moment, when all looks hopeless, a brilliant entomologist (Michael Caine) steps forward to save the day. Apparently, he has seen *The Invasion of the Bee Girls* and therefore realizes that in addition to their murderous tendencies, these killer bees are absolute maniacs when it comes to sex. Caine devises a sonic alarm system that "sounds like the mating ritual of the queen bees." Several loud speakers are dropped into the Gulf of Mexico and the bees, hearing this new version of the old siren's song, zoom down into the water toward their decoy queen. The Air Force then violates every rule of fair play by spreading oil over their little yellow-and-black bodies, then setting the entire mass aflame as the victorious scientists hug one another in jubilation.

Even with this less-than-inspired plot, the film might have been saved by the spectacular special effects Irwin Allen promised to deliver. Instead, we are treated to killer bees that resemble colored Styrofoam pellets, thrown carelessly toward their victims. To show the terrifying swarm flying in formation, it looks as if the cameraman sprinkled some nutmeg over his lenses. The reaction of the zombie-like extras to this buzzing horror is about what one would expect. There are innumerable shots of various victims running wildly in slow motion, flapping their arms like penguins trying to fly and, in one case, even bumping into a telephone pole.

The film's all-star cast does plenty of bumping and thrashing of its own, as these venerable actors and actresses try to deliver

the lines screenwriter Sterling Silliphant has given them. Immunologist Henry Fonda, for instance, is forced to comment on the bee situation by declaring: "They're more virulent than the Australian brown box jellyfish!" Richard Widmark, Michael Caine, Katharine Ross, Fred MacMurray, Olivia de Havilland, Slim Pickens, José Ferrer and Richard Chamberlain all have similar struggles. Many critics amused themselves by trying to decide which of these stars turned in the most embarrassing performance. Their consensus: Katharine Ross, whose entrance line ("I need an antitoxin!") set the tone for her entire part.

Much of the action of this film takes place in a town called Marysville—one of those quaint, cardboard villages that thrive on every Hollywood backlot. This particular town is obviously inhabited by a cult of bad film fanatics because the local movie house is playing Irwin Allen's previous towering turkey, *The Towering Inferno*. This modest allusion to his own earlier work is illustrated by not one, but two (count 'em—two!) posters for *Inferno* outside the theater. Given the disastrous reception accorded to this film, it is highly doubtful that Allen's future movies will be decorated by advertisements for *The Swarm*.

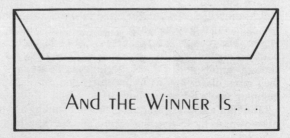

And the Winner Is...

... THE SWARM

Not only did this $12-million disaster cost more than all the other bee movies combined, but its script guaranteed it a place in the pantheon of all-time bad films. There are an abundance of lines in *The Swarm* to warm the heart of even the most jaded connoisseur of cinematic mess-terpieces. Among them:

RICHARD WIDMARK: "I'm going to be the first officer in U.S. battle history to get his butt kicked by a mess of bugs!"

RICHARD WIDMARK: "Houston on fire. Will history blame me—or the bees?"

AIR FORCE PILOT: "Oh my gosh! Bees! Bees! Millions of bees! They're all around me! Bees! Bees!"

School teacher OLIVIA DE HAVILLAND makes an announcement to her students over a public-address system: Attention! A swarm of killer bees are (*sic*) coming.

RICHARD WIDMARK (as a general on Bee patrol): "I always credit my enemy, no matter what he may be, with equal intelligence."

In view of the fact that the military's first dozen attempts to wipe out the deadly insects are miserable failures, this assessment may not have been far from the mark. We can only assume that these clever bees, if they were ever to make films about crowds of murderous people who came to raid their honeycombs, would come up with products a good deal more frightening and convincing than *The Swarm*. Small wonder that this bumbling bomb has proven to be one of the leading vote-getters in our national Worst Films Poll.

Producer–Director Irwin Allen points with pride to the buzzing hordes that are supposed to terrify the audience.

The Worst Casting of All Time

And the Nominees Are...

Roger Daltrey as Franz Liszt
in *Lisztomania* [1975]

It might seem a bit eccentric to ask Roger Daltrey, the baby-faced, blond-haired rock star and member of "The Who," to play the great nineteenth-century pianist and composer Franz

Liszt. Writer-director Ken Russell, however, insists that the choice of Daltrey is perfectly logical.

Lisztomania marked Russell's tenth essay in musical biography. "The past attracts me because when dealing with it you don't have to be historically accurate," the director lucidly explains. In speaking specifically of *Lisztomania*, he adds: "It's pure fantasy based on fact rather than straight factual biography." With statements like these, Russell's sense of proportion seems to have vanished right up his aesthetic.

As an excuse for the director to indulge his penchant for bizarre and disconnected images, his biography of Liszt is a great success. As a movie, it stinks. Russell's film defies any connection between the composer the audience may know and the one-dimensional carricature that appears onscreen. It depicts Liszt as an oversexed rock idol victimized by a vampiric Richard Wagner, who wears a sailor hat bearing the name "Nietzsche." It's always a pleasure to see profound philosophical questions so tastefully and responsibly handled. The director even asked Rick Wakeman to rework Liszt's music into a contemporary pop idiom to make it more "relevant."

Fondly recalling his work on the project, award-winning cameraman Peter Surshitzky told *American Cinematographer:* "We did have one scene in Hell that might be considered striking, shocking or even vulgar. We had a group of girls pulling along a ten-foot phallus." Yes, that *might* be considered striking, shocking or even vulgar—especially since the gigantic organ in question had been attached to Roger Daltrey.

In the face of these enormous difficulties, our hero struggles manfully with his role but is hardly prepared for the demands placed on him by Russell. As John Simon reported in *The New York Times*, Daltrey performed "with a face as long as a mule and a talent considerably shorter." The star himself could see his part in perspective, since *Lisztomania* marked the second occasion on which he had worked with the temperamental Russell. Previously, he played the title role in Russell's free-form adaption of The Who's celebrated rock opera, *Tommy*. "Liszt is a lot like Tommy spiritually," observed the introspective rock star-turned-actor, "but you couldn't get a more opposite person physically. Liszt is a more difficult part for me, because I have lots of dialogue, which I didn't in *Tommy*, because the character was deaf, dumb and blind."

For the future, we recommend that Mr. Daltrey stick to

playing characters who are deaf, dumb and blind and who possess sexual organs of normal size.

Harpo Marx as Sir Isaac Newton in *The Story of Mankind* [1957]

Like Ken Russell, producer-writer-director Irwin Allen has a special approach when it comes to putting historical characters on the screen. "Telling history on the screen can be like a bad joke told twice. You first have to find a handle, a gimmick,"

he told the *Los Angeles Times*. "Where we can't do justice to a time and place we won't brush them off summarily. We just won't use them." With these idealistic goals in mind, Allen seemed to hit upon the perfect "gimmick" to "do justice" to Newton's discovery of the law of gravitation: he would ask Harpo Marx to portray the great British scientist. To supplement this comic master stroke, Allen would show a whole bushel of apples falling on Newton's unsuspecting head—rather than the single small fruit indicated by tradition. Harpo goes through his brief slapstick routine in a tired, listless style as if he is embarrassed by the whole concept.

The misuse of Harpo is only one of the many inspired casting ideas used by Allen for this dreary film. *The Story of Mankind* also features Peter Lorre as Nero, Virginia Mayo as Cleopatra, Dennis Hopper as Napoleon, Francis X. Bushman as Moses, and Hedy Lamarr as Joan of Arc. Obviously, part of the problem here is that Allen couldn't decide whether his free-form adaptation of Hendrik Willem Van Loon's best-selling history of the world was meant to be taken seriously or not. There is, after all, a long trial sequence in heaven with Vincent Price as the devil pleading for the destruction of the human race. Had he presented his case somewhat later, he could have used this wretched film as a prime piece of evidence.

For Mr. Allen, this project may be seen as a useful warmup for his later contributions to the wonderful world of worst cinema, in particular his ever-popular classic *The Swarm*. (*See: The Most Badly Bumbled Bee Movie of All Time*.)

For Harpo, and for Sir Isaac Newton, *The Story of Mankind* is only a small, sad blot on their otherwise brilliant careers.

Jack Palance as Fidel Castro in *Che!* [1969]

Critic Leonard Maltin in his book *TV Movies* described *Che!* as "one of the biggest film jokes of the 1960's," but added: "You haven't lived until you see Palance play Fidel Castro." The choice of an actor known more for his high cheekbones than his expressive range seemed to go along with the casting of Omar Sharif in the title role as Che Guevara; with Palance as his co-star, Sharif faced no danger of being outclassed. In his most successful previous parts Mr. Palance had portrayed

a sneering gunfighter in *Shane*, and a punch-drunk fighter in TV's classic production of *Requiem for a Heavyweight*. In rendering Castro for the multitudes, the innovative star seemed to combine elements of both these previous triumphs.

Through it all, he showed an admirable concern for artistic integrity. During production of the film, *Time* magazine reported that Palance "asked for script changes reducing the 'buffoonery' of Castro as originally characterized." Judging from the finished product, the actor failed to get his wish.

After the film's release, critics unanimously panned Mr. Palance's mannered impersonation of the Cuban leader. *New Films* declared: "As Castro, Jack Palance sporting a fake nose, outsize glasses, and a cigar, comes off as a bit of a fuddy-duddy revolutionist, sounding oddly like someone impersonating Jimmy Cagney." Francis O. Beerman reported in *Film and TV Daily* that "Palance's style is not always a happy one and most of his acting is accomplished by squinting his eyes and gesturing with his hand. He also chomps a pretty fervent cigar." Tom Ramage, in *Boston After Dark*, decided to give the star the benefit of the doubt: "Palance's performance raises the possibility that his portrayal is meant as pure camp."

Shortly before Twentieth Century-Fox unleashed this cinematic Bay of Pigs on the unsuspecting public, Palance commented to the press: "If this picture is just an attempt to capitalize on the name of Guevara and make a lot of money, then it's criminal, and I'd be sorry to have been associated with it."

On this count, at least, he has no need to apologize. The $5-million project actually *lost* money and proved itself one of the more notable financial disasters in the studio's history.

Ginger Rogers as Dolley Madison in *Magnificent Doll* [1946]

According to Irving Stone, distinguished novelist and the screenwriter for *Magnificent Doll*, Dolley Madison single-handedly saved the presidency from the power-hungry Aaron Burr and so made America safe for Jeffersonian Democracy. This original thesis is supported by the casting of David Niven as the villainous Burr, Burgess Meredith as the level-headed James Madison, and Ginger Rogers as the Magnificent Dolley.

Magnificent? Well, Ms. Rogers plays a vivacious Quaker widow who runs a boarding house. Her star lodgers are Burr and Madison. Against this cozy backdrop of domestic intrigue our drama of early American politics slowly unfolds. Burr will not only lose the Presidency but finish second in the race for the lady. Or is it the other way around? Let's try again: Madison will triumph and win the lady and the Presidency. Or is it the other way around?

Part of the confusion is due to the script, which bears only the slightest resemblance to historical fact. Nor does the presence of Ginger Rogers contribute to the credibility of the tired melodrama. As Howard Barnes wrote in the *Herald Tribune:* "Miss Rogers was a bad choice for the central part. Neither in looks nor in temperament does she succeed in giving one the impression that she might be a Virginia Belle, forced into a Quaker marriage, early widowed and destined to be a President's wife." In *The New York Times*, Bosley Crowther reported: "In the role of the magnificent Dolley, Miss Rogers wears her Lilly Daché hats and her Vera West gowns with more attention than she seems to be giving her lines." She is a lovely lady, who dances divinely with Fred Astaire, but in this picture she is definitely out of step. Critic Alton Cook in the *World-Telegram* adequately summed it up. "Dolley Madison was one of the most intriguing figures of early American history," he wrote, "and it seems a shame to make a movie that will give unwary audiences an idea that she was anything like this Ginger Rogers creation. Above everything else, neither Mrs. Madison nor her career were dull."

John Wayne as Genghis Khan in *The Conqueror* [1955]

With his drooping Fu Manchu mustache, his greased yak's wool hairpiece and his crudely stenciled oriental eyebrows, John Wayne might also have qualified for The Most Ludicrous Racial Impersonation in Hollywood History, but we didn't want this one film dominating too many different positions in the

Hall of Shame. As the Scourge of Asia, the Duke spends more time subduing his red-haired, fair-skinned Tartar bride (Susan Hayward) than conquering the world. As the plot line begins to sag, a troupe of exotic dancing girls arrives on the scene, providing entertainment that combines the worst elements of a Las Vegas review and the half-time show at a high school football game. Sauntering through this low-grade chop suey in his classic Western stride, John Wayne makes no attempt to alter his familiar mannerisms in order to portray a twelfth-century Mongolian chieftain. "The Conqueror is a Western in some ways," he told the press. "The way the screenplay reads, it is a cowboy picture and that is how I am going to play Genghis Khan. I see him as a gunfighter." Historians might disagree—and critics might howl at Wayne's performance—but the picture did please the one person most concerned with its success: the producer Howard Hughes. The legendary billionaire personally supervised the production for his RKO Radio Pictures and found himself entranced by the results. Eventually, Hughes sold RKO and its more than 700 films for $25 million. A few years later he bought back just two of those films for some $12 million. The two he chose were *Jet Pilot* (another embarrassing John Wayne effort) and *The Conqueror*. On lonely evenings, the eccentric plutocrat showed the film over and over again, thrilling in glorious solitude to the familiar story of Genghis Khan. For reasons of his own, he refused to show his masterpiece on television—a decision that no doubt pleased John Wayne and all his loyal fans.

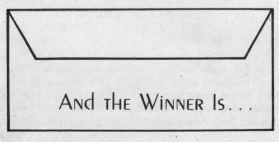

AND THE WINNER IS...

. . . John Wayne as Genghis Khan

Who came up with the brilliant idea of wasting John Wayne in this laughable role? The Duke himself deserves full credit.

Long before this picture got off the ground, he had committed himself to an RKO project with former actor Dick Powell directing. One afternoon, Wayne walked into Powell's office and happened to pick up a script that was lying around called *The Conqueror*. It was a case of love at first sight: the Duke immediately insisted that he had found the story he wanted to film.

For more than twenty years after its release, the resulting fiasco remained all but forgotten by everyone in the world except Howard Hughes and a handful of diehard bad-film devotees. Then suddenly in 1979, shortly after John Wayne's death, *The Conqueror* burst once more into the headlines. A number of researchers linked Wayne's fatal cancer—as well as the tragic illness suffered by several other principals on the project—to a radiation leak in the Utah desert near the place the battle scenes were filmed. This theory provided a heartbreaking footnote to a film which could stand as some sort of monument to Hollywood stupidity and bad taste.

The Worst Performance by a Politician

A NUMBER of Hollywood personalities—including Ronald Reagan, George Murphy, Helen Gahagan Douglas and Shirley Temple—have used their movie prominence as the basis for careers in politics. Since turnabout is supposed to be fair play, it is hardly surprising that a number of frustrated politicians have traveled in the opposite direction—attempting to leap from statecraft onto the silver screen. Their dreary record suggests that holding down even the most exalted public offices—such as the mayoralty of Riverside, California—is no guarantee of acting ability.

And the Nominees Are...

Julian Bond in *Greased Lightning* [1977]

For Julian Bond, the Georgia state legislator, the role of "Russell" in *Greased Lightning* should have been a piece of cake. He played a young lawyer and civil rights activist who labors to register black voters in the rural South. This character closely paralleled Bond's real-life activities in the sixties as a leader of the Student Non-Violent Coordinating Committee (SNCC). His awkwardness onscreen, however, teaches us once again that it is no simple matter to transmute life into art. To paraphrase the late Dorothy Parker, Mr. Bond's emotions as an actor run the gamut all the way from A to B. Someone seems to have taught him how to register astonishment by raising one eyebrow, so he resorts to that reaction again and again, even when it is totally inappropriate. Leading man Richard Pryor fares somewhat better as Wendell Scott, the first black driver

Julian Bond (holding his jacket) thrills to a stockcar race in Greased Lightning.

to earn a place on the national racing circuit, but his lively efforts are not enough to save this dismal, predictable Hollywood biography. At least the experience proved enlightening for Bond, who shared some of his profound discoveries with reporters who spoke with him during shooting. "There's a thin line between politics and theatricals," he observed. Unfortunately, that line did not turn out to be thin enough for Julian Bond to cross.

The Honorable Ben H. Lewis, Mayor of Riverside, California, in *Bug!* [1975]

Director William Castle, the genius of gimmickry who gave the world such startling new technologies as "Percepto" and "Emergo" (*See:* The Most Inane and Unwelcome Technical Advance in Hollywood History) decided to shoot his cockroach epic, *Bug!* in the pleasant desert city of Riverside, California. The film tells the heartwarming story of flying cockroaches who belch fire from their rear-ends and spell out threatening messages with their bodies in the manner of a Super Bowl half-time show. The residents of Riverside were so deeply honored that this distinguished production had chosen their community as its location that many of the townsfolk wanted parts in the film. One aspiring thespian who made his screen debut in this fashion was the ebullient Ben Lewis, mayor of the town. His participation in the project helped to insure full cooperation from the city government as Castle merrily staged his glorified insecticide commercial in Riverside and its environs. It is not known whether Mayor Lewis hired an acting coach to prepare him for his brief moment of glory in the film, but one clever exchange between neophyte actor and veteran director has been preserved in the publicity material released with the movie:

"I imagine the movies, like politics, are a fascinating business," the mayor wittily observed one day during filming.

"And precarious," added director Castle. "You're only as good as your last picture."

"Same thing goes for politics," chirped his honor, "where you're only as good as your last election!"

Thanks to outstanding civic cooperation, the filmmakers finished their work in short order and quickly returned to Tinseltown. In the months that followed, Riverside awaited the film's release in a fever of excitement. At *Bug!*'s debut, however, many local residents noticed that something had gone terribly wrong; all the scenes featuring their beloved mayor had been cut from the final version of the film. Apparently, some painful sacrifices had to be made for the sake of cinematic art, and Mr. Lewis's bravura performance was held to be expendable. Well, Ben, that's show biz...If you wait patiently for twenty years or so they're bound to shoot another film in Riverside.

John V. Lindsay in *Rosebud* [1975]

During his years as a U.S. Congressman and two-term Mayor of New York, John Lindsay provided a favorite subject for columnists and pundits who wrote endlessly of his "charisma" and "star quality." Surely, the man who advanced the hilarious "Fun City" concept during some of the darkest days of Gotham history had the makings of a flamboyant actor. Though his overall performance as mayor had garnered decidedly mixed reviews, a number of experienced observers considered the slim, handsome aristocrat to be a hot Hollywood property. Director Otto Preminger, for one, felt he had achieved a major coup when he signed Lindsay for a substantial part in the forthcoming action spectacular, *Rosebud*. The plot of the movie concerned a band of Palestinian terrorists, so desperate that they don't even have time to shave. These baddies kidnap a group of rich teenage girls onboard a yacht. One of the girls is the daughter of an influential U.S. Senator. Now: which of these parts do you think John Lindsay played? A Palestinian terrorist? A spoiled teenage girl? A luxury yacht? Aw, come on, you knew the answer all the time—they cast Big John as the worried U.S. Senator. Unfortunately, Lindsay handles the demands of the part about as successfully as he negotiated contracts with New York City employees. He moves with the

John Lindsay tries (in vain) to take acting lessons from his co-star Peter O'Toole in Rosebud.

natural grace of the Tin Man of Oz and speaks with the easy spontaneity of Walt Disney's electronic effigy of Abe Lincoln. Like Julian Bond, he seems to have mastered only one facial expression, but in Lindsay's case it's a troubled, brow-furrowed look, supplemented by one emphatic gesture: the pounding of a fist into a palm. Lindsay repeats this motion so awkwardly and so often that we suspect he is trying to crack a particularly stubborn walnut. Fortunately, Lindsay's on-screen virtuosity blends in perfectly with the rest of the film. As John Barbour of *Los Angeles* magazine enthused after *Rosebud*'s release: "I thought *At Long Last Love (See:* The Worst Musical Extravaganza in Hollywood History) was as bad a film as I'd ever seen; but then here comes this turkey. Otto Preminger has turned the tragedy of the Middle East into an asinine travesty even Tom Laughlin wouldn't have a kind word for." *Time* magazine's Richard Schickel singled out Lindsay's debut for special commendation, and discovered an admirable consistency in the man's career: "John V. Lindsay plays a U.S. Senator pretty much as he played being mayor of New York City—like a B-picture leading man."

Leon Trotsky in *My Official Wife* [1916]

In preparing a World War I spy melodrama called *My Official Wife*, the Vitagraph studio in New York hired emigré director Emil Vester to provide some authentic Russian atmosphere. One crucial sequence depicted a band of embittered revolutionaries gathered in a basement meeting place, and Vester decided to use authentic "nihilist types" as his extras in this scene. To recruit these bearded bombers, the filmmakers simply walked into a Second Avenue café and offered its habitués $5 a day for their work in a feature film. Among the volunteers who jumped at the chance for a screen appearance was the revolutionary leader Leon Trotsky. He had spent nearly a year in forced exile in New York editing the Russian language journal *Novy Mir* (New World) and the job with Vitagraph offered a welcome supplement to his meager salary. Reportedly, Trotsky overacted in his big scene, mugging at the camera and glowering ferociously at his associates. Fortunately, he did not have a speaking role since *My Official Wife* was a silent picture.

Leon Trotsky overacts shamelessly as a revolutionary nihilist in My Official Wife (1916).

In the best Hollywood tradition, the hopeful star changed his name for the purpose of his movie career. His real name—before he had even taken the alias of "Trotsky"—had been Lev Davidovich Bronstein. He now shortened that original surname to appear on the studio roster as "Mr. Brown." A few months after filming his debut, Trotsky had to cut short his promising career to return to Russia as a leader of the revolution. The movie people never forgave him for this unconscionable desertion. Some sixty years later, the film industry avenged itself by bringing out a revolting bomb based very loosely on episodes in Trotsky's life and called it appropriately enough, *The Assassination of Trotsky*. To play the part of the one-time Vitagraph extra, Joe Losey cast Richard Burton (*See:* Life Achievements Awards: The Worst Actor of All Time). Now, talk about overacting . . .

And the Winner Is. . . .

... John Lindsay in *Rosebud*

Since inspiring the gratitude of all New Yorkers by his retirement from the mayor's office, Lindsay has tried his hand at a number of alternative professions including novelist, Presidential hopeful, sportscaster, talk-show regular, and movie star. Concerning the last named career, it is worth recalling the inspired words of William Castle as addressed to Riverside's plucky Ben Lewis: "You're only as good as your last picture."

Only as good as *Rosebud?*

While Mr. Lindsay waits for his next movie role, we had best move on to another subject. Having explored Hollywood's unhappy adventures with working politicians, it is time to examine other peculiar forms of life and their role in cinema history, as we proudly present the coveted award for...

The Worst Two-Headed Transplant Movie Ever Made

ON APRIL 12, 1959, a wire-service story reported that American surgeon Dr. David Gurewitz had witnessed bizarre transplanting operations in the Soviet Union. Among other useful achievements, the Russian doctors managed to graft a dog's head onto the body of another dog, creating a two-headed canine which thrived for several days. No explanation was offered as to the purpose of this experiment, or for Hollywood's subsequent fascination with the idea of two-headed transplants. Suffice it to say that the attempts of several producers to exploit the dramatic possibilities of this concept, have provided us with an enduring rebuttal to the argument that two heads are better than one.

And the Nominees Are . . .

The Incredible Two-Headed Transplant [1971]

What happens when the head of a vicious homicidal maniac is transplanted onto the enormous body of a drooling, mentally-retarded hulk? If you have ever sat awake at night with this haunting question gnawing at your innards, then this movie is for you. Bruce Dern is featured here as a ghoulish mad-scientist in a role that has even less to offer him than his previous turns in Grade Z motorcycle movies. The good doctor Dern shrieks, giggles, rolls his eyes, and creates a two-headed monster whose most attractive feature is its neatly pressed blue overalls. To

John Bloom and Albert Cole put their heads together for an intimate scene in The Incredible Two-Headed Transplant.

no one's surprise, the cunning homicidal head (Albert Cole) soon bullies the pathetic retarded head (John Bloom) and takes over all the flesh inside the overalls. Since that is not enough for him, he begins lusting after Dern's curvaceous wife (Pat Priest). The Mad Doctor is prepared to sacrifice everything for the Sake of Science, so he places his wife in a cage as an offering to the monster. The lady's virtue is rescued in the nick of time when a mine shaft conveniently collapses on the evil Dr. Dern, his aging assistant Max, and that Incredible Two-Headed Transplant Monster.

American International Pictures realized that the plot line of its new masterpiece was somewhat "thin," so they decided to beef up the film's appeal with cameo appearances by some third-rate media personalities. The ineffable Casey Kasem, America's most widely syndicated disc jockey, played one of Bruce Dern's sane, one-headed friends. The late Larry Vincent, known to millions as "Seymour," the caped host of late-night horror films on TV, showed up as Dern's gardener.

When the film was released the *Hollywood Reporter* proudly declared "the acting is on the high school level" but neglected to mention that the special-effects department had not yet graduated from kindergarten. For the most part, it seems that the two-headed effect was simulated by asking Albert Cole to walk directly behind John Bloom while sticking his head over Bloom's left shoulder. Advertisements for this saga warned that "ONE WANTS TO LOVE! ONE WANTS TO KILL!" without revealing that members of most audiences, after seeing the film, will all want to kill. The entire production is perhaps best summed up by the title of the stirring theme song used on the soundtrack: "It's Incredible!"

The Manster:
Half Man And Half Monster[1962]

The combined filmmaking forces of Japan and the United States pooled their talents and resources to produce this feature—which set back the cause of international understanding by at

The Manster emerges from its lair to threaten Japanese-American co-operation.

least five years. A nefarious Japanese chemist (Satoshi Nak-amura) develops a powerful serum that causes its user to sprout an extra head. An overly-curious New York newspaperman (Peter Dyneley) stumbles into the mad doctor's laboratory and wins the privilege of becoming guinea-pig-of-the-month. While his wife and editor scream in horror, and the audience yawns in boredom, this mild-mannered journalist is transformed into a "manster." This new look for the Fall features two beastly noggins, each one with its own set of furry eyebrows and crooked teeth. It is apparently a well-known law of nature that all two-headed monsters develop homicidal tendencies, and our hard-boiled reporter with the double nose for news is no ex-ception. After the normal quota of bloody mishaps, our fun-loving manster and his evil creator are destroyed in the crater of an erupting volcano. According to the credits, this film was directed by George P. Breakston *and* Kenneth G. Crane, but it is not known whether this team represented the industry's first two-headed director.

The Thing with Two Heads
(Alternate Titles: *Beast with Two Heads*
and *The Man with Two Heads)* [1972]

One of the most famous "message" pictures of the 1950s, *The Defiant Ones*, featured Tony Curtis and Sidney Poitier as two escaped convicts bound together by an unbreakable chain. It made a powerful statement about racial relations and the way blacks and whites are stuck with one another, like it or not. *The Thing with Two Heads* carries the same idea one step further: what if the proud black and the white bigot are not merely chained together, but are forced to share the same body? Following its "success" with *The Incredible Two-Headed*

The Thing with Two Heads shares an intimate evening with its girl-friend, Chelsea Brown.

Transplant, American International Pictures decided that this premise would provide the perfect excuse for yet another cinematic double-header.

Ray Milland plays a brilliant doctor who is suffering from terminal cancer and harbors a pathological hatred for blacks. Since he is a pioneer in the technology of brain transplantation, he has decided to trade in his disease-ridden body for a healthy, robust, up-to-date non-cancerous model. The only problem involves his color preferences for this spiffy new corpus—ivory white, antique white, off white, or at worst, hot pink, are his favorites but none of them seem to be available on the show-room floor. At death's door, the doctors goes under anesthetic and hopes for the best. As it turns out the only resting place that can be found for his severed head is the brawny bull-neck of former pro-footballer Rosey Grier. Grier plays a hulking black convict who has been unjustly condemned to die and who submits to this bizarre experiment as a means of saving his... uh... head. When Milland comes round after the operation, imagine his surprise to discover that he has suddenly developed a natural sense of rhythm. Though he plans to kill off Grier's head and to later have it surgically removed, he is still less than thrilled at riding along aboard those broad black shoulders. After all, how will it look on the beach to see a dark body with a pale, light-skinned face? People might think that the doctor had been wearing his bathing trunks over his head.

Rosey Grier takes advantage of all this confusion by grabbing a gun from the police guard who has been assigned to the hospital bed. He makes a break for freedom, but his reunion with his girlfriend (Chelsea Brown) is spoiled by the prying eyes of that other head on his shoulders. The police are in hot pursuit anyway. As the pressbook for the film eloquently describes what follows: "The chase now becomes a mad melee of narrow escapes, screeching rubber, flying dust and tortured metal as motorcyclists scatter before the ghastly apparition on wheels of the two-headed body and squad cars crash and pound across the hills in pursuit of the fugitives."

At long last, Milland decides to make a citizen's arrest: he takes control of the body and socks his other half in the jaw, knocking him out. Watching Rosey Grier deliver a vicious right hook to his own jaw is one of the unquestioned highlights of the film. With the black head unconscious, our white, honky doctor now runs to his laboratory to prepare his surgical tools for removing that unwanted growth on his neck.... Just as he is about to make the incision, Rosey's long-suffering girlfriend arrives with a clean-cut young black doctor in tow. These two help the Big Man regain control of his own body and it is the white head that is neatly detached, then attached to a life-support system. Rosey and his girlfriend ride off into the sunset while the mad doctor, or what's left of him, grumbles and snarls as he begins the search for another body. Any volunteers?

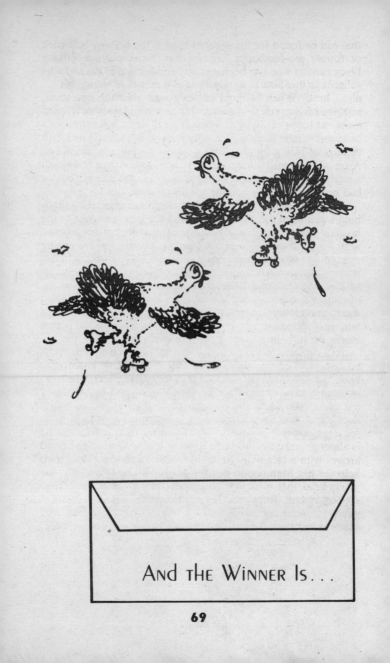

And the Winner Is . . .

... The Thing
With Two Heads

The producers of this one were more confused than any imaginable two-headed monster. They couldn't decide whether they were making a serious statement about racial prejudice, a horror science-fiction film, a motorcycle yarn, or an action-escape-adventure saga. When they saw the finished product they realized they could only advertise it as a comedy, with special appeal to the blaxploitation market. The tag line read—"The doctor blew it—He transplanted a WHITE BIGOT'S HEAD on a SOUL BROTHER'S BODY! Man, they're really in deeeeep trouble!" American International found itself in such deeeep trouble when it came to marketing the film that it recommended that local theater owners try various ingenious promotional gimmicks, such as framing "a large ear of corn which has two big bites out of it and post with the caption stating: BITTEN BY 'THE THING WITH TWO HEADS.'" The distributor further suggested that two football helmets be sewn together as specially designed for The Thing with Two Heads, with the hope that this reminder of Rosey Grier's record as a football player would help the public to forget his prowess as an actor. Not even a reference to his later and most distinguished career, as a master of needlepoint, could have saved this picture.

The Worst Rodent Movie of All Time

A RODENT is a gnawing mammal, small to medium in size, such as a rat, mouse, chinchilla, chipmunk, guinea pig, squirrel, porcupine or beaver. There are 2,000 species within the order Rodentia—more variety than in any other order of mammals. Rodents are accordingly well represented as the subjects of thoroughly wretched motion pictures. There is something about these furry little critters that has inspired the absolute worst in a number of imaginative filmmakers.

For the purposes of this book, we have broadened the strictly scientific definition of "rodent" to include some members of the order Insectivora—such as moles and shrews—who bear a certain resemblance to their mousey colleagues. We hope that this liberty will not offend zoological purists. There is also heated controversy as to whether rabbits and hares should properly be classified as rodents, but here we side with those who seek to have them admitted into the distinguished rodent family.

Before introducing the astonishing nominees in this category, a few other notable rodent films deserve brief recognition. These include Willard *and* Ben, *two recent dramas about hordes of trained, man-eating rats; Joan Rivers's comedy* Rabbit Test; *and an offbeat porno film called* Pray for Rosemary's Beaver. *In many another category these films would have been bad enough for selection as full nominees but here, with the competition particularly fierce among our little gnawing mammals, they rate only a dis-honorable mention. Only the very worst—the undisputed dregs—can compete for this coveted honor.*

And the Nominees Are...

A giant rat attacks dog-food magnate Ralph Meeker in The Food of the Gods.

The Food of the Gods [1976]

Producer Bert I. (*Attack of the Puppet People*) Gordon noted the popularity of films like *Willard* and *Ben*, dealing with packs of deadly killer rats, and went on to enlarge the original concept: what if the rodents in question were four feet high? *The Food of the Gods*, based (very loosely) on "a portion" of H. G. Wells' novel, attempts to answer that question.

On a secluded island in British Columbia, a farmer and his wife (John McLiam and Ida Lupino) discover a mysterious white substance that looks like vanilla custard. Without thinking twice, these hayseeds feed the goop to their barnyard animals and, SHAZAM!, the farm is suddenly invaded by giant rubber worms, a huge rooster head, hawk-sized wasps, and enormous rats. Ms. Lupino, who obviously subscribes to the theory that Big is Beautiful, decides that these unexpected

72

guests are blessings from God. McLiam then names the psychedelic custard "Food of the Gods" and stores it in jars labled "F.O.T.G." just in case anyone has forgotten the film's title.

The plot thickens with the presence of a football star (Marjoe Gortner) who is visiting the island with his two buddies on a deer-hunting expedition; little do they know they can get in some giant rat-hunting on the same trip. Throw in an hysterical pregnant woman and her husband for good measure, add a pinch of Ralph Meeker as a dog-food manufacturer who hopes to make money from "F.O.T.G.," include a teaspoonful of Pamela Franklin as his sex-interest scientist assistant and, voilà!—you have Le Royal Mess de Bertrand Gordon. The heroic Marjoe rescues the few survivors at the end but somehow, that mysterious muck "F.O.T.G." finds its way onto the counters of a food chain. The last shot of the movie shows an unwitting child happily slurping away at a glass of contaminated milk.

And as we say a fond farewell to our enchanted isle of robust rodents, let us linger for a few brief moments to savor one of this film's genuine distinctions: its dialogue. At a particularly touching moment, as they are about to be devoured by the rampaging rats, Pamela Franklin breathily confesses to Marjoe Gortner: "This may sound crazy to you, but I want you to make love to me." In another, less intimate setting, Ms. Franklin conducts the following exchange with Ralph Meeker:

PAMELA: I think you're the most selfish man in the world!

RALPH: So why do you work for me?

PAMELA: Because jobs for Lady Bacteriologists are not easy to find!

If she has a tough time finding work, imagine what it's like for the poor people who wrote, directed and produced this film?

The Killer Shrews [1959]

What, precisely, is a "killer shrew"? The script explains that it is a mutant created when some bumbling scientists attempt genetic experiments on "the flesh-eating Blarina Shrew." Actually, these furry little fiends have their chromosomal structure

A ferocious collie with artificial fangs plays the title role in The Killer Shrews.

so radically altered that they wind up looking like mangy collies that have been fitted with Halloween masks. This cleverly devised "special effect" fooled absolutely no one: virtually every review of this film mentions that the vicious shrews are portrayed by tail-wagging canines.

The hapless geneticists who created these horrifying creatures are working to solve "the worldwide population problem" at a remote laboratory. No, they do not suggest man-eating shrews as an interim solution—they are simply trying to teach the quickly reproducing little buggers how to use modern birth-control techniques. During their experiments, they make several profound scientific statements, such as: "There is an extremely high content in the shrew's saliva!" A young charter-boat captain (James Best, star of Jerry Lewis's abysmal *Three on a Couch*, who is here groomed to resemble Elvis Presley) arrives to deliver some goods, but decides to stay when he "gets a load" of one of those hot scientists. This lady zoologist (apparently, they are easier to place than Lady Bacteriologists) is a voluptuous Swede played by Ingrid Goude, Miss Universe of 1957. On this point the casting seems particularly puzzling, as the buxom blonde *shikseh* is supposed to play the daughter of Yiddish-accented Baruch Lumet (the actor-father of director Sidney Lumet).

In any event, before we have time to ponder these problems, the shrews get out of hand. They begin surrounding the laboratory and attempt to burrow holes under the walls so everyone gets a good long look at their "horrifying" faces and ridiculous porcelain fangs. It looks as if Best, Goude and Lumet are going to be eaten alive; as if this weren't bad enough, it's raining outside so that all of Ms. Goude's laundry is undoubtedly getting soaked. Finally, Lumet and Best devise a "human tank" to help them escape a fate worse than death. (Don't snicker—it's no fun being chewed to death by a dog wearing a mask.) This life-saving technological innovation consists of a number of empty barrels tied together. Each one of the brave survivors inhabits one of the barrels and they crawl away in unison until they've escaped the shrews. Since the killer shrews can't get at their human snacks through the metal barrels, the monsters decide to eat each other. The immortal last line of the film is uttered by James Best, while kissing Ingrid Goude. As our manly hero declares to his aging scientist, father-in-law to be: "You know something, Doctor, I'm not going to worry about overpopulation just yet."

One of the Mole People enjoys a delectable human snack.

The Mole People [1956]

Written by a gentleman named Laszlo Gorog, this Universal-
International feature was paired on double bills with the Beverly
Garland clunker, *Curucu, Beast of the Amazon* (in which the
title monster turned out to be a frustrated native in a gorilla
suit). *Cue* magazine raved: "Science fiction in *Curucu* and *The
Mole People* reaches its lowest common denominator—which
is to say, approximately age six and a half." The story concerns
a pair of enterprising archaeologists (John Agar and Hugh Beau-
mont) who are looking for a lost underground civilization in
the Himalayas. As they burrow their merry way through an
underground tunnel, an earthquake upsets their plans and causes
them to tumble all the way down to the lost city of Sumeria.
This plastic metropolis is ruled by a solemn albino named Elinu
(Alan Napier—Batman's butler on the popular TV show). As
it turns out, Elinu is not the only albino in town—all of the

locals are shrouded in thick layers of chalk in a futile attempt to make them look like grown-up descendants of Casper the Friendly Ghost. Unfortunately for our intrepid archaeologists, the entire city boasts only one curvaceous albino-ette (and she seems to have been sneaking some sun on the side). Since all of the inhabitants of Sumeria (except the girl, Cynthia Patrick) are bald and irritable, they sentence their hairy, jolly visitors to death. As the *Los Angeles Times* reports on the rest of the action: "Things are pretty nip and tuck until Agar defeats the whitewashed villains with—and you don't have to believe this if you don't want to—a flashlight. Like the story line, the Albinos can't stand much illumination."

So where do the Mole People come in? They are the monstrous servants of the Albino People—they carry out most of the killing for them and can't protest since each Mole Person is mute. They don't look much like moles—or even like killer shrews—but then again, we're supposed to suspend disbelief, right? The huge saucer-like peepers of these pointy-headed creatures could hardly be further from the tiny slit-eyes nature provided for real moles, but the imaginative costume designer decided he likes it better this way. John Agar resolves to use these unfortunates in planning his escape, and so rallies this oppressed minority to rebel against their imperious masters. The revolution is in full swing when an enormous earthquake (another one?) ends all the fun, destroys the evil civilization and thrusts our two adventurers through a hole in the earth's surface. They blink at the sunlight, astonished at their deliverance, and are deeply grateful (as is the audience) that the long ordeal is over.

The Nasty Rabbit [1965]

A Russian master spy (Mischa Terr) arrives in the United States onboard a top-secret nuclear submarine. He is dressed as a cowboy and accompanies a talking rabbit that wears a vial of lethal bacteria around its neck. When released, this rambunctious rodent is supposed to infect every citizen of America with some of its deadly serum. Our Russian No-goodnik is being watched by other spies from several countries, including Sweden's seductive Cecelia (Melissa Morgan), Japan's Colonel

Kobayashi (John Akana), Mexico's most formidable secret agent, Gonzales (Ray Vegas), Germany's Heinrich Krueger (Harold Bizzy), and Israel's Maxwell Stoppic (portrayed by a midget named Little Jack Little). Despite his diminutive stature, the "Israeli" easily offers the most offensive characterization in the film—he speaks in an American-Jewish—not Israeli— accent and offers several utterly tasteless jokes about Nazi extermination camps. Eventually, this "international cast" makes its way to a dude ranch, where the guests are entertained by rock-and-roll singer Arch Hall, Jr. This musician is so thoroughly and obviously without talent that one wonders, even on a film of this caliber, how he got the part. That question is answered by a glance at the credits: this film was produced by Fairway International, whose president, Arch Hall, Sr., had to find work for his unemployable son. (Lady Bacteriologists aren't the only ones who have a hard time.) In any event, the elder Arch Hall also wrote this script—such as it is—which calls for Junior to play the part of an FBI agent in addition to belting out his romantic ballad, "Jackie." In the end, young Arch manages to capture the nasty rabbit of the title and to deactivate his vicious vial of serum. In promoting the film in the trade papers, Arch Hall, Sr., invited the public to "See My Hare-Larious Tale Made for People of All Espion-Ages." *Variety* offered a suitable response, declaring the "Company which has stressed sex and violence in previous efforts turns to comedy with tragic results."

Night of the Lepus [1972]

Ads for this film proclaimed:

HOW MANY EYES
DOES HORROR HAVE?

HOW MANY TIMES
WILL TERROR STRIKE?

"They were born that tragic moment when Science made its Great mistake. . . . Now, from behind the shroud of night they come, a scuttling, shambling horde of creatures destroying all in their path."

78

Bumbling scientist Janet Leigh works with a laboratory rabbit in Night of the Lepus. *Little does she know that this harmless bunny will soon be transformed into a four-foot-high man-eater.*

What are they? Oversized cockroaches? Mutant lizards? Lady Bacteriologists? Well, guess again, because these particular creatures are gigantic, voracious, merciless, bloodthirsty, rampaging . . . rabbits.

Rabbits? That's right. "Lepus" is the Latin word for rabbit. Originally, the film was titled *Rabbits* but that was considered too prosaic. Another ad for this saga warned viewers of "The Terror of the Monster Rabbits—Out to Destroy Everything in their Path . . . They Multiply, They Weigh 150 pounds, They're Four Feet Tall—and They Kill . . . Dynamite Won't Stop the Hopping of these Giants."

Amazing as it seems, the producers have come up with the most ludicrous concept in cinema history (with the possible exception of Attack of the Killer Tomatoes—*See:* Worst Vegetable Movie of All Time), and they are 100 percent serious about it. This film was based on the novel *Year of the Angry Rabbit* by one Russell Braddon. *Night of the Lepus* tells the story of an Arizona rancher (Rory Calhoun) who uses cyanide to kill off the coyotes that have been menacing his stock. No sooner have the coyotes departed than his ranch is overrun by millions of hungry rabbits (mmm . . . must be an ecological lesson in there somewhere). This time he is reluctant to use poison, so he plans to bore the rodents to death by bringing in a husband and wife scientist team (Stuart Whitman and Janet Leigh). These dedicated experimenters plan to shoot the bunnies up with hormones and to stop them from doing what all rabbits do best—thereby protecting the film's PG rating and saving Rory's ranch at the same time. Unfortunately, their adorable little daughter (Melanie Fullerton) blows the whole project by taking a pet bunny injected with the experimental serum and releasing it on the prairie. Before long this single prolific mutant begins breeding a whole new strain of rabbits, more than four feet high and with a sweet tooth for Grade D actors. The man-eating hordes devour a truck driver, an old prospector, and various anonymous tourists before the national Guard and the Deputy Sheriff (in that order) arrive on the scene. This local lawman (Paul Fix) devises an ingenious method to destroy these pernicious pests: he rigs up a railway crossing with high-voltage electricity. If the dumb bunnies can be persuaded to walk across those deadly tracks, then quicker than you can say "What's Up, Doc?" the sweet smell of fried rabbit will pervade the prairie. The only problem is these heavy hares are smarter than they look: they decide that they prefer watching teenagers necking in a local drive-in to volunteering themselves for the world's largest platter of Welsh rarebit. The crafty Deputy Sheriff, however, outwits these marauding rodents by utilizing all the headlights of the cars in the drive-in to frighten the rabbits toward the ambush at the rail crossing. There, they are either burned to death or machine-gunned by National Guardsmen waiting for them at the other side, and civilization, as we know it, is saved once again.

Among this film's many delights is one of the most unintentionally hilarious lines ever spoken. As the heroic Sheriff attempts to warn the patrons of the drive-in of impending doom, he comes up, frantically shouting: "There's a herd of killer rabbits heading this way!" There are very few audiences that will be able to keep a straight face through that one. This movie does carry one important message that should be welcomed by true rodent fanciers everywhere: rabbits, even when photographed in slow motion close-ups to make them look huge and menacing, will inspire fear in absolutely no one.

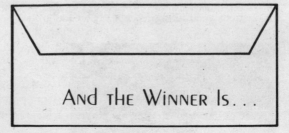

And the Winner Is...

... The Food of the Gods

This was a particularly tough decision, but after lengthy deliberations, we agreed to give the nod to F.O.T.G. in appreciation of its rare combination of ridiculous script, bad camera work, pretentious advertising, poor acting, nonexistent direction, and laughable special effects. On this project, producer Bert I. Gordon genuinely managed to put it all together. As Arthur Knight described the film in *The Hollywood Reporter:* "While normally a friend to man, I found myself surprisingly undistressed when the rodents consumed John McLiam . . . I was positively delighted when they finally got to Ralph Meeker . . . But most of all, I wished that these ugly mutants might have gotten to Bert Gordon. Not that it would have done much good. The process work is so crude that anyone over five could see that the wasps were animations, ths rooster a large-scale dummy, and the rodents were plain, ordinary rodents swarming around doll-sized Volkswagens, campers and cottages. *The Food of the Gods* is not only sick, but sickening."

Incidentally, it should be noted that all of Gordon's films deal with some sort of enlargement or shrinkage. In addition to this chilling tale of oversized rodents, Gordon gave us *The Amazing Colossal Man* (1957), which tells the story of a bald colonel who grows ten feet a day; *War of the Colossal Beast* (1958), which was its sequel; *Attack of the Puppet People* (1958), which concerns itself with the plight of shrinking men and women; *The Cyclops* (1957) about a Mexican He-Man who is turned into a murderous giant by radiation; and *The Magic Sword* (1962), which stars the celebrated screen giant Richard Kiel, who is best known as the character "Jaws" in the recent James Bond Films. According to vague rumors, Bert Gordon's most recent project describes the drama and heartbreak in the mysteriously shrinking job market for Lady Bacteriologists.

The Worst Performance by a Novelist

And the Nominees Are...

Jimmy Breslin in
If Ever I See You Again [1978]

Jimmy Breslin, author of such diverting volumes as *The Gang That Couldn't Shoot Straight* and *Can't Anybody Here Play This Game?* (the story of the New York Mets' first disastrous season), continued his quest for the perfect loser by appearing in this film.

If Ever I See You Again represented the ultimate in self-indulgence for Joe Brooks, the successful composer of TV commercial jingles who co-wrote, produced, directed, scored and starred in the film. His previous credits include the Academy Award winning song "You Light Up My Life." If Ever I See You Again amounts to little more than a 93-minute commercial for a new song, for which the title is taken. The story concerns itself with a character named Bob Morrison, a successful composer of TV commercial jingles who bears a remarkable resemblance to Joe Brooks and is, in fact, played by him. Unhappy with his lack of creative freedom in developing the definitive dog-food song, Bob heads out to Hollywood to score a movie. While in California, he reestablishes contact with an old girlfriend played by Shelly Hack.

Where does Mr. Jimmy Breslin fit into this idyllic and wistful tale? He plays the part of Mario Marino, the central character's "Music contractor." Mario Marino—and a "con-

Jimmy Breslin requests another cheeseburger from Director, Co-star Joe Brooks in If I Ever See You Again.

tractor"? It sounds as if our friend Mario never gets any closer to the real music business than carrying a violin case. Breslin furthers this impression by playing the part in the best Chíco Marx style, full of broad gestures and wildly modulating speech patterns. To show that he means business, Jimmy appears to have gained forty pounds for this role and bears a certain resemblance to one of those huge, inflatable dummies in the Macy's Thanksgiving Day Parade. As it turns out, Mario/Breslin is actually a legitimate musician with a heart of gold inside all that protective flesh. His cute, alliterative Italian name is just one of Joe Brooks' clever little jokes. George Plimpton, another renowned writer who makes an appearance in the film (apparently Brooks had a hard time finding professional actors who would work for him), plays a character with a name problem that is even more severe. Plimpton's role is an advertising executive known as Laurence Lawrence. Or was that Lawrence Laurence?

In any event, as William Wolfe wrote in *Cue* magazine: "For the record, Jimmy Breslin was enticed away from his typewriter long enough to play Brooks' music contractor. I hope his job at the *Daily News* is secure."

Breslin himself observed: "Until Brooks came along, everybody saw me in the same role—a reporter who hangs around in saloons. Oddly enough, my boozing days are over; I'm now a teetotaler." But that was said before this movie was released.

Truman Capote in *Murder by Death* [1976]

In his innumerable talk-show appearances over the years, the irrepressible Truman Capote has shown small regard for thespian intelligence. Before making his dramatic debut in Neil Simon's *Murder by Death*, in fact, he once told a national audience: "Actors are stupid, but I'm not stupid..." At least he doesn't have to worry about contradicting himself, since his role in the film proves that he's no actor either.

Nonetheless, Capote prepared for his Hollywood excursion with some absolutely shameless bouts of self-promotion. "What

Truman Capote as eccentric millionaire Lionel Twain in Murder by Death.

Dom Perignon is to champagne, I am to acting," he told *People* magazine before beginning work on the film, but added, "You must realize that I happen to be a particularly good fan of mine." He turned out to be such a good fan that all he can offer the film is a second-rate imitation of himself. His cold-blooded, wispy-lispy approach couldn't even qualify as legitimate over-acting. It is merely a sideshow that distracts audience attention from a frequently entertaining film. Frankly, Paul Lynde does a far better Capote impression. As John Simon wrote in *New York* magazine: "Hitherto, I thought Zsa Zsa Gabor was unique among 'performers' in not even being able to play herself on screen; now Capote has snatched these sorry laurels from her."

In the movie, Capote plays the part of an eccentric millionaire named Lionel Twain who dresses outlandishly and has a peculiar speech impediment. The only missing detail is a penchant for sucking gas from helium-filled balloons, and it would be an absolutely made-to-order role. Furthermore, Mr. Twain invites the world's greatest detectives to his mansion to solve a murder which has not yet taken place—the murder of one of his guests. Anyone who has seen Capote in one of his late-night TV slots knows that he's still in character (assassinations, that is). How then could he fail?

The answer emerged in a totally uncharacteristic display of humility during a talk-show conversation (of course). "Just recently," the writer confessed, "I found out there was also something else I couldn't do—which was act."

At least he might have expressed it more elegantly. How about: What Boone's Farm Apple Wine is to Chateau de Rothschild 1967, Truman Capote is to acting . . . ?

Norman Mailer in *Wild 90* [1967]

The limitations that Truman Capote now recognizes in himself have no place whatever in the self-confident universe of Norman Mailer. This is the same man who once picked a public fight with a professional boxer in order to demonstrate his pugilistic prowess and came out, despite black eye and badly battered face, insisting that he won. With an ego of these epic proportions, Mailer felt no hesitation in taking on the Hollywood establishment and showing those losers once and for all how a truly "artistic" movie ought to be made.

Norman Mailer reviews fan mail for his remarkable performance in Wild 90.

In his first "film," which he funded himself à la Francis Ford Coppola (and, please, the comparison ends there), he spared every expense in his efforts to bring the public an unquestioned masterpiece. His total budget came to an incredible $1,600, but he undoubtedly spent more than that in his subsequent attempts to distribute the film to art theaters across the country. His finished product is a grainy, barely audible strip of celluloid, which features Mailer, two nonactor drinking buddies and an assortment of extras sitting and walking around (but mostly sitting) in a Brooklyn warehouse for 90 minutes. Ergo, the title, *Wild 90*, although 90 minutes in any Brooklyn warehouse, particularly if you're cooped up with Norman Mailer, can seem like an eternity. Wild it isn't, but the producer-director-star needed a better title than the original, *The Maf Boys*.

The story—such as it is—concerns itself with three hoodlums who are planning their next job. Mailer plays the part of "The Prince" who is the recognized leader of this fearsome crew. Most viewers have found the film to be utterly pointless, but one prominent writer in *Esquire* magazine saw it as a priceless cinematic gem. That writer was (surprise!) Norman Mailer, posing as a coolly objective critic of his own work. "The dialogue was sensational," he modestly reported, and then went on to quote several examples.

> BUZZ CAMEO: I ain't gonna get killed here.
>
> THE PRINCE: Look. You're gonna get killed, or you're not gonna get killed. But you don't know shit. You don't know when you're gonna get killed or how you're gonna get killed, and just shut. Shut.

Or, how about:

> BUZZ CAMEO: I'm goin' down to the beach.
>
> TWENTY YEARS: (to Cameo): Ya know there's one thing about singin'—it leaves ya hoarse.
>
> THE PRINCE (to Cameo): If you leave, ya know what you are? You're the prunes.
>
> BUZZ CAMEO: Prunes? You're the dunes.
>
> THE PRINCE: Yeh. You're the real prunes.

"Yes, where was the scriptwriter?" Mailer asks. "Where was he? And the answer is that no hat could fit his head, for he did not exist. The dialogue had come out of the native wit of the actors."

When Mailer speaks of "native wit" we suspect he is referring to aborigines. For during the course of those "wild" 90 minutes, according to *Newsweek,* "Norman belches, yawns, kicks a crate, brushes his hair, shoots off his mouth constantly, swills Bourbon, barks at a barking German Shepherd until the poor dog backs down." Surprisingly enough, this glorified home movie received reviews in several national publications. Not surprisingly, the content of those reviews turned out to be thoroughly negative. As Stanley Kaufman summed up the situation in *The New Republic:* "I cannot say that Mailer was drunk the whole time he was on camera. I can only *hope* that he was drunk."

Erich Segal in
Without Apparent Motive [1972]

Erich Segal is best known to bad movie buffs as the author of two novels (*Love Story* and *Oliver's Story*) which provided the basis for saccharine screen adaptations. Less celebrated, but equally worthy of attention, are his special contributions as an actor.

In 1972, near the height of his novelistic success, this former Classics professor showed off his linguistic prowess by appearing in a French language murder mystery. The film's title, *Without Apparent Motive*, adequately describes the decision to cast Segal in a pivotal role.

The story is a rather standard multiple-killing murder mystery, with Jean-Louis Trintignant playing Humphrey Bogart playing Sam Spade. Segal plays Hans Kleinberg, a character described in the pressbook as "an offbeat astrologer connected somehow with the victims." Unfortunately, offbeat isn't the same as offscreen, and consequently one of the victims is the movie itself. Apparently, the only qualification Segal needed for his part was an ability to speak French. But mastering the French tongue isn't the same as being French, nor is it the same as being an actor, as proven by Linda Lovelace not long

Erich Segal plays a corpse in his most convincing moment in Without Apparent Motive.

ago. Gary Giddins commented in *The Hollywood Reporter:* "Erich Segal, with his arms flapping and eyes bulging in a vapid impersonation of what he thinks Frenchmen are like, is awful." Fortunately, he is felled by an assassin's bullet before he gets too much of a chance to act. Hopefully, he'll stay down. Love may mean never having to say you're sorry, but Segal owes plenty of apologies for his eminently lamentable screen debut.

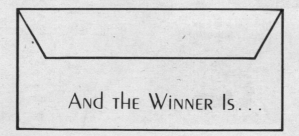

AND THE WINNER IS. . .

... NORMAN MAILER
IN *Wild 90*

Mr. Mailer unquestionably deserves The Bird because he takes himself so much more seriously than the other nominees. His novelist-actor colleagues also knew when to quit (namely, after a single screen appearance) but Norman went on to two other cinematic triumphs. These additional films—*Beyond the Law* (1968) and *Maidstone* (1970)—continued the noble tradition begun in *Wild 90*. All action onscreen is totally improvised; plot and direction are virtually nonexistent. *Maidstone*, a film about a highly unconventional candidate for President of the United States (played by Norman Mailer, naturally), featured a particularly noteworthy conclusion. Actor Rip Torn, who took part in this fiasco, suddenly lost his temper at Mailer and jumps at the director-star with a hammer. The camera duly records this attack, as well as Mailer's response, which was to bite Torn's ear until he drew blood. Fortunately, this wound did not amount to a permanent mutilation, or else Torn might have become a candidate in our next category...

The P. T. Barnum Award for the Worst Cinematic Exploitation of a Physical Deformity

IN 1932, Tod Browning directed the film Freaks—*a brutal view of life in a circus sideshow. The use of reallife "freaks" in all of the key roles gave the movie a sense of conviction and immediacy that horrified contemporary audiences. Reactions to the film were so strong, in fact, that British authorities banned it in the United Kingdom for nearly thirty years.*

It is highly ironic that many other films that trivialize human deformities are shown everywhere without protest. These movies have no power to produce either horror or pity. They represent the worst kind of cinematic exploitation and can inspire only disgust in a sensitive viewer.

And the Nominees Are...

The Brute Man [1946]

This is the last in a series of films about "The Creeper"—a horribly deformed behemoth who flies into a rage and strangles his victims because they scream in horror at his face. The police seem powerless to solve these crimes, until they make use of a blind girl (Jane Adams) who has befriended the monster because she is unable to see his fearsome physiognomy.

The film stars Rondo Hatton, a remarkable Hollywood personality whose real-life story would have made a far more

Rondo Hatton (right), "The Ugliest Man in Pictures," plays the title role in The Brute Man.

compelling film than the tawdry thriller enacted here. Hatton, "The Creeper," featured in more than 100 films, was a tragic victim of acromegaly, a rare disease which causes enlargement of the bones of the head. Known as "The Ugliest Man in Pictures," Rondo as a young man was twice voted the most handsome boy in his high school class at Hillsborough, Florida. Later, he was named captain of the University of Florida football team, though he weighed just 136 pounds.

Then came World War I and he was gassed on the Western front. That was the presumed cause of the disease that put him in the hospital for 10 out of the next 28 years. The size of his face bones doubled. His weight went to 204 pounds with the gain coming from extra cartilage in the face, feet and hands. It required several operations and four sets of teeth before he could chew. His cheekbones were surgically removed and replaced by metal braces. For several years he was blind and the pain was like a migraine all over his body.

When he first came home from the hospital after his disease, his parents didn't recognize him. Former girlfriends would cross the street when they saw him for fear he'd ask them for a date. So Hatton retreated from the world into hospitals, lying in bed for years and feeling sorry for himself. Finally, he resolved to change his life and take his fate into his own hands. "In a veteran's hospital," he recalled, "you see so many guys so much worse off than you are that . . . well, if there's anything left in you, you quit feeling sorry for yourself."

Determined to return to normal life, Rondo got a job as a sports reporter in Tampa. That's where he met his wife, May, a woman of great natural beauty. She'd been married once before to a very handsome man and had learned the hard way that you can't judge character by physical appearance.

In 1938 his condition took a turn for the worse, and the doctors recommended that he try the dry climate of Southern California. For a time, the deterioration of the bones in his feet left him so badly crippled that he couldn't walk. While lying in the Los Angeles V.A. hospital without a job, he first conceived the idea of letting Hollywood exploit his terrible face. He initially played bit parts and made little impression, since audiences automatically assumed that his appearance had been created by gifted makeup artists. Finally, after playing The Creeper in Universal's *House of Horror*, Rondo made it to the big-time. With Boris Karloff leaving the studio, Universal needed a replacement horror star. They signed Hatton to a seven-year contract and began a huge publicity buildup. This studio drum-beating presented Hatton as a born monster, "a freak of nature," with little hint at the suffering and heroism in his past. After all, if people knew the truth about Hatton they might have been forced to take him seriously as a human being, rather than simply gawking at him as an object of curiosity. *Brute Man* represented only Rondo's second film under his star contract, but it was also the last time he was to appear on the screen. Shortly after the movie's release, he died of a heart attack.

Chained for Life [1950]

Long ago, P. T. Barnum discovered that gullible Americans could be persuaded to part with their hard-earned dollars for even a brief peek at Chang and Eng, the original Siamese twins. The producers of this film obviously concluded that they could enjoy similar success by exhibiting a contemporary set of Siamese twins, Daisy and Violet Hilton, on the silver screen. They do indeed provide many glimpses of the two girls who are "chained for life," but offer very little in the way of plot, characterization or action. The story—about one sister being judged guilty of murder and her innocent twin having to face the consequences—is only a feeble excuse for this old-fashioned freak show. In addition to listening to the nontalented twins singing three bad songs, we are treated to trick sharpshooters, weird clowns on collapsing bicycles, a smiling accordianist named Tony Lovello, and a Roumanian gypsy who sits at a player piano and sings madly and passionately about nothing at all. Harry L. Fraser directed, based on the screenplay by Nat Tanchuk. They later joined forces for a sequel to *Chained for Life*, also starring the Hilton Sisters. It bore the intriguing title *Torn by the Knife*.

Little Cigars [1973]

The "Little Cigars" of the title rather crudely refers to five midget gangsters with a yen for a tall, busty blonde (Angel Tompkins). She is the former mistress of an underworld honcho who runs away from him and falls in with the mini-mob. With Angel as the sex interest, three of the midgets stage a medicine show while the other two rob cars. Gradually, the curvaceous Miss Tompkins inspires the little fellows to bigger things, including a cross-country crime spree. At one point she is caught during a supermarket robbery but is promptly rescued by her bitty-buddies. In one climactic scene, the midgets prove that height has nothing to do with stature by killing the two full-grown mobsters who are chasing their beloved den mother.

Out of gratitude, Angel starts an affair with the leader of the midgets (Billy Curtis) and persuades him to desert his pals. The two lovebirds run off with all of the gang's ill-gotten gains,

*Angel Tompkins and her
midget boyfriend, Billy Curtis,
in a touching love scene from
Little Cigars.*

and we suspect that Angel is only manipulating her paramour
for selfish reasons. But no! True love wins out: the other midgets catch up with the two of them, take the money back, and
Angel and Billy nonetheless ride off together toward the sunset,
materially poor but spiritually enriched by their touching romance.

For those who find midgets irresistibly "cute," and love
dirty jokes about small men mating with big, tall girls, this
film may have some appeal. But for the rest of us...well,
perhaps *Boxoffice* magazine, trying to be generous, summed
it up best in its review of *Little Cigars:* "Only limited appeal
to the curious. If properly exploited the film can really entertain
large audiences who certainly won't be overly familiar with the
sight of midgets committing assorted mayhem."

The Terror of Tiny Town [1938]

Once again, midgets are the victims here (Hey, come on fellas, pick on somebody your own size!), but this time they are definitely exploited in a big way. This musical Western was enthusiastically billed as the only film in Hollywood history with "an all-midget cast." This is not precisely accurate, since we do see one full-sized announcer at the beginning of the film just for the sake of comparison. "The Terror" described in the title is actually a bite-sized baddy named Haines (portrayed by the midget star, Little Billy), who incites a feud between two Western families so that he can take over both their ranches. The Hero (Billy Curtis—who later starred in *Little Cigars*) spends most of the film galloping around the countryside on-board a Shetland pony trying to spread goodwill between the potentially warring families. In the end, after numerous musical numbers and shoot-'em-ups, Billy Curtis succeeds in blowing up the evil Little Billy with a stick of dynamite. Before this inspired denouement, we are able to enjoy innumerable midgets walking under saloon doors, drinking from beer steins bigger than their heads, and chasing one another under—rather than around—the furniture. For good measure, a penguin wanders onto the set and waddles inexplicably through one scene. Perhaps the producers are attempting to give us The Bird. In the last analysis, the whole show is stolen by Nita Krebs, the Terror's gun moll, who is a barroom thrush with a breathy accent somewhere between Marlene Dietrich's and Boris Karloff's. She warbles out one sensuous ballad that begins, "Let's go way up on the hill/You can be Jack and I'll be Jill." Perhaps the torrid musicality of this midget mademoiselle might give contemporary producers the idea for an X-rated novelty item—but let's not get into that. The problem is that for even the most kinky viewers of this film, it becomes tiring after a while to watch the little people slamming into huge doors, riding horses the size of puppies, or falling backwards when they fire off their huge six-guns. We get the point after about three minutes and can only begin thinking of new possibilities for specialty horse operas. just imagine the sort of Western you could make *à la Tiny Town* if, instead of a troupe of midgets, you used a truckload of amputees, or what kind of showdown you could stage with an all-blind cast.

The leading lights from the all-midget cast in The Terror of Tiny Town *pose for a prerelease promotional still.*

And the Winner Is...

... The Terror of Tiny Town

This American classic has aged remarkably well: after 42 years it remains in a class by itself in terms of bizarre tastelessness. Like all great ideas, the concept for *Tiny Town* came to producer Jed Buell in a blinding flash. One afternoon a subordinate quipped to Buell, "If this economy drive keeps on, we'll be using midgets for actors," and the visionary producer immediately saw the potential in that suggestion. To realize his dream, Mr. Buell ran advertisements in newspapers around the country proclaiming, "Big Salaries for Little People." He collected midgets from every corner of the United States, using agencies, advertisements and radio broadcasts. A squad of fourteen midgets arrived from Hawaii. Eventually, he secured the services of some sixty midgets, averaging 3'8'' in height.

The film, which cost Buell just over $100,000 to produce, turned out to be a modest financial success, and the ambitious filmmaker naturally planned a sequel. On July 20, 1938, *Weekly Variety* ran the following news item:

PEE-WEES TO MAKE SERIES OF PICTURES
Sol Lesser has closed a deal with Jed Buell for a series of films using midget cast utilized in Buell's *Terror of Tiny Town*. Second picture to be started within thirty days will be based on lumber camp, with a grown-up heavy portraying mythical Paul Bunyan. Upon completetion of this one Buell is leaving for Europe to round up additional midgets for future productions.

Unfortunately for bad-film aficionados, these plans amounted to nothing, though the irrepressible Buell did persevere in making two more novelty Westerns: *Harlem on the Prairie (See:* The Worst Blaxploitation Movie Ever Made) and *Little Covered Wagons*, which featured a dozen dancing chimpanzees in the leading roles.

The Worst Musical Extravaganza in Hollywood History

THE FIRST talking motion picture—The Jazz Singer—was also the first movie musical. Since its release in 1927, Hollywood has been consistently fascinated by combinations of musical and dramatic entertainment. Gene Autry serenaded his horse, Allan Jones crooned for the Marx Brothers, and "tuneful interludes" turned up in the most unlikely and unwelcome places. It is only in the last two decades, however, that American moviegoers have been subjected to a steady diet of syrupy, overproduced, empty-headed multimillion dollar musical spectaculars. In many respects The Sound of Music *(1965) blazed a trail along this primrose path—making so much money for floundering Twentieth Century-Fox that it inspired a host of imitators. Many of the blockbuster songfests that followed were dull and poorly conceived, but even* Doctor Dolittle *(1967) and* Star! *(1968) look like high art when compared to the very worst of the overblown musical genre.*

And the Nominees Are...

At Long Last Love [1975]

Peter Bogdanovich wrote, produced and directed this $6-million excuse to showcase 16 vintage Cole Porter songs along with the dubious talents of the *auteur's* roommate, Cybill Shepherd. Bogdanovich, who had previously achieved box-office success with his conscientious tributes to old Hollywood forms *(Paper Moon, What's Up Doc?)* this time attempts to recapture

101

Eileen Brennan, Cybill Shepherd and Madeline Kahn dance away their troubles in At Long Last Love.

the charm of the Fred Astaire-Ginger Rogers musicals of the 1930s. The problem is that Burt Reynolds and Cybill Shepherd are not Astaire and Rogers. In fact, they are not even Marge and Gower Champion. What they are, in the words of Vincent Canby of *The New York Times*, are two stars "who have between them four left feet." Nor do the principals in this film demonstrate even the slightest singing ability, a situation that was only exacerbated by Bogdanovich's incomprehensible insistence on recording all his musical numbers live. This unusual process leaves his tone-deaf stars exposed to the world, without even the fig leaf of postproduction dubbing. In one memorable scene, as Cybill Shepherd "sings" "I Get a Kick Out of You," she waltzes herself around her living room and accidentally gets lost behind a curtain so that she has to beat her way out to get back to the camera's view. In another inane number, Cybill and Burt enjoy a midnight dip in an elegant pool, and can think of nothing better to do than to spit water at each other. Perhaps the best definition of the Bogdanovich version of subtle humor is provided by the knee-slapping sequence in which Reynolds, in his boxer shorts, inadvertently sprinkles shaving lotion in his eyes, causing him to stumble into the next-door room in which Shepherd, in curlers, is cosmetically applying cucumber slices to her face. An actor named Peter Dane, whose role as a cardsharp was cut from the final film, shared with us his tender recollections of this joyous production: "Nobody had recorded a live musical since the days of Aristophanes . . . We were stuck in a hotel room because Bogdanovich didn't know what to do with us. Cybill kept crying, 'The lights are so hot! I can't stand them!' during all her dance numbers."

The film proved such an unmitigated disaster after its release that Bogdanovich felt the need to apologize publicly. On January 30, 1976, he rented a page in *The Hollywood Reporter* to print an open letter addressed "To Whom It May Concern." In the text of this ad, he thanked his music and soundmen for "contributions that were unique technically and far beyond the call of duty." He went on to say: "All this was to prove the perhaps lame-brained theory of the director that musicals ought to be done entirely live. Whether he was right or wrong is beside the point." It is hard to disagree with this last statement; considering the vapidity of the script and the dull clumsiness of its stars, not even the dubbed voice of Marni Nixon could have possibly saved *At Long Last Love*.

Lost Horizon [1973]

Few films have been accompanied by more elaborate or misleading media hype than this sodden remake of the 1937 Frank Capra classic. As a public service, we offer a counterpoint, between the lines of one of the extravagant ads for the film, and supply down-to-earth descriptions of the wretched reality:

The Adventure of "Lost Horizon" is as breathless as it is spectacular . . . You are there in the awesome wilderness of the snows at the top of the world!

The sequences of actors trudging through enormous Himalayan snowdrifts were actually filmed in Bronson Canyon near Los Angeles, a favorite locale for the makers of low-budget sci-fi and Western films. In order to convert the dry, sandy California landscape into the icy peaks of Asia, the producers used tons of artificial snow, but failed to convince anyone at all. The special effects—even with a rented polar bear wandering aimlessly through the set—could hardly be more laughable. We have seen more convincing winter scenes in second-grade Christmas pageants.

The Excitement of "Lost Horizon" holds all your senses nerve-taut . . . the escape from the rebels and the airplane crash are spell-binding moments of entertainment!

The costumes of the aforementioned rebels could, according to film-critic Judith Crist, "kindly be called comic." To register their displeasure at the departing plane, these disgruntled extras—no doubt embarrassed by their plastic loincloths and bandoliers—shake their fists in the air like a chorus line of disco dancers.

The Beauty of "Lost Horizon" is a faraway wonderland of epic proportions, re-created with artistry and authenticity.

Even for the ambitious Ross Hunter, producer of this epic, it must have been a great challenge to reproduce the mythical Shangri-La with "authenticity." On what inspired vision did he base his architectural conception? Judging from the final set used in the film, Hunter was most likely looking at a Holiday Inn somewhere in Arizona at the time that he hit on the proper solution. All that is missing from this Himalayan "wonderland" is the putting green and the Olympic-sized pool. *Newsweek* suggested that this version of Shangri-La "resembles the valley of the Jolly Green Giant—a fitting showcase for a film that is so much spinach."

The Stars of "Lost Horizon" come through as colorful and real characters . . . the rich and vivid roles you will remember them for always!

And oh, how they wish we would forget! Charles Boyer (as the 210-year-old High Lama); John Gielgud (as Chang, his chief-of-staff); Peter Finch (as a painfully earnest American diplomat); and Sally Kellerman (as an aggressive, obnoxious *Newsweek* photographer) all embarrass themselves in this musical flopbuster. The worst fate, however, is reserved for Liv Ullman. She is offered here as Ross Hunter's answer to the Julie Andrews role in *The Sound of Music*. Playing a sweetsie-

Liv Ullmann, as a creative French teacher, leads her students in their daily lesson about the meaning of life in Lost Horizon.

neatsie French teacher, she is supposed to lead a crowd of adorable schoolchildren as they sing and dance their way into our hearts. Actually, these talentless urchins move their lips out of synchronization with the music and dance as if they had been recruited from a nursery-school play. Their inane production numbers—including a would-be show-stopper called "The World Is a Circle"—only make the situation worse. Wasting the talents of the luminously beautiful and prodigiously gifted Ms. Ullman on this sort of nonsense amounts to a criminal plundering of a great natural resource. Where's the Environmental Protection Agency when we really need them?

The Music of "Lost Horizon" lives and breathes freshness . . . The ten new Burt Bacharach-Hal David songs will make you dance with joy!

Various intense physical reactions have indeed been reported in response to the music of this film, but "dancing with joy" is not one of them. Bacharach's bouncy, monotonous score offers all the sparkling sophistication of the background music in a baby-food commercial. The inane lyrics, frequently straining to provide philosophical profundities, suggest a neurotic adolescent on twenty tabs of Seconal presenting with great intensity his hackneyed theories of cosmic consciousness. This is never more true than in the meaningful "Living Together, Growing Together" sequence, in which scores of Tibetan monks walk in slow procession with swinging teapots in front of them. The flavor of this unforgettable scene calls to mind an international yo-yo tournament convened with high solemnity in San Francisco's Chinatown.

Ross Hunter's musical production of "Lost Horizon" is backed by the strongest merchandising campaign in the history of the industry!

On this one point, at least, we will offer no argument. It is true that an enormous advertising and promotional effort attempted to sell this ridiculous film to a skeptical public. Among the items created to tie-in with this massive assault on good sense and good taste were *Lost Horizon* wristwatches, costume jewelry, belts, shirts, loungewear, scents, dresses, soundtrack albums, hanging planters, pillows, paint-by-number sets, looms, scented candles, cookbooks, and coloring books.

None of it seemed to work, however, as the film became one of the greatest financial disasters in the history of Columbia Studios. No wonder that *Lost Horizon* became known to Hollywood insiders by the affectionate nickname "Lost Investments."

Sgt. Pepper's Lonely Hearts Club Band [1978]

One of the top vote-getters in our national poll for "The Worst Film of All Time," this lame-brained $12-million spectacular offered less of a plot than *At Long Last Love*. In place of a story line the producer of the film—rock impresario Robert

The Bee Gees, Peter Frampton, and George Burns plead with the audience to accept their bloated cinematic cheeseburger in Sgt. Pepper's Lonely Hearts Club Band.

Stigwood—presents 29 Beatles songs stitched together with only the flimsiest attempts at logical connections. The female lead, for instance, is named "Strawberry Fields" in order to provide an excuse for the Lennon-McCartney classic "Strawberry Fields Forever." A romantic scene in a haystack is interrupted by the sudden appearance of the sun from behind the clouds, giving the cue for "Here Comes the Sun." And so it goes. Each of these numbers is presented in the fragmented style of the old *Ed Sullivan Show*, with a new guest artist coming onstage and playing his heart out in between commercial breaks. Actual commercials, as it turns out, would have provided a welcome relief from the insufferably cute and cloying texture of this film. The Bee Gees plus Peter Frampton (the peachy-cheeked heartthrob of every red-blooded prepubescent American girl) make up the central foursome known in the film as Sgt. Pepper's Band. They are obviously intended as a late seventies answer to the Beatles themselves, but they are a far cry from the boys from Liverpool in terms of both musical and acting ability. As Frampton candidly confessed after the film's release: "I learned a lot—what not to do—from *Sgt. Pepper*. I would love to be an actor held in high esteem like Robert De Niro—but I think one walk on the screen and everyone would laugh."

Concerning the film and its mastermind, Robert Stigwood, scriptwriter Henry Edwards enthused: "Can you believe it? Whoever thought it could be done? Robert is a genius. Who else could make a movie with a screenwriter who never had written a movie before, a director who never had directed a musical, and stars who never have acted." Add to this formula for disaster a set that consists of a twenty-foot hamburger superimposed on Andy Hardy's old hometown from the M-G-M backlot; costumes that resemble a cub-scout honor guard, and the colorful likes of Alice Cooper, Aerosmith, Earth, Wind & Fire, Steve Martin, George Burns, Keith Carradine, David Bowie, Connie Stevens, Curtis Mayfield, Minnie Riperton and Tina Turner, and you end up with a winning prescription for a sweet-sixteen party for a spoiled and slightly feebleminded teeny-bopper. Near the end of the film, producer Stigwood attempts atonement for his previous messterpiece (*Jesus Christ Superstar—See:* The Worst Performance by an Actor as Jesus Christ) in which he offended many sensibilities by casting a black actor as Judas. This time he gives us a black messiah in a gold lamé suit (Billy Preston) who revives Peter Frampton's love interest from the dead and magically turns all the villains into nuns, monks and cardinals by singing: "Get Back! Get Back! Get Back to Where You Once Belonged!" The grand finale uses some 200 rock stars—each one wriggling mugging and trying to steal the scene—in the most expensive choir in Hollywood history. As a parting shot, we glimpse an Astroturf lawn with the words "THE END" spelled out in red, white and blue letters. That patriotic touch seemed tailor-made for a film that takes place in Heartland, U.S.A.—the perfectly logical hometown for the three Australian Bee Gees and the British Peter Frampton. Where's the American Legion when we really need them?

The unanimously hostile critical response helped warn audiences away from this film, and except for the mammoth sales of the two-record soundtrack, the Stigwood organization would have suffered an unprecedented financial disaster. According to most reliable estimates, the film itself has brought in less than one-third of its expected gross of $35 million. *Rolling Stone* magazine reported one typical New York screening, attended by screenwriter Henry Edwards, at which the audience "greeted the film with boos and barfing noises." "I would have preferred another response," Edwards philosophically observed, "but better to have done the film than to be a booer. I feel home free." At last report, the screenwriter is working on a projected biography of Timothy Leary.

Song of Norway [1970]

Director Andrew L. Stone seems to specialize in dull and saccharine musical entertainments. In addition to this sentimental biography of composer Edvard Grieg, he has crafted such unforgettable toe-tappers as *The Great Waltz* (1972) and *Never Put It in Writing* (1964). *Song of Norway* represents his most lavish and ambitious production, featuring Edward G. Robinson as a "lovable" piano salesman named Krogstad, and the "electrifying" star of the Norwegian stage, one Toralv Maurstad, as Mr. Grieg himself. And who do you think plays the lovely Mrs. Grieg? Come on, guess. We'll give you a hint: she has the dramatic intensity to make Julie Andrews look like Irene Papas. That's right—it's Florence Henderson—the female Peter Frampton for the Geritol generation.

109

Florence Henderson steals the show as Mrs. Edvard Grieg in the uplifting Song of Norway.

The film is based loosely on the 1944 stage hit by Robert Wright and George Forrest with songs adapted from the music of Edvard Grieg. As our eyes thrill to the magic of flat-footed actors romping around Danish and Norwegian locations, our ears tingle to the sound of 45—that's right, 45—musical numbers, and 25—yup, 25—songs. So, you may ask, what could be so bad about looking at pretty Scandinavian countryside and listening to the romantic strains of Grieg? If you see this picture you will understand. Just listen to these reviews:

"The movie is of an unbelievable badness; it brings back clichés you didn't know you knew—they're practically from the unconscious of moviegoers. You can't get angry at something this stupefying; it seems to have been made by trolls."

PAULINE KAEL, *The New Yorker*

"Godawful . . . The musical numbers, when not downright ugly, are ludicrous, containing all the conventions of staging that made *The Sound of Music* so easy to hate. Grieg having apparently lived a life of exemplary dullness, the only issue Stone can trump up for dramatic purposes is his thwarted desire to create an indigenous national music for Norway—hardly a matter to keep us on the edge of our chairs. In the ineptitude of his writing, Mr. Stone matches the clumsiness of his direction, unconsciously creating a double parody of both the operetta and biographical forms— truly an amazing work of unintentional humor."

RICHARD SCHICKEL, *Life*

Cinerama Releasing entertained high hopes for this film. One trade paper asked: "Is this to be the successor to all-time box-office champ *Sound of Music?*" The answer, accompanied by Bronx cheers and brickbats from all quarters, was a resounding "No!" Not even the most ardent Florence Henderson fans bothered to get up from their rocking chairs for this one.

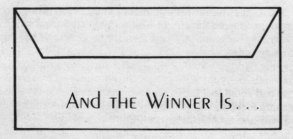

AND THE WINNER IS. . .

... AT LONG LAST LOVE

This celebrated stinker stands as something of a milestone in Hollywood history: few films have ever been able to unite the critics as enthusiastically and entirely as this one. It's not that we revere critical opinion, but at times their reviews are too pungent and colorful to omit. Imagine yourself in the position of producer-director Peter Bogdanovich, receiving printed responses to your beloved creation such as the following:

"A shameful failure."

PAULINE KAEL, *The New Yorker*

"One of the Ten Worst Films of 1975."

VINCENT CANBY, *The New York Times*

"May be the worst movie musical of this—or any—decade."

JOHN SIMON, *Esquire*

"If this Peter Bogdanovich fiasco were any more of a dog, it would shed."

JOHN BARBOUR, *Los Angeles* magazine

"To get the good out of the way first, let me say that this film is an atrocity. Now for the bad: for me, it's the kind of movie one waits years to avoid."

JOHN KOBAL, *Film*

"Turkey of the Year Award."

MICHAEL GOODWIN, *Take One*

"The most perverse movie musical ever made."

FRANK RICH, *New Times*

"One of those grand catastrophes that make audiences either hoot in derisive surprise or look away in embarrassment."

JAY COCKS, *Time*

"This is failure so dismal it goes beyond failure."

HOLLIS ALPERT, *Saturday Review*

Notices such as these led the star of the film, Mr. Burt Reynolds, to deliver himself of a classic understatement. "I think we bombed," he shrugged, and moved on to other triumphs.

Duilio del Prete, Cybill Shepherd, Burt Reynolds, and Madeline Kahn show the precise, disciplined balletic skills that endeared them to audiences and critics alike.

The Ecclesiastical Award for the Worst Performance by an Actor or Actress as a Clergyman or Nun

And the Nominees Are...

The Reverend Pat Boone in *The Cross and the Switchblade* [1970]

This Heav-ee Message movie, from a studio called "Responsible Entertainment," describes the adventures of a real-life minister named David Wilkerson who moves to Harlem to bring Peace and Love to warring Black and Puerto Rican gangs. Boone plays the holy hero as the best-dressed cleric in ghetto history, with not a hair out of place and his gleaming ivory choppers beaming out reassurance at every opportunity. Valium would seem to be the secret weapon in the arsenal of this preternaturally patient preacher man. At one point, a hot-blooded gang leader shows his contempt for Boone by striking him and spitting in his face (perhaps he has seen some of Boone's earlier screen work, such as *April Love* [1957] or *All Hands on Deck* [1961]). The star takes this criticism philosophically. He not only manages to control his temper—but fails to display any emotion at all (You see how effectively all those years of milk addiction can soothe your jangled nerves!) The Chicago *Sun-Times* hailed his performance as "unintentionally hilarious," while Kevin Thomas of the *Los Angeles Times* observed: "That Boone is so unsympathetic a personality throws the film hopelessly out of kilter: You're against him even if you're all for helping the kids." As one irate member of the black gang summed it up in denouncing the Reverend Pat: "Oh man, you ain't real!"

The Right Reverend Clark Gable in *Polly of the Circus* [1932]

In one of his most embarrassing roles, "The King" plays an idealistic minister who scandalizes his congregation by marrying a winsome trapeze artist named Polly (Marion Davies) who performs for the local circus. Seeing that this union has ruined hubby's chances for ecclesiastical advancement, that noble lass sees only one way out: she will pretend not to love him, return to the circus, and then do away with herself by performing her Chevy Chase imitation in midair. Gable and a friendly bishop manage to track her down; while standing below the trapeze, they plead with Polly to spare herself and generally make themselves look foolish. She goes forward nonetheless with a suicidal attempt at a triple somersault but the Lord, understandably, smiles on the preacher's wife. She not only succeeds in her gravity-defying feat, but through this display of prowess (and divine favor) convinces the town gossips that she is, after all, a suitable mate for a man of the cloth.

And what a man of the cloth Gable makes! He plays the minister as an overgrown altar boy. The beatific smile he affects for this part looks greasy and obsequious—as if Uriah Heep had taken Holy Orders. In one scene, Davies informs Gable that whenever he is around, her "heart goes bumpety-bump"; actually, this observation might more accurately apply to organs of digestion than to those of circulation. The screenwriter has gone to great lengths to show that Gable, despite his Holy-Joe aura, is really a down-to-earth "regular guy." He eats peanuts, just like we do; he enjoys the circus, just like we do; he drinks soda pop just like we do; he loves Marion Davies, just like we do . . . or at least like William Randolph Hearst does, whose funds helped to finance this ridiculous picture. The Chicago *Tribune* wrote of the film that: "Mr. Gable is so smugly gentle as the saintly prelate that those of us who admire him can only hope that he will be permitted once more to do what he is best

The Right Reverend Clark Gable swings with co-star Marion Davies in Polly of the Circus.

117

at and will again be seen as a sinister, rather than a noble, fellow." (Rhett Butler, sinister? Well, at least he wasn't holier-than-thou...he used the word "damn" didn't he?) In a biography of Gable, René Jordan enthused: "That his career survived *Polly of the Circus* is again proof of his indestructible power."

Dr. Elvis Presley directs his smoldering sexuality at that glamorous nun, Sister Mary Tyler Moore.

Sister Mary Tyler Moore in *Change of Habit* [1969]

Yes, Ms. Moore is badly miscast as a sister of mercy, but not nearly so badly as her co-star, Elvis Presley, who is expected to play a dedicated young M.D. who has pledged to bring medical care and rock 'n roll to the poor, deprived youth of the ghetto. Naturally, the two of them fall in love, but when Elvis declares his passion for the vivacious nun she raises her eyebrows and archly observes that she is "already involved." Meanwhile they manage to do all kinds-a-fun-things-together, like riding a merry-go-round, jogging in the park, and providing a miraculous cure to a pathetic and autistic six-year-old. To get her mind off ol' Liver Lips and his sexy sideburns, Sister Mary throws herself into the nun business with renewed enthusiasm. She works with two giggly colleagues (Barbara McNair and Jane Elliot) who help give this team the same dedicated intensity of the "Three Little Maids from School" in *The Mikado*. During her romantic interludes with Presley, Ms. Moore seems to recall the Doris Day character from innumerable 1960s bedroom romps. She is the attractive virgin (she's a nun, after all!) offering sweetness and smiles, and fighting—but not too hard— to protect her virtue. To help publicize the film's release, Ms. Moore told an interviewer: "I must admit I enjoyed doing these scenes in a habit and I'd be anxious to do another such role . . . But of course, I wouldn't want to become stereotyped as a nun in films." Based on her ridiculous performance in *Change of Habit*, Mary Tyler Moore has nothing to worry about.

The Reverend Mickey Rooney in *The Twinkle in God's Eye* [1955]

What better way for Mickey Rooney to rehabilitate his public reputation as a hard-drinking ladies' man than to play the part of the courageous minister in a film advertised as "a religious Western"? The grown-up child star felt so much enthusiasm for this inspirational project that he not only starred in it, but also produced the film and wrote the title song. Once upon a time, Mickey specialized in characters with simple desires: all he wanted in life was an innocent hug from Judy Garland. This time, our hero has moved on to bigger and better obsessions: he wants to build a church. Rooney plays a fearless preacher who plans to "clean up" the tough Western town of Lodestone, and in the process must defy the cynical saloon owner (Hugh

The Reverend Mickey Rooney in a moment of intense piety.

O'Brian), a barroom thrush (Colleen Gray), and other hard-bitten but lovable characters. According to the preposterous plot, Mickey comes by his vocation honestly: his mother, while pregnant with our hero, had her life saved when her Bible stopped a stray Indian arrow. With this sort of background, is it any wonder that the Reverend Mick possesses miraculous powers? He can stay aboard a bucking bronco when all other cowpokes have been thrown, and his potent prayers succeed in single-handedly saving a group of miners caught in a cave-in. The news of this miracle arrives while Rooney is still kneeling, enunciating the last words of his prayer of deliverance. This climactic scene would suggest that for his favorites, the Lord is willing to perform as dutifully and promptly as a short-order cook—one platter of rescued miners, comin' right up, Reverend! Rooney plays his part with the smug assurance of the vulnerable little guy who, though subject to taunts and abuse from the bullies of the world, knows that his enormous big brother is following just behind him to even the score. Frequently, the minuscule stature of this preacher on the prairie distracts the audience—try as he may to infuse his role with "reverence," Rooney cannot help coming across as "cute." More than once, he reminded us of the deadpan midget cowboys in *The Terror of Tiny Town* (*See:* The P. T. Barnum Award for the Worst Cinematic Exploitation of a Physical Deformity).

Father Frank Sinatra in
The Miracle of the Bells [1948]

It's easy to imagine the logic that led the producers of this dismal film to cast Sinatra as an adorable Polish Catholic priest. The argument probably went something like this: "Bing Crosby's *número uno* when it comes to playing priests, right? And what's Crosby? He's a crooner, right? Well, we can't get Der Bingle for a miserable little picture like this one, so why don't we go after Sinatra. He's a crooner too, and his career's been in a tailspin. He'll be perfect, and the bobby-soxers'll eat it right up!"

Sinatra does bring certain assets to his role. The costume department has provided him with a handsome cassock and his

Father Frankie Sinatra pleads for heavenly guidance in Miracle of the Bells.

acting coach has equipped him with a vaguely troubled expression meant to suggest spiritual depths. *The New York Times* reported that "Frank Sinatra appears frightened speechless (and almost songless) by the task of playing a priest . . . the picture is so weighted with mawkish melancholia that it drips all over the screen." The story is based on a best-selling novel by Russell Janney about a young star (Alida Valli) from the coal country of Pennsylvania, who dies shortly after completing filming on a big studio production of *Joan of Arc*. The studio boss (Lee J. Cobb) wants to shoot the film over with another star, because there won't be enough public interest in the dead girl. (This is obviously the same sort of sharp thinking that led to the major decisions behind *The Miracle of the Bells*.) Press agent Fred MacMurray wants to persuade the studio to go ahead with the original film so the public will see "the fine acting" of the late lamented starlet. He enlists the help of Sinatra—the parish priest in the girl's hometown of Coaltown, Pa. (You could never guess the chief industry of the village, could you?) To show their support for this holy cause, all churches in Coaltown ring their bells for three days without interruption. This does wonders for the hearing of all the local inhabitants (they hadn't heard of noise pollution back in '47) and wins enough publicity so the studio releases *Joan of Arc* in its pristine form. In the triumphal, upbeat finale to this picture, we get to see the funeral of the now-celebrated star in the little coal miner's church over which Father Frankie presides. The House of God is packed with humble, decent folk, who loved her, etc., etc., and so forth. Then, miracle of miracles, two statues turn to face the coffin! Skeptics say it is only a slight earthquake, but we know better. So does Sinatra, who rolls his eyes to the heavens in gratitude. Apparently, the Lord is a big fan of the newly released picture, and hands us a miracle as His own sort of positive review. *The Miracle of the Bells* got reviews of an entirely different kidney. *Cue* magazine succinctly observed: "The picture can be reasonably described as nauseating."

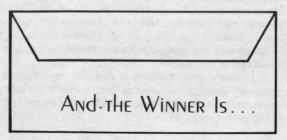

And·the Winner Is...

. . . Sister Mary Tyler Moore
in *Change of Habit*

With her whining voice, cutie-pie makeup and flirtatious manners, Sister Mary sweeps the field in this category. She has received powerful assists not only from co-star Presley, but from the screenwriter and director who created a vehicle that fairly cries out for bad acting. In the climactic sequence of events, a ghetto youth tries to rape our heroine. She is rescued by Dr. Elvis, but something in this encounter has finally aroused her as a woman. (Germaine Greer—where are you when we really need you?) Her devoted admirer once more asks the nun to leave Holy Orders and marry him. To prove his sincerity, he leaves her alone to make up her mind while he goes over to lead a big folk-rock mass that she has helped to organize. Mary comes into the church just in time to see Elvis uplifting the mass and the masses with one of his big hits "Let Us Pray!" She is undecided at the fade out whether to choose Elvis or Jesus, though we receive hints that the Man from Memphis is winning out.

In movie terms, that would probably be the right choice, especially considering some of the miserable performances by actors as Jesus Christ over the years, which brings us, naturally, to our next category . . .

THE WORST PERFORMANCE by AN ACTOR AS JESUS CHRIST

SINCE the beginning of the motion-picture industry, Hollywood moguls have noted the worldwide popularity of Jesus Christ and tried to capitalize on it for their own ends. The problem was that many of these attempts provoked charges of blasphemy and bad taste. Cecil B. De Mille seemed to find a successful formula in his silent classic, King of Kings, *but that film nearly ruined the career of its star, H. B. Warner. After his appearance as the Man from Nazareth, producers felt uncomfortable casting him as a mere mortal.*

The advent of talkies only intensified the problems: to offer the public a walking, talking Jesus seemed to be asking for trouble. So began the holy tradition of presenting Christ in Biblical epics as a long-haired bitplayer with his back turned to the camera (as in Ben Hur). *The stars invariably stared at his flowing locks, listened to his golden words, and breathlessly asked one another, "Was that . . . ?"*

Not until the 1950s, with the production of a church-sponsored film called Day of Triumph, *did Jesus show his face in full view in a major Hollywood talking production. This is one movie breakthrough that should never have been made. What followed was a series of mindless assaults on religious sensibility. Christ may forgive the stars and producers of these films but we, the viewing audience, cannot.*

And the Nominees Are. . .

Director-Star Robert Elfstrom pauses to contemplate the sorrows of mankind in the Johnny Cash production The Gospel Road.

Robert Elfstrom in *The Gospel Road* [1973]

Who, you may ask, is Robert Elfstrom? The pressbook for this film answers that question by describing him as "the famed Swedish filmmaker, Robert Elfstrom." Famed? Well, it's true, he does have a previous film credit—for a documentary called *Johnny Cash: The Man and His Music*. Not coincidentally, Cash produced *The Gospel Road* and persuaded his friend Elfstrom to direct it in addition to playing the part of Jesus. This bit of uninspired but economical casting causes us to see the Saviour as a big-boned, clumsy, flat-footed Swede who looks horribly uncomfortable in his long robe and sandals. To indicate Christ's deep spiritual nature, Elfstrom wears that amazed, blissful, slightly perplexed expression that is colloquially known as "spaced out"—in fact, he resembles nothing so much as a zombified panhandler fresh off Berkeley's Telegraph Avenue.

Fortunately, Elfstrom is denied a speaking part; Johnny Cash steals all of Christ's best lines, as he wanders around the Israeli landscape, interrupting the action of the film to read from his Bible or sing a song. Cash presents eight new songs in the film, including: "I See Men as Trees Walking," "He Turned the Water into Wine" and "Lord, Is It I?" *(sic)*. Cash also wrote the screenplay and, after a worldwide search, cast his wife, June Carter Cash, in the plum role of Mary Magdalene. He took the entire endeavor with the utmost seriousness. As he declared in a "Personal Letter to Theatre Exhibitors": "The film is my life's proudest work. It's the reason I'm on this earth." Cash believed with a perfect faith that other committed Christians would share his enthusiasm for *The Gospel Road* and for Robert Elfstrom as Jesus. He therefore arranged a special advance screening for pastors and church officials in Atlanta. As *Variety* reported the decidedly mixed response: "One complaint was that there was 'a little too much guitar,' and another was that Jesus and his apostles 'looked like hippies' . . . His apostles are an assortment of ragged, unkempt men, as if Christ selected them from a ghetto area inhabited by street people." To these objections, Cash wittily shot back: "I guess that's because Christ was sort of a hippie in his day." The film received its California benefit premiere at the "John Wayne Theatre" at Knotts Berry Farm, where the audience responded enthusiastically. *The Gospel Road* also proved to be a big hit in Norway.

Jeffrey Hunter in *King of Kings* [1961]

This film became known in the industry as "I Was a Teenage Jesus" because of the casting of Jeffrey Hunter in the title role. Hunter, the boyish star of a host of horse-operas, had won a large following among prepubescent girls for his clean-cut good looks and dreamy blue eyes. In *King of Kings* he completed the image by donning a blond wig and shaving his armpits for the crucifixion scene. When asked by interviewers how he got the part, Hunter fumbled pathetically for convincing answers. He told Louella Parsons: "Christ was a carpenter and thirty-three years old and I am thirty-three, and I suppose my physical measurements fitted the description in the New Testament." Had Hunter discovered a little-known passage in the Gospels lost to the rest of the world all these years? Perhaps so, since he plays Christ with a thin, reedy, tentative voice and a manner that is passive and withdrawn. When in doubt as to what to do

Siobhan McKenna as the Virgin Mary in a poignant domestic scene with her son, Jesus (Jeffrey Hunter), in King of Kings.

next, he simply turns his baby blues toward the far horizon as if waiting for guidance. Unfortunately, director Nicholas Ray provided precious little of that in this $8,000,000 production. During filming in Spain, Hunter's co-star Robert Ryan (who plays John the Baptist) told the press that "everyone is going to be amazed when they witness Jeff's performance." This proved a remarkably accurate prediction. *Time* magazine, for example, welcomed the film as "Incontestably the corniest, phoniest, ickiest and most monstrously vulgar of all the big Bible stories Hollywood has told in the last decade . . . Christianity, which has survived the Turkish onslaught and the Communist conspiracy, may even survive this picture; but individual Christians who try to sit through it may find themselves longing for extreme unction."

Judas (Carl Anderson) stands behind his Savior (Ted Neeley) 1000% in Jesus Christ Superstar.

Ted Neeley in *Jesus Christ Superstar* [1973]

In preparing the big-budget film version of this celebrated rock opera, the producers toyed with a number of unconventional casting ideas. Originally, Mick Jagger was supposed to take the part of Jesus. Then David Cassidy was proposed, and finally, John Lennon. After all, hadn't Lennon stunned the world years before with his announcement that the Beatles were more popular than Christ? When none of these big-name rockers panned out, the producers finally settled for Mr. Ted Neeley— a third-rate warbler from Ranger, Texas, who had done his time in L.A. supper clubs and Grand Ol' Opry warm-up bands before landing this, his big break. Neeley was so conscious of this rare opportunity to display his acting skills, that he is on the verge of hysteria most of the time he appears onscreen. His performance is enough to make us wish that the filmmakers had gone with John Lennon—or even Ringo Starr. As Paul D. Zimmerman observed in *Newsweek*, Neeley's "Jesus often recalls Charles Manson." He shrieks, pouts, grits his teeth, rolls his eyes, and twitches intermittently. As Bruce Williamson of *Playboy* enthusiastically declared, Neeley's "portrayal of Christ ought to fix him permanently in public memory as the Screamin' Jesus." In one memorable scene, he grimaces and whines as hundreds of lepers, covered with slimy rag outfits, crawl out from their caves begging to be healed. His obscene and idiotic portrayal is only occasionally overshadowed by Carl Anderson's performance as Judas. At one point, this black singer-actor, dressed in a sparkling white disco outfit, boogies down to the beat of the song "Jesus Christ Superstar" while his dancing soul sisters in silvery bikini tops magically appear behind him. To complete this feast for the eyes, a series of bright neon crosses appear, and begin waving back and forth in time to the music. Small wonder that *Newsweek* granted this film immediate recognition as "one of the true fiascos of modern cinema."

Donald Sutherland in
Johnny Got His Gun [1971]

Jesus makes only a few brief appearances in this interesting antiwar film, but it is enough to establish Sutherland as a solid contender for the Golden Turkey. Once again, we see Christ as a hip, blissed-out child of the sixties, and once again this Middle Eastern Messiah is inexplicably graced with flowing blond hair. Sutherland's performance is full of shrugs and grunts which are apparently meant to prove that Jesus is a mellow, modern guy who is acquainted with the techniques of method acting. In one scene, the faceless, armless, legless hero of the film (Timothy Bottoms) imagines himself in a decorated coffin holding a conversation with Christ while his father (Jason Robards) displays him as a sideshow attraction. To make the unfortunate young man feel at ease, the Son of Man plays a hand of cards with him and then observes that miracles are made in heaven, not on earth. Eventually, He becomes convinced that this entire interaction is "a bummer" and delivers a line that's certain to make even the most hard-hearted audience groan: "Perhaps it would be better for you to go away now. You're a very unlucky young man and perhaps it rubs off." This film marked the directorial debut of screenwriter Dalton Trumbo, one of the Hollywood Ten. He proudly told interviewers that his friend, Sutherland, worked purely for his love of the part, without even a penny of financial renumeration. There can be no question that the producers got their money's worth.

AND THE WINNER IS...

... Ted Neeley in

Jesus Christ Superstar

Neeley richly deserves this award, but it should be recognized that he received plenty of help from his director, Norman Jewison. In an interview in *Playboy*, Jewison spoke movingly about his approach to this classic bad film:

"We could have been vulgar. We could have played this for cheap. Nothing simpler. Guaranteed socko at the box office. We could have been really filthy. But we weren't. For instance...half the apostles are gay, right, and what about Jesus and Judas?...A big, wet smackeroo, right on the lips. How about that? Oh yeah, we could have been vulgar all right. We could have milked it for every grab in the book. But we didn't. Instead, we decided to make it beautiful...We made it into a spiritual experience and it's beautiful, and Jesus is beautiful, the kids are beautiful, it's going to be a beautiful film. People are going to see it in drive-ins and neighborhood nowhere theaters and they're going to be moved by it. People who were never moved by this story before. People who always thought that Jesus Christ was some kind of schmuck. They're going to see something beautiful and they're going to cry. They won't be able to help themselves. When you really come to think of it, we're doing Him a favor."

What more can we say? Father, forgive them, for they know not what they do.

The Worst
Blaxploitation Movie
Ever Made

FIRST the good news: in the 1970s, Hollywood at long last discovered a large, enthusiastic audience for films about black Americans. Now the bad news: most of the movies designed for that audience were violent, simple-minded and utterly lacking in craft or inventiveness. Needless to say, this recent explosion of "Blaxploitation" films has provided an unexpected bonanza for all true connoisseurs of the very worst in motion-picture art.

And the Nominees Are . . .

Abby [1974]

The pivotal character in this wretched melodrama is not Abby herself, but her father-in-law. As played by William Marshal, star of the *Blacula* films, this gentleman is a bishop, amateur archaeologist, and affirmative-action exorcist. While on a dig in Nigeria, he releases an African demon named Eshu who proceeds to possess the lovely Abby (Carol Speed). To show that the gap between blacks and whites is closing fast, Ms. Speed then proceeds to her best Linda Blair imitation, with a deep-voice transformation (courtesy of Bill Holt); hideous makeup job; glazed, cat's eyes contact lenses; a broadened, somewhat coarser vocabulary; and the ability to vomit white foam, make the furniture romp around the room, and throw her husband from pillar to post like a rag doll. If all of this sounds

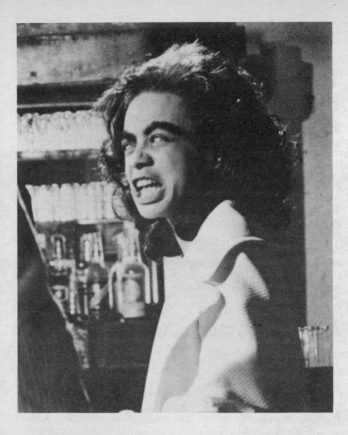

vaguely familiar, you can forget it; any *real* resemblance between this film and *The Exorcist* is destroyed by *Abby*'s incredibly low-production values, inane dialogue ("Whatever possessed you to do that?") and miserable acting. To give the plot a unique twist, the climactic exorcism takes place on the dance floor of a discotheque. Before the film's release, Carol Speed was considered a major discovery: she sings the movie's theme song ("My Soul Is a Witness") as well as playing the title role. Unfortunately, as the Los Angeles *Herald-Examiner* observed: "Many of her dramatic highlights leave the audience possessed with laughter."

Blackenstein [1973]

The production of this film was treated as an event of solemn and monumental importance by its producers, American International Pictures. *Blackenstein* marked the hundredth film in the company's history, and studio head Samuel Z. Arkoff soberly intoned: "We plan to devote our full resources to making this hundredth picture particularly outstanding." Sure enough, the finished product bears many of the AIP's distinctive touches—shoddy lighting, ripoff story line, laughable makeup, shameless overacting, and so forth. The plot, such as it is, concerns the lovable idiosyncracies of a young black medic named "Dr. Stein." To prove that he is a true soul brother despite his Jewish-sounding name, the good doctor uses real African zebra legs in his experiments, grafting them onto his unsuspecting female victims. At one point Ivory Stone, his former student, approaches this dedicated healer with a winning proposition: how would he like to sew her dismembered fiancée back together? The resulting creature, according to *Players* magazine, is "a cross between the original Frankenstein and the Saturday morning cartoon feature Magilla Gorilla."

Originally, the executives at AIP planned two sequels to this masterpiece: *The Fall of the House of Blackenstein* and *Blackenstein III*. One look at the final print of *Blackenstein* convinced them to abandon all plans for follow-ups to their "classy," classic hundredth film.

Boss Nigger [1975]

In this horse-opera, former pro-footballer Fred Williamson rides into a bigoted, lily-white Western town and, much to the horror of the inhabitants, installs himself as the straight-shooting black sheriff. Sound familiar? It's the same plot as in Mel Brooks' *Blazing Saddles*, but this time around it's supposed to be taken seriously. Every moment of this dismal "legend" is absolutely predictable, including the obligatory titillation of interacial sex. Naturally, it is the town's white liberal school marm (Barbara Leigh) who goes ga-ga over the he-man sheriff, and, in the process, makes several inspiring speeches about human brotherhood. "I judge a man by his deeds, not by his color," she declares. When asked by an interviewer how he hit upon this particular plot twist, screenwriter-co-producer-star Fred Williamson explained: "I'm riding through the West there in this all-white town, and there are no black women, and I can't make love to my horse." The *Los Angeles Times* described *Boss Nigger* as "an amateurishly made, incompetently acted, patronizing movie that seems like a spoof of a bad Western." Nevertheless, it helped to establish Fred Williamson as one of the kings of Blaxploitation cinema. Among his other hits are *The Legend of Nigger Charley, Bucktown, That Man Bolt, Black Caesar*, and *Hell Up in Harlem*. In 1978, he made his directorial debut with a putrid action picture, based on his own screenplay, called *Mean Johnny Barrows*. Williamson obviously entertains aspirations to become the black Sylvester Stallone, but we don't think he's enough of a heavyweight to last fifteen rounds with Apollo Creed.

Harlem on the Prairie [1937]

This pioneering Blaxploitation Western was the work of producer Jed Buell and director Sam Newfield, the same men who gave us that all-midget classic *The Terror of Tiny Town*. (*See:* The P. T. Barnum Award for The Worst Cinematic Exploitation of a Physical Deformity.*) Apparently, Buell and Newfield felt that blacks were nearly as cute as midgets. Billed as "the World's First Outdoor Action Adventure with an all-Negro Cast," it starred former L.A. policeman Maceo B. Sheffield and a waitress from Yuma, Arizona, named Connie Harris. Throughout the film, blacks are treated as the objects of humor, with plenty of watermelon, fried chicken, and several scenes showing their superstitious fear of "spooks and ghosties." Despite this horribly patronizing attitude, the film proved wildly popular in the more than 800 theatres across the nation that catered especially to black audiences. Though charitably described by *Variety* as "a quickie," the film made a bundle for its producers and showed the crying need for quality black cinema. As *Time* magazine observed, this minstrel show of hidden gold, heroic sheriff, damsel in distress and villainous villain, could appeal only to "the artier white houses."

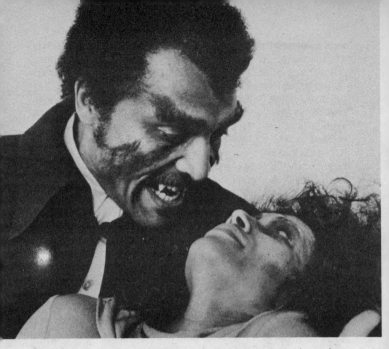

William Marshall as Blacula in Scream, Blacula, Scream *bares his fangs and offers a glimpse of his fillings.*

Scream, Blacula, Scream [1972]

The "dreaded vampire" Blacula rises from the dead once again to terrorize a multiracial group of victims. As the film opens, Blacula (William Marshall) is in a state of "eternal rest"—his first film having opened a few months earlier in 1972. This tranquil slumber is interrupted by a crude voodoo ceremony performed by a super-cool ghetto youth, and Blacula is so deeply irritated at being called out of retirement that he sinks his fangs into the young man's neck. After a long, loving glimpse of our hero's blood-stained, bewhiskered jowls, we watch the change that has come over his victim: Presto! here's an apprentice vampire. Unfortunately, our hero's youthful follower is not entirely delighted with this change of circumstances. In one of the film's many notable lines, he comments, "Aw man, you're jivin' me! Look, man, I don't mind bein' a vampire an' shit, but this really ain't hip!"

To show that he's not an absolutely hopeless square, Count Blac shows up at a red-hot party, where he droolingly watches Pam Grier cut herself on a broken champagne glass. Before the party's over, he lures her to an upstairs bedroom for a brief, after-dinner snack. Ms. Grier then joins the growing gang of vampires that Blacula and his assistant are assembling under one roof. These are not your old-fashioned, ghoulish vampires with a ghostly pallor, but a new, hot-to-trot crowd with disco pants, platform shoes, bright red hats, plaid shirts and dark glasses. The local police are outraged at this sort of flashy dressing—not to mention all the unsolved murders with two fang marks in the neck—and they decide to raid the vampire headquarters. They arrive with sharpened stakes ready for proper application, and the entire confrontation is a blessing in disguise for our hero. Throughout the film, the weary-eyed Star of the Undead has hoped for a way to return to his "eternal rest." In a final act of love during the police assault, Pam Grier finds a way to oblige him. Snipping off a lock of Blacula's hair, she stuffs it into a voodoo doll, then stabs the toy with an arrow four times. While this rhythmic ritual is going on, Blacula shouts up at the ceiling and the audience is presented with a freeze frame of his horrified yet relieved countenance. The appropriate "eerie music" for this masterpiece wells up triumphantly at the close. Curiously enough, this bizarre pastiche of voodoo chants and bongo drums was prepared by one Bill Marx, Harpo's adopted son. Bad films, as you may have noticed, make strange bed-fellows.

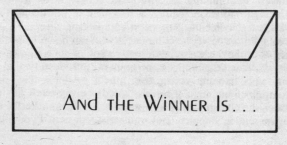

And the Winner Is . . .

... SCREAM, BLACULA, SCREAM

There are many reasons we could offer to explain this choice, including the film's florid title (wouldn't *The Return of Blacula* or *Blacula's Revenge* have been more than sufficient?); the incomprehensible editing (which renders the plot senseless unless you carry a scorecard into the theater); the outlandish misuse of William Marshal (a talented actor who had won earlier praise for his Shakespearean roles on the New York stage); and its ridiculous script (which is a wild and wooly combination of ghetto argot, California psycho-babble and the Transylvanian vampire idiom developed by the late Bela Lugosi).

All of these elements contributed to our decision to hand The Golden Turkey to *Scream, Blacula, Scream,* but we will freely admit that another more personal factor also influenced our choice. The circumstances under which we saw this particular film only enhanced our appreciation of its many putrid attributes. The Arcade Theatre, adjacent to "skid row" in downtown Los Angeles, is an ideal setting for viewing the very worst in cinematic "entertainment." The Arcade offers continuous triple features, beginning at nine each morning and ending at 6 A.M. the next day. This leaves only three brief hours for the theatre's distinguished patrons to stumble down the streets of downtown L.A., waiting for the cinematic cycle to begin anew.

As we walked into the brightly lit foyer, our tickets were taken by a hulking security guard nearly seven feet tall. His presence no doubt helped to insure a restful evening for the audience members. The most enthusiastic spectator the night we paid our visit was a large rat who ran down an aisle to the front of the theatre to get a better view of the action on screen.

Scream, Blacula, Scream began at exactly 4:49 A.M.; it was the final feature on the long day's program. The audience participation in the film was exemplary: during the voodoo scenes, mild ripples of laughter could be heard, but these soon gave way to a mighty and consistent chorus of snores. A high-

140

light in the screening occurred when an elderly woman just in front of us came down with a hacking case of the coughs midway through the picture. A teenage girl to our right then politely commented: "Hey, bitch, why don't you take your ass home and cough!" The senior citizen registered her irritation with a witty riposte. "F—— you, bitch!" she declared. The boyfriend of the teenage girl then shot out of his seat and went for the lady with the coughs, as the action in the theater became far more absorbing than the action onscreen. The gigantic security guard soon arrived on the scene to restore order, brandishing his billy club and urging the audience "To shut the hell up and watch the f——ing movie!" No sooner had the guard returned to the ticket counter, than the elderly woman, in between coughs, managed to get in the last word: "She got no business callin' me a bitch!"

At the end of the film, as the freeze frame of William Marshall's howling face was immortalized on the screen, the theater lights went up suddenly, even before the credits had finished. At that moment the towering security guard went storming up and down the aisles, rattling his billy club expressively against the walls, announcing to the satisfied patrons: "Awright. LESSGO! Closin' Time! Lessgo! Lessgo!" As we made our way briskly to the exit, we noticed one happy customer, clutching a small bottle inside a brown paper bag, and singing cheerily along wth the film's closing song. He knew the lyrics perfectly, and we could only conclude that he had seen the film so many times in the course of the night just past (and the night before? and the night before that?) that the words had permanently imprinted themselves on his memory. We can imagine no more eloquent and persuasive tribute to the enduring qualities of this extraordinary motion picture.

The Biggest Ripoff in Hollywood History

HOLLYWOOD appears to be running out of new ideas. In the last few years, the number of remakes, sequels and readily-recognizable spinoffs of established winners has easily exceeded the tally of truly original concepts. Every blockbuster success inevitably spawns a host of shabby imitations. The Exorcist begat Abby, The House of Exorcism, Beyond the Door and The Manitou; Jaws begat Tentacles, Tintorera the Tiger Shark, Mako-Jaws of Death, Barracuda and Orca (see below); Star Wars begat Star Crash, Laserblast and Battlestar Galactica (see below). If handled competently and professionally, these derivative entertainments might have been endurable, or even enjoyable; after all, Ecclesiastes dictated long ago that "there is nothing new under the sun." Unfortunately, these ripoffs are generally characterized by shoddy workmanship and an unashamedly sleazy approach, and so deserve the most virulent sort of condemnation.

And the Nominees Are...

Battlestar Galactica [1979]

Everyone knows that the feature films we pay good money to see will eventually find their way to TV. But what about taking a has-been TV show and screening it at your local theater? What about asking the public to shell out $4.50 per head for a few spliced-together network episodes that have already aired on the tube? It sounds like an impossible dream, but producer Glen A. Larsen made this particular nightmare into a reality

with his manipulation of *Battlestar Galactica*. What's more, he got away with it, and in so doing provided new proof for H. L. Mencken's classic rule: "Nobody ever went broke underestimating the intelligence of the American public."

As a TV series on ABC, *Battlestar Galactica* proved to be a resounding dud. *Time*'s television critic called the program "perhaps the most blatant ripoff ever to appear on the small screen." The borrowing from *Star Wars* in every detail became so painfully obvious that not even the four-year-old minds for which the series apparently aimed could fail to notice the resemblance. Faced with enormous production costs and mediocre viewer response, ABC canceled the program during its first season. This left Universal Studios—producers of the show—with a glitzy and expensive property on its hands and nothing to do with it. At this point, producer Larson (a onetime member of "The Four Preps" singing group) rode to the rescue. Under his inspired guidance, the studio souped up the first two hours of TV footage with the wonders of the technological marvel "Sensurround" during the scenes of rockets launching or exploding. Larson also included the death scene of the show's traitor, John Colicos, which TV viewers had not been able to watch until the third episode. Finally, Universal had 120 minutes of "film" ready to unleash on theatrical audiences first in Canada, and then in the United States. As Mr. Larson deadpanned: "I think our story is very fresh, and we've made our own breakthroughs." The movie achieved an astonishing level of public acceptance and even became the basis for a computer controlled special effects attraction on the Universal Studios Tour called "The Battle of Galactica."

Everyone seemed delighted by the film's unexpected success—everyone, that is, except George Lucas and Twentieth Century-Fox, who sued Universal Studios and ABC-TV for their obvious plagiarism from *Star Wars*. Demonstrating enough gall to be divided into three parts, the Universal legal department responded by filing a counterclaim insisting that *Star Wars* itself had "infringed on copyrights" held by Universal on the Bruce Dern movie *Silent Running*. Now wait a second— *Silent Running* is an environmental message movie about a botanist trying to save earth's last vegetation in his space green-

A Cylon from Battlestar Galactica *is fashionably attired in interstellar galoshes.*

house. Yes, it does feature two anthropomorphic drones, but aside from that the two films are about as similar as *The Philadelphia Story* and *Animal House*. Universal, realizing the tenuous nature of its claim, filed another countersuit charging that *Star Wars* had also infringed on copyrights held by the old Buck Rogers serials.

While this legal tangle awaits resolution, several producers are charging forward to follow the path blazed by *Battlestar Galactica* and to invade neighborhood theaters with glorified TV shows. Most notable among these pending attempts is the projected *Gong Show Movie*, based on the ever-popular half-hour of humiliation and nausea starring Chuck Barris. We will wait for the estate of Ted Mack, creator of the original "Amateur Hour," to file an immediate counterclaim.

The Greek Tycoon [1978]

Initially intended as a straightforward film biography of Aristotle Onassis, this project began life with the working title *The Tycoon*. The producer, a former Athens journalist named Nico Mastorakis, anticipated full cooperation from the Onassis family and even offered Jacqueline Kennedy $1 million to play herself. When Christina Onassis, Ari's daughter and heiress, denied legal consent for the film to proceed, the ingenious Mastorakis simply changed the names in his script and altered minor details to create a work of "fiction." He also changed the title to *The Greek Tycoon*. "We're not doing a film about Aristotle Onassis," Mastorakis explained. "It's a personification of *all* Greek tycoons." It is well known, of course, that *all* Greek tycoons marry the widows of martyred Irish Catholic Presidents of the United States as does Anthony Quinn in the film: Mastorakis can therefore justify his claim that any *specific* resemblance to the life of Onassis is "purely coincidental." To demonstrate the sweeping originality of the producer, *The Greek Tycoon* introduces a novel plot twist involving the younger brother of murdered President "James Cassidy," who happens to be Attorney General and nurses White House ambitions of his own. Though this far-fetched plot premise is hardly credible (after all, the opposition party would never permit a President to appoint his own brother as Attorney Gen-

Anthony Quinn plays an Aegean shipping magnate, James Franciscus is a handsome young President of the United States, and Jacqueline Bisset portrays the elegant First Lady, who loves both of them in the highly imaginative The Greek Tycoon.

eral!), it demonstrates the fertile imagination of the screenwriters.

Jacqueline Bisset seemed the ideal choice to play the former First Lady in the film—after all, she had the same first name as as the real-life socialite her character "coincidentally" resembles. "My role is not Jackie Kennedy," Ms. Bisset passionately declared to the press, "it's people like her. I can identify with that, too. I know many in that world . . . Honestly, I can't think of anything in the film anyone could object to . . ."

Ms. Bisset must have been stunned when the reviewers welcomed *The Greek Tycoon* as an historic lowpoint in terms of artistic integrity. Jack Kroll wrote in *Newsweek:*

"The Greeks have a word for it, and the word for *The Greek Tycoon* is Yecchh!...foul and sleazy...abominably produced...wretchedly directed...detestably written...poorly photographed...awkwardly edited...slurpily scored ...and pathetically acted by actors who probably need extensive debriefing before they can reenter the human race."

Vincent Canby in *The New York Times* wondered:

"How do they get away with it?...a film that plagiarizes real lives more outrageously than any other film in recent memory, and though plagiarism isn't nice, it isn't this that is worrisome but the fact that so little is done with the stolen goods...If *The Greek Tycoon* had one tenth as much style and imagination as it has chutzpah, it would be the *Citizen Kane* of junk movies, which it isn't...I've no doubt that *The Greek Tycoon* will make a bundle, but be forewarned. Though it's only 106 minutes long, it's a numbing experience, like being forced to read the collected works of Louella Parsons."

Though his last comment is no doubt unfair to Louella Parsons, Mr. Canby's prediction proved accurate: the film *did* make a bundle and ended up as one of the biggest movie hits of the summer of '78.

King Kong [1976]

In his $24-million monkey-shine, producer Dino de Laurentiis managed to ripoff two quality films at once. The first victim was the original *Kong*, the 1933 classic which had its plot distorted just enough to make it laughable. De Laurentiis also paid close attention to *Jaws*, which had demonstrated the enormous box-office potential of gigantic animals that are both deadly and fascinating. With his new *Kong*, de Laurentiis planned to go Spielberg & Co. one better. "Nobody cry when Jaws die," he explained to *New West* magazine. "But when the monkey die, people gonna cry. Intellectuals gonna love Konk; even film buffs who love the first Konk gonna love ours. Why? Because I no give them crap. I no spend two, three million

The big ape bites the dust in the grand finale to the 1976 remake of King Kong.

dollars to do business. I spend 24 million on my Konk. I give them quality. I got here a great love story, a great adventure. And she rated P.G. For everybody."

Well, not exactly everybody. In fact, *King Kong* emerged as one of the top vote-getters in our readers' poll for The Worst Film of All Time. Before its release, however, nearly everyone expected a tremendous success. Initially, Universal Studios fought de Laurentiis for the rights to remake the 1933 RKO General movie, and both companies signed contracts with different parties at RKO. It seemed for a while that the world would endure two remakes of the *Kong* story: Universal's *The Legend of King Kong* (which provided an ideal vehicle for the studio's wonder-of-science, "Sensurround") and the Dino de Laurentiis *King Kong*. Finally, de Laurentiis persuaded Universal to close down their production by offering them a percentage of the profits on his final work of art. Investors considered Barbra Streisand for the old Fay Wray role but, fortunately for her, she turned them down. The producers settled for Jessica Lange, an inept fashion model with no previous acting experience. The lines given her by Lorenzo Semple's simple-minded script did not help her cause. After she is captured by the gigantic gorilla, she begins punching his Naugahyde nose and yells: "Put me down! You male chauvinist pig ape!" When Kong loses his temper, she apologizes: "I didn't mean that! I swear I didn't! Sometimes I get too physical; it's a sign of insecurity, you know? Like when you knock over trees."

How did de Laurentiis intend to present his monster monkey onscreen? Carlo Rambaldi, his special effects man from Italy, joined with Glen Robinson to construct Dino's dream: a 40-foot high, six-and-a-half-ton robot. Electronically and hydraulically controlled, it had an arm span of 20 feet. Its insides consisted of 3,100 feet of hose and 4,500 feet of electrical wiring; 4,000 pounds of Argentinian horse tails were used for the covering on Kong's hairy body, and some of the horse tails went through a massive tinting process to keep the color uniform. Glen Robinson bragged about his technological marvel: "Our Kong is fully functional. He wiggles his arms, rolls his neck, twitches his ears, rolls his eyes, bends both legs, pulls his mouth back to show his gums, rotates on his hips, thrusts out his legs and, when he has to, smiles."

This monster 40-foot robot toured various American cities

like a circus attraction; newspapers carried advertisements asking people to come see the filming of *King Kong*. For the ape's death scene, New Yorkers gathered at the bottom of the World Trade Center twin towers. According to studio publicity, it was "the largest crowd ever to appear in a motion picture, 45,000 New Yorkers..." Many of the fans made off with patches of Kong's horse hair and one grabbed an eye. Little did they know how worthless these souvenirs would become.

Released in Christmas of '76, *Kong* opened at 2,200 U.S. theaters simultaneously. Paramount gave it "the biggest saturation of commercial product ever seen for an American film." Jim Beam offered up a mixture of grenadine and orange juice as "The King Kong Cocktail." King Kong peanut Butter Bars hit the market—consisting of three measly butter cups. Sedgefield Jeans came up with the most inane gimmick of them all. For every pair of pants purchased, the buyer would receive a keychain of Kong's hair—absolutely free!

With all this ballyhoo, the film wound up making money for it producers, but far, far less than expected. Despite the disappointing public response, de Laurentiis forged ahead with his plans for a sequel. Originally called *King Kong in Africa*, this prospective film was locale-shifted to the States and became *King Kong II*. Dino de Laurentiis told columnist Mary Murphy about his plans:

> "I am think about. Maybe I no do. But I tell-a you what ingenuity we plan and you tell me what you think. Kong a lay dead, and—how you say—scientist come and take apart, and Kong come like Frunkensteen—you know Frunkensteen—and he come crazy bad. He kill everyone. And Dwan (Jessica Lange) is now a big-a time movie star and she say, 'Hey, Kong, remember me?' She jumps in his hand, he picks her up, put her to his face, smile and then...womp, he eat her. You like, Mary?"

Ms. Murphy declined comment.

Orca [1977]

Here's a whale of a bad movie, from the same folks who gave the world *King Kong*. By following up his simian shenanigans with one of the worst fish stories ever told, Dino de Laurentiis clearly earned the proud title by which he is known to industry insiders: "Dino de Horrendous." In describing his new project to interviewer Murphy, he ventured: "In my opinion, this-a film is a battle between brain of fish and brain of man." If the "brain of man" came from either de Laurentiis or his associates, the battle would clearly have been a mismatch.

Richard Harris, star of the film, declared to the press: "I get really offended when people compare it with *Jaws*. It's going to make that movie look like an anemic sprat alongside it. It's enormous in the true meaning of the word. Enormous and truly grand and majestic and beautiful. The characters are real people, three-dimensional people whose lives become inexorably laced into that of a brace of mammoth mammals of the sea."

The critics failed to appreciate the "majesty" and "beauty" in the way that Harris had hoped. In fact, Charles Champlin

Orca the killer-whale neatly divides an unsuspecting home in an effort to secure the munchies inside.

of the *Los Angeles Times* announced: "A lousier movie may get made one of these months or years, but it will have to wrest the trophy from the dead and icy grasp of *Orca*...It is not easy to remember a major commercial filmmaking enterprise that violates so many of the customary concerns for characterization, motivation, narrative coherence, credible dialogue or credibility in any aspect."

Meanwhile, *New York* magazine's John Simon reported that "for nasty snickers, this movie is as good a dog as any in these dog days... Among the screenplay's lush absurdities, my favorite is Charlotte Rampling's invitation to a ghoulish looking Richard Harris, as the ice closes in on them: 'Come, let me warm you.' Personally, I'd prefer an iceberg."

The title derives from "*Orcinus Orca*"—the proper name for the species "Killer Whale." Also, "Orca" just *happened* to be the name of Robert Shaw's boat in *Jaws;* de Laurentiis no doubt assumed that the carryover would bring him good luck.

Charlotte Rampling, playing a pretty marine biologist, narrates the film. To show just how much of an "anemic sprat" *Jaws* really was, the action opens with a shark attack. Rampling's assistant, Robert Carradine, is about to be gobbled up when suddenly, out of the blue (sea), a heroic killer whale appears and chomps the Great White into little bits and pieces. Take that, Peter Benchley.

Richard Harris, captain of a crew that makes its living capturing aquarium specimens, fails to understand that Orca the recently sighted heroic whale—covets the title "Man's Best Friend." With neither sensitivity nor skill, he pursues the creature in an attempt to bring the noble beast into captivity. When shipmate Keenan Wynn misses Orca and instead harpoon's the whale's pregnant wife, poor Mrs. Orca lets out an almost human shriek; in fact, her expressive delivery constitutes the best acting in the film. The pregnant she-whale is then strung up over Harris's deck, and the dying mammal politely aborts her fetus. Captain Harris, who hates the sight of whale fetus on his deck, washes the bloody mess into the sea. After this horrifying act takes place, we enjoy a close-up of Orca's glaring eyeball. (This ubiquitous eye bit occurs time and again throughout the film.) With both his wife and his future child killed before his eye, the sensitive whale becomes embittered against society and turns into a juvenile delinquent.

The rest of the film becomes a sort of *Moby Dick* in reverse.

The whale puts a bounty on Harris's head and tries to live up to his personal credo, "I always get my fisherman." But first, Orca is going to have some fun. Reading the name on his adversary's boat, "The Bumpo," and confusing it for a new Marineland ride, the whale rams into the ship several times. At one point, Keenan Wynn takes a peaceful stroll ondeck, when suddenly the big fish jumps out of the water, grabs Wynn in its jaws, and pulls him below the surface for a heart-to-heart talk. In another memorable scene, Orca knocks over a house (honest to God!) and manages to tilt it so that his victims come sliding down into his jaws. The beauteous Bo Derek is wearing a cast on one leg, and so hops around the collapsing house to escape her fate as an in-between-meal snack. Richard Harris tries to hold on to her hands and keep her from sliding into Orca's gullet, but to no avail. The whale ignores her shapely uninjured leg, and proceeds to munch on the one with the cast. Those crispy-crunchies are always the best, you know.

After eating Keenan Wynn, knocking over a house, and chewing off Bo Derek's leg, Orca remains bent on destruction. The killer whale proceeds to collapse a pier, start a fire (by knocking over the town's reserve gas tanks) and persuades Charlotte Rampling that Richard Harris should come out and fight like a man, er, a whale, or something. Forced out to sea by Ms. Rampling and the disgruntled townfolk in this scenic Canadian village, Captain Harris and his men follow Orca to the frozen coast of Labrador. The whalers try to smash the beast with underwater bombs, but the explosions only wound and anger the whale. In retaliation, Orca pushes an iceberg into the ship and then slams the craft into a solid wall of ice—an action that turns the entire crew into bloody ice cubes, except for Ms. Rampling and Mr. Harris.

Being a good sport despite his energetic play during this grudge match, Orca decides to permit Richard Harris one last night of love with his fellow survivor. Their home-away-from-home on a deserted ice floe offers none of the comforts of an X-rated motel, but at least the price is right. After sex comes violence (naturally) as Orca bursts suddenly through the ice and throws Harris against an iceberg, knocking him out cold and leaving him as a bloody mass of near-frozen meat. The champ, without taking a bow, then dives back into the water for his statement to the press. As the icebound Charlotte Rampling looks helpless and lost, waiting for the movie to end, a helicopter suddenly appears on the horizon. The credits go up, and Ennio Morricone's romantic ballad "My Love, We Are One" wafts its way across the soundtrack. What does this soupy love song have to do with what we have just seen? Does it describe the romance of Harris and Rampling? of Orca and Mrs. Orca? Or perhaps it concerns Orca and Harris (after all, S and M is very big these days). The best idea, however, is that de Laurentiis has inserted the song to subtly prepare us for a romantic sequel. How about: *King Kong's Daughter Courts the Son of Orca?* We can hardly wait for his future offerings.

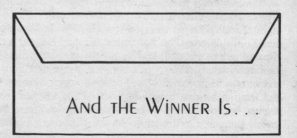

And the Winner Is...

. . . King Kong

Not only did this blundering blob of a movie make a mockery of its 1930s model, but it also ripped off the gullible public with a deceptive and ingenious promotional gimmick.

The intensive hype surrounding the film concentrated on that marvel of modern science, Dino's 40-foot-high gorilla robot. What few viewers realized was that the ape they saw onscreen actually had no connection with this mechanical monster. What they were seeing was very simply a man in a monkey suit. That's right—as any fan of the Japanese Godzilla movies could have told you—that was a normal sized gent dressed up as King Kong walking around miniature sets. The actual Kong robot appeared on film for less than ten seconds, during the Shea Stadium sequence just before the big ape breaks loose. The stiff movements of his arms and the blank, staring expression on his face make him look entirely different from the Kong we see during the rest of the movie.

So much for the bad news. Now the good news: the de Laurentiis family did its bit for racial brotherhood in the casting of this title part. Civil Rights groups went absolutely wild when Dino's twenty-one-year-old son Federico (supposedly "executive producer" of the film) advertised in Hollywood's trade papers for a "tall, well-built black man" to play the monkey. Federico later explained that an Afro-American muscleman would eliminate the need for extra padding in the suit. In the face of mounting protests (and cries of "reverse discrimination" from white gorilla specialists) Dino overruled his bad boy and hired Rick Baker to impersonate the ape. Baker, one of the best makeup artists in the business, had long experience in designing monkey suits and frequently played gorillas himself. In *The Thing with Two Heads (See:* The Worst Two-Headed Transplant Movie Ever Made) he even appeared as a laboratory primate with an experimental extra head. Reflecting on his experience as The Man Who Would Be Kong, Baker said: "*King Kong* offered the one chance to do a really perfect gorilla suit. With the money and the time it could have been outstand-

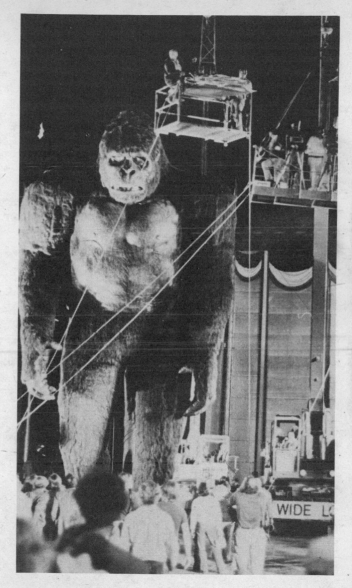

ing. Unfortunately, it wasn't. There were compromises and enforced deadlines. A once in a lifetime opportunity was lost."

Some special effects professionals took a much stronger stand concerning the ape's shortcomings. Jim Danforth resigned from the Academy of Motion Picture Arts and Sciences to protest a special award given to *King Kong* for "special visual effects." Danforth declared: "In my opinion, the effects are a joke...absolutely terrible...the conception, design and planning of the effects in general are just the worst they can be...I went to great lengths to point out that Rick Baker was not in any way in my opinion to be considered 'a special visual effect.' No more than Bert Lahr could be considered a special effect when he played the Cowardly Lion in *The Wizard of Oz*."

Unlike Bert Lahr, poor Rick Baker never received proper recognition for his performance in the film. If he had, the credit line, "AND FEATURING, Rick Baker as KONG..." might have qualified for our next category.

The Worst Credit Line of All Time

WHEN A MOVIE concludes and the long string of credits rolls onto the screen, many viewers will get out of their seats and head for the parking lot. Discerning collectors of cinematic oddities, on the other hand, will remain in place and pay close attention to what these written announcements are trying to say. Some of the credit lines we have noted in the past are every bit as idiotic as the films to which they are appended.

And the Nominees Are:

Cat Women of the Moon [1953]
"...And featuring
THE HOLLYWOOD COVER GIRLS
as
The Cat Women"

Dawn of the Dead [1979]
"...Music by Dario Argento and THE GOBLINS"

Exorcist II: The Heretic [1977]
"Tap Dance Routine Choreographed by Daniel Joseph Giaghi"

The Greek Tycoon [1978]
"The characters in this film are fictitious and any resemblance to persons living or dead is purely coincidental."

Robot Monster [1953]
". . . Automatic Billion Bubble Machine by N. A. Fisher Chemical Products, Inc."

Solomon and Sheba [1959]
"Orgy Sequence Advisor—Granville Heathway"

Superman [1978]
". . . Cheerios by General Mills"

This chilling effect in Robot Monster *was provided by N. A. Fisher Chemical Products, Inc.*

The Swarm [1978]
"The African killer bee should not be confused with the hard-working, industrious American honey bee, which provides us with honey and pollinates our flowers."

The Taming of the Shrew [1929]
"By WILLIAM SHAKESPEARE
with additional dialogue by Sam Taylor"

What's Up Front [1965]
"Bras by Frederick's of Hollywood"

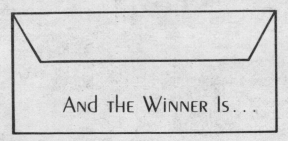

And the Winner Is...

"Additional dialogue by Sam Taylor?"

Actually, the finished script shows Taylor's touch far more conspicuously than it does Shakespeare's. This early talkie with Douglas Fairbanks and Mary Pickford marked a new low point for both stars. "I have no qualms in admitting that Katherine was one of my worst performances," Miss Pickford confessed. "Instead of being a forceful tiger-cat, I was a spitting little kitten."

Under the circumstances, the producers might well have listed the name of contemporary screenwriter Sam Taylor ahead of William Shakespeare, but alphabetical order dictated that the Bard should receive top billing.

Mary Pickford restrains Douglas Fairbanks from punishing the author of a highly dubious credit line for their first film, The Taming of the Shrew.

The Most Unerotic Concept in Pornography

And the Nominees Are...

Candice Rialson allows her better half to make one of its triumphant media appearances in Chatterbox.

Chatterbox [1976]

The makers of *Deep Throat* earned millions by telling the story of a young lady whose vaginal equipment had somehow found its way into her throat. The writer-director of this film (Tom De Simone) simply reverses that concept by creating a character who has an extra voice box inside her vagina. The plot develops with all the thrills and fascination of a two-headed transplant movie (*See:* The Worst Two-Headed Transplant Movie Ever Made) as the vagina in question (named Virginia, naturally) develops a will and personality distinct from its (her?) mistress. Penelope (Candice Rialson), the unfortunate victim of this sloppy bit of anatomical engineering, is dumped by her boyfriend when her better half complains out loud about his performance. Escapades include a sojourn in jail with a basketball team and sessions with a psychiatrist to help Virginia overcome her emotional problems. With her self-confidence restored, she makes several hit appearances on TV talk shows; the theory, apparently, is that Virginia makes an even more interesting late-night guest than Truman Capote (*See:* The Worst Performance by a Novelist).

The Erotic Adventures of Pinocchio [1976]

Pinocchio, as you'll recall, was an adorable marionette magically come to life, whose nose grew a few inches every time he told a lie. In this contemporary retelling of the classic fairy tale, "It's Not His Nose That Grows"—as the ads for the film smugly announce. These same promotional materials include a picture of good ol' Pinoc', surrounded by seven adoring women wearing bras and panties. These admirers have focused their drooling attention on a gigantic proboscis that bears a striking resemblance to an erect male member. The director of photography for this Chris Warfield production was the great Ray Dennis Steckler—beloved by bad-film buffs for his contributions as a producer-writer-director in the 1960s. During that decade he gave the world such cinematic experiences as *Rat Fink a Boo Boo* and *The Incredibly Strange Creatures Who Stopped Living* and Became Mixed Up Zombies. (*See:* The Worst Title of All Time.) We are pleased to see that as recently as 1976 Mr. Steckler could still find work as a cameraman on this Pinocchio project—a film in which he should feel entirely at home.

Him [1974]

This innovative film, designed exclusively for gay audiences, goes into excruciating detail concerning the erotic career of Jesus Christ. The ads for the film show the face of The Savior (with a cross glistening in one eye) while the headline inquires "Are You Curious about HIS Sexual Life?" Filmmaker Ed D. Louie satisfies that curiosity by showing us that the Son of Man was a voracious homosexual. (After all, why did he spend all that time hanging around with the Apostles?) The central character of the film is actually a young gay male in contemporary America whose sexual obsession with Jesus helps him to understand the "hidden meaning" of the Gospels.

Percy [1971]

If Myron Breckenridge lost it, then why not have Hywel Bennet get it back? This big-budget, soft-core feature from producer Betty Box (that's right, Betty Box) tells the story of the world's first penis transplant. It all starts when Bennet, playing the part of a London antiques dealer, is separated from his heart's delight by a shard from a falling chandelier. He is rushed to the hospital where transplant surgeon Denholm Elliott (who is whistling a little ditty he calls "Penis from Heaven") accomplishes the graft with the generously proportioned bequest of a recently deceased organ donor. When the operation is pronounced a success, the nurse declares: "Let's see how it stands up in the light of day."

This sort of smirking double entendre is typical of the entire film, and is generally delivered with such pained archness and raising of eyebrows that any traces of humor are totally obliterated. We follow our hero as he sets out in pursuit of all the lovely ladies who have enjoyed the services of "Percy" in the past. These sex objects include Britt Ekland, Margaret Scott,

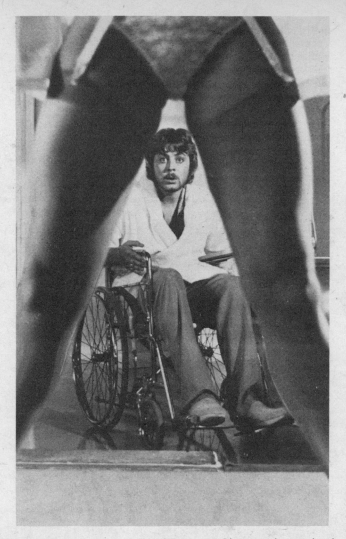

Hywel Bennet prepares to test the success of his recently completed organ transplant operation in Percy.

and Elke Sommer doing a feeble Zsa Zsa Gabor imitation. As a subplot, we have a touching love affair between a Lesbian leather girl and a comely stripper, with the macho half of this combo becoming the recipient of the next transplant from our surgeon's bag of tricks.

And the Winner Is. . .

... *Him*

For sheer tastelessness, this film has no equals. In one scene, our homosexual hero goes to his local priest to confess his erotic fixation on Jesus Christ. The priest sits in the confessional, listening to the young man breathlessly elaborating his perverted fantasies, while taking advantage of the situation to reach under his cassock and masturbate grotesquely on camera. This charming episode surely marks one of the absolute low points in the history of American cinema. Those pathetic few who might want to see *Him* ought to come to the theater dressed in plain, brown paper wrappers, that hopefully cover their eyes along with the rest of their faces.

The Worst Performance by an Animal

And the Nominees Are...

Blue Boy the Hog in
State Fair [1962]

After winning a prestigious role in this third movie version of the Rodgers and Hammerstein musical, George, an 800-pound Hampshire hog, had his name legally changed to "Blue Boy" to correspond to his onscreen identity. To this day, Mr. Boy has the distinction of being one of the fattest porkers ever to appear in motion pictures. His big scene occurs when he is required to gaze affectionately at his owner (Tom Ewell) while that dedicated farmer caresses the pig's massive black back on the eve of the State Fair. Ewell whispers sweet nothings into Blue Boy's ear, then is so emotionally transported by this intimate scene in the barn, that he begins to serenade the prize hog. Blue Boy is supposed to look touched as Farmer Ewell sings:

> Sweet Hog of mine!
> Warm and soft Affection lies
> In your teenie-weenie eyes . . .
>
> Sweet Hog of mine!
> Sweet Hog of mine!
> Other friends may drift away;
> Tell me that you'll always stay!

Blue Boy the Hog demonstrates his emotional range in the grand finale of State Fair.

Unfortunately, Mr. Boy is not a graduate of the Actors Studio. Director José Ferrer must have tried desperately to get some emotion out of the animal, but the huge pig simply sits back in his stall and grunts. Even while his co-star Ewell sings his heart out, Blue Boy looks off in another direction, thinking of new pigpens to conquer and all the other places he'd rather be. As the camera comes in close for a profile (of all things!) the noble hog merely blinks an eye and twitches his nostrils. At the conclusion of the film, Blue Boy wins a "Grand Champion" blue ribbon, sending Ewell, his wife (Alice Faye), and his son (Pat Boone) into paroxysms of delight. Obviously, the judges based their decision on the pig's sheer enormity rather than on his acting ability. The tender porcine love scene in *State Fair* did, however, make a lasting impression on actor Tom Ewell. "I'll never be able to eat a pork chop again without thinking of Blue Boy," he sighed.

Dinky the Chimp in
Tarzan and the Great River [1967]

Chimpanzees are among the most intelligent animals on earth and they *can* act, as demonstrated by their colorful roles in numerous motion pictures. One particularly gifted chimp named Bonzo showed enough natural acting ability to thoroughly upstage his co-star, Ronald Reagan, in the 1951 romp *Bedtime for Bonzo*. Unfortunately, the difference in theatrical flair between the immortal Bonzo and the pathetic Dinky is comparable to the talent gap between Sir Laurence Olivier and Burt Reynolds. Dinky, playing the classic role of "Cheetah" in which many of his fellow-creatures have distinguished themselves, proves a hopeless disgrace to his species.

The plot of the movie concerns Tarzan's journey to New

Dinky the Chimp advises supporting actor Jan Murray on his poker hand during a quiet moment in Tarzan and the Great River.

York to rescue Cheetah and Baron the Lion from the zoo in which they are imprisoned, so the love interest between man and monkey is absolutely crucial to the story. Former L.A. Rams linebacker Mike Henry, the fourteenth man in Hollywood history to play Tarzan, does his best to snuggle up to his simian co-star but finds his advances repulsed at every turn. Dinky appears consistently hostile and uncomfortable, as if he can't wait to escape from Henry's massive arms. Perhaps the chimp resents the fact that the football star received a higher salary and more prominent billing than he did. In any event, Dinky tries his best to show his contempt for Tarzan. Watching him snarl and grit his teeth, we keep waiting for a surprise ending to reveal that Henry's character is actually an unscrupulous villain posing as the real jungle man and that Dinky is the only one perceptive enough to spot the impersonator. For Mike Henry, this conflict on the set proved a painful ordeal. As he told a reporter who interviewed him on location near Rio de Janeiro, "I took this job to find out if the movie people really had fun. Now that I know, I'm getting the hell out!" Concerning his co-star, Dinky, Henry commented: "Performances of animals are so unpredictable—you never know when one is going to turn on you. Football was never like this. In fact, I'd rather face those big guys on that line from the Green Bay Packers, Chicago Bears or Detroit Lions any day. At least I have a good idea what they will do. But animals—shucks, you never know."

Gocha the Russian Circus Bear in *The Bear* (Alternate Title: *The Talking Bear*) [1961]

The star of this French comedy is a 7'4", 550-pound bear who has more natural ham on his body than Blue Boy the Hog. Every time he appears onscreen, Gocha tries to overwhelm us with cuddly adorableness. His limited talents include juggling balls and sipping French champagne, and somewhere along the line the film-makers must have realized that this wouldn't provide enough material for even a ten-minute short, much less a feature-length movie. Their solution?—Hire a man in a bear-skin suit to act as a stand-in for Gocha. This way they can expand the star's abilities to include riding a motorcycle, playing cards, riding on an airplane, driving a car and changing the tire. Director-screenwriter Edmond Séchan (cinematographer for the prize-winning short *The Red Balloon*) devised a complex plot to make the most of the situation. The story involves a kindly zookeeper (Renato Rascel, composer of the hit tune *"Arrivederci, Roma!"*) who trades places with his caged bear so that the animal can experience one blissful night of love with a polar bear-ette in a neighboring zoo. (Yes, we know they're not married, but remember this is a *French* comedy.)

How did a Russian bear stumble into a French movie? Gocha, who was six-years-old at the time of this, his first and last film appearance, had been found in the Siberian forest by hunters when he was only two-months old. A youngster named Ivan Fedorovich cared for him in his parent's home, and Ivan eventually became the bear's trainer. He started out too small for The Great Circus, but eventually became the star of the Russian troupe. Branching out on his own, Gocha toured the world with a clown named Popov until a group of Frenchmen, figuring that bears worked cheap, decided to use him in a movie. He received $600 a day for his film assignment, which was clearly more than he deserved. Joseph E. Levine's Embassy Pictures picked up the American distribution rights and dubbed the film into English. Gocha is given a goony baritone voice that makes him sound like a hulking half-wit on tranquilizers. In general, his performance resembles the antics of a pet dog who enthralls his master by rolling over or picking up a bone, but proves an absolute bore to the rest of the world. Sure, it's fun to watch the bear juggle balls for a few moments, but when he goes on and on with the tricks, the experience becomes painfully tiresome. It would be entirely appropriate if the dopey voice allotted to him suddenly bellowed out: "Wait a second! Watch me ride a bicycle! You ain't seen nothing yet! Wanna see me sweep my cage with a broom? Okay—here goes! Oops, wait—wait a second—now you gotta watch me carry my own luggage onto an airplane half my size! Ha-ha! You're gonna love this!"

Enough already! It's like watching Jerry Lewis reincarnated as a bear, trying to steal the show, which is his to begin with, by writing, directing, acting, singing, etc. Francis Blanche, who played the zoo's director in the film, said of his furry colleague: "He speaks better English than I do, but—*sacré bleu*, what a ham! He—how do you say it—overact!"

Realizing that their final product had thin appeal, the American distributors of *The Bear* recommended a hard sell to theater owners. Ads featured a picture of Gocha, carrying a broom and a bouquet of flowers, saying: "If you and your cubs can bear (get it?) 90 minutes of uncaged, unforgettable fun—I'm for you." Some of the inane selling slants suggested by the pressbook included:

LANGUAGE SCHOOL
Tie-in with a language school, such as Berlitz, using the talking bear angle. Copy should read: "If a Bear Can Be Taught Another Language, So Can You!"

CRITICS
Be kind to your critics. Send them fancy jars of honey from *The Bear* and maybe they'll be sweet to you. Better still, get a pretty model to dress in leotards and a *brief* bear costume and send *her* around to the papers with the honey.

If the distributors come through with our honey in the near future, we will consider deleting *The Bear* from subsequent editions of this book. Oh, and by the way, we would prefer tight black leotards, please.

Muki the Wonder Hound in *Dog of Norway* [1948]

Republic Studios had great hopes for their canine star of the late forties, offered as a poor man's (or at least a poor producer's) answer to Lassie. Instead of a collie, the geniuses at Republic picked an obscure breed known as "Norwegian Elkhound" and tried, in its publicity, to educate the public as to the many virtues of these heroic dogs.

"Norwegian Elkhounds are loving, kind, expressive, and particularly good with children," a studio press release explained. "For thousands of years, they have enjoyed an honored place at Viking campfires. They are absolutely fearless when it comes to hunting game—including bear, raccoon, squirrel and the Norwegian 'Elk'—our equivalent of a 'Moose'... One of the breed's many advantages is

Muki the Wonderhound strikes a heroic pose in a promotional shot for Dog of Norway.

its astonishing absence of unpleasant 'doggy odor'... Their uncommonly keen minds are well represented by the movie star, Muki—a hound that enjoys an IQ of at least 180 in canine terms."

According to the studio, this genius hound understood the meaning of 63 different words and responded to more than 40 different commands. Particularly remarkable were the bitch's feats of consumption, since Muki could crack eggs, peel bananas or slice tomatoes at will. Unfortunately, Charles Kaufman, director of *Dog of Norway*, felt called upon to display every aspect of this virtuosity in endless sequences of the creature stuffing itself—at times while wearing a clean white bib with its name embroidered on it.

In addition to eating, "The Wonder Hound" also knew how to bark. Oh, could it bark! According to Werner Altschuler, the veteran trainer who prepared Muki for her first starring role: "We wanted to teach her to bark back at people, as if she were taking part in conversation, but she learned the trick too well. As it turned out, whenever people started talking while Muki was on camera, she began barking away. We couldn't stop her. Sometimes you can't even hear the lines in the film, but the director thought it was cute."

Director Kaufman, a Republic in-house hack who had previously specialized in low-grade Westerns, also thought the dog's co-star was cute. "Little Hershel Feldstad," the press release explained, "is a tow-headed Norwegian tyke who wills his way straight into your heart." Little Hershel is actually well cast in this film because he, like Muki herself, enjoys a chubby face and stumpy body. Apparently, the only acting he has been able to master is the skill of crying on camera—well, at least Muki can peel bananas. Little Hershel sheds plenty of tears during the idiotic plot, which finds him lost in the "midst of the great forests of Norway"—actually, Republic's backlot. His parents (Constance Moore and Fortunio Bonanova) give up hope of finding him, but his devoted pal Muki escapes from her kennel and waddles forth into the woods to perform the rescue. In the process of returning home they encounter a friendly hermit (George "Gabby" Hayes) and a group of helpful trolls, who are played by apparent rejects from *The Terror of Tiny Town*. (*See:* P. T. Barnum Award for the Worst Cinematic Exploitation of a Physical Deformity.)

Finally, Hershel and Muki run into a band of evil hunters (all of whom wear dark mustaches) who plan to kidnap the poor boy and hold him for ransom. Unfortunately for them, they have not reckoned on the superb intelligence of "the Wonder Hound." At night, Muki picks up a shotgun in her mouth, sets it up against a rock, and squeezes the trigger with her snout. One baddie bites the dust and the others scatter to the winds, knowing they are hopelessly outwitted.

Plans called for a whole series of films starring Muki the Wonder Hound, including *Muki, The Littlest Stowaway* (about her journey to America), and *Muki Goes to College* (about her adventures in a laboratory at a great Norwegian University). "Once Muki catches on," declared director Kaufman, "the children of America will see Lassie for what she really is. Just another dumb dog. This hound, on the other hand, is so intelligent it's frightening."

Apparently, her awesome intellect managed to frighten everyone away from the theaters, for *Dog of Norway* turned out to be a notorious dog—er, turkey—in financial terms. Even by Republic's low standards the film proved an embarrassment. Plans for Muki's future career were abruptly canceled, and the one-time star retired to a "canine hotel" in Santa Monica, California. There, she became even more grotesquely fat than before and concentrated on teaching her fellow hounds how to peel bananas.

Scuttlebutt the Duck in *Everything's Ducky* [1961]

1961 was apparently a big year for talking animals: first came Gocha the Bear, who was shortly followed by Scuttlebutt the Duck. This comedy concerns the misadventures of two bumbling, blubbering sailors (Mickey Rooney and Buddy Hackett), who befriend an intellectual duck who has memorized the last great formula of a dead missile scientist. The main problem with Scuttlebutt's approach to this role is that he constantly tries to scuttle off camera. The Duck—like a fondly remembered politician from Grand Rapids—fails to convince us that he could walk and chew gum at the same time, let alone talk. For the most part he looks at his surroundings with all the intelligent comprehension of a lobotomized turtle. Frequently, he even forgets to clack his bill when he is supposed to be speaking. Trying to build public enthusiasm for this film, Buddy Hackett recounted to reporters his favorite scene in the movie: "The duck wants to play tennis but I talk him out of it by telling him, 'You'd look so stupid jumping over the net with those short legs.'" The film ends with Scuttlebutt, Rooney, and Hackett locked together in the nose cone of a satellite as it circles the earth. The two blubber boys fall into each other's arms, yelling for Scuttlebutt to save them. As

Mickey Rooney, Buddy Hackett and Scuttlebutt the Duck (center) drowning their sorrows in Everything's Ducky.

James Powers wrote in the *Hollywood Reporter*, what follows is "a fadeout that seems to come for no reason except that time has run out."

The talking duck performs basically the same stunts that Gocha executed in his cinematic showcase: talk, drink alcohol (Scuttlebutt prefers martinis in place of Gocha's champagne), and run away from his pursuers (scientists want to remove the duck's brain for study). Scuttlebutt was so uncomfortable during the shooting that he had no less than 12 stand-ins to help him with his role (the filmmakers decided against using a man in a duck suit). Producer Red Doff talked about his star and explained: "We want him to be nice and fresh for his many close-ups. He has his own little trailer and a set of tailored wool sweaters to keep him warm when he gets out of the cold water." Needless to say, a star of Scuttlebutt's magnitude was hard to find. "I put out a casting call, or rather a duck call," said Doff, "for weeks before the picture started. But it wasn't long before my office was swimming with hammy ducks whose owners wanted their pets to break into movies. It was Ralph Helfer, though, who brought in the right bird." The songs in this fowl extravaganza included "Everything's Ducky," "Moonlight Music" and "The Scuttlebutt Walk." We were working on some stupid line about the relationship between ducks and turkeys, but with no interest in scoring paltry (poultry?) points, we will restrain ourselves.

And the Winner Is. . .

... Dinky the Chimp

The advertisement read: "TARZAN ... in barehanded combat with a wild jaguar ... escaping vicious man-eating piranhas ... trapped by a blazing volcano ... braving the savage tribes ..." For some unknown reason, the lyrical copy writer forgot to mention the most formidable danger of them all—namely, Dinky the Chimp. Onscreen, the animal may have been a dull and irritating presence, but off-camera he was about as much fun as the proverbial barrel of monkeys. Described by Tarzan historian Gabe Essoe as "a cantankerous veteran former," Dinky previously played Cheetah to Mike Henry's Tarzan in *Tarzan and the Valley of Gold*. Henry had been mildly dissatisfied with his co-star's performance in that 1966 film, but in *Tarzan and the Great River* the former football star received the shock of his life. We'll let Henry describe the incident himself:

> "In the second week of shooting, we were working with Dinky the Chimp, who seemed uneasy in his new environment. I was to run over to the chimp and pick him up and kiss him. When I did, he lashed out at me and ripped my jaw open. It took twenty stitches to put my face back together. I was in a 'monkey-fever delirium' for three days and nights. It took me three weeks to recuperate."

Following the on-camera slashing incident, the temperamental animal star suffered a more or less complete nervous breakdown. The filmmakers decided that he had to be destroyed. Unfortunately, Dinky had never joined the Screen Actors Guild so the union made no attempt to plead for his life. After he passed on to his reward, a stand-in chimp joined the production to shoot Dinky's unfinished scenes.

Mr. Henry, after having his face torn to pieces while trying to kiss a monkey, would make only one more Tarzan movie *(Tarzan and the Jungle Boy)* before hanging up his loincloth. Following the mishap with Dinky, Henry filed two lawsuits against Banner Productions (producers of the Tarzan series).

Former football star Mike Henry with Dinky the Chimp, his late lamented co-star in Tarzan and the Great River.

The first suit asked $800,000 for "maltreatment, abuse and working conditions detrimental to my health and welfare." A second legal action demanded $75,000 as compensation for the "human error" involved in the chimp's attack. "Although the chimp chittered nervously just before that particular shot," Henry recalled, "and I cautioned the director about it, he instructed me to do as I was told and go ahead with the scene. And that's when I got bit."

Though the teeth of a chimpanzee can leave painful and bloody wounds, they are nothing when compared to the deadly bite of a man-eating vegetable, as you will soon discover...

181

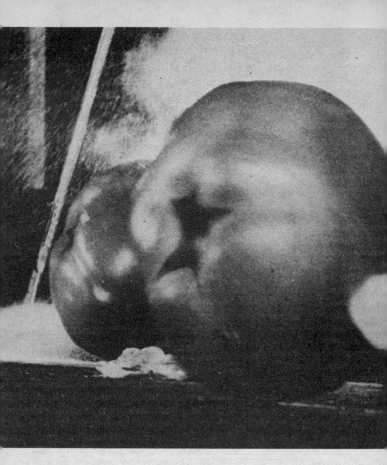

Gigantic man-eating tomatoes run wild in the streets of San Diego.

The Worst Vegetable Movie of All Time

And the Nominees Are...

Attack of the Killer Tomatoes [1978]

This chilling saga was greeted by Kevin Thomas of the *Los Angeles Times* as "hopelessly inane." An anonymous reviewer in *Variety* went so far as to question whether it deserves consideration as a vegetable movie in the first place. "There's always been confusion about whether tomatoes are a vegetable or a fruit," he wrote. "In this instance, a third classification is in order. *Attack of the Killer Tomatoes* is a turkey." The plot, such as it is, concerns rampaging tomatoes, reaching monstrous heights, who wreak horrible revenge on housewives, drinkers of Bloody Mary's and corrupt politicians who misappropriate agricultural allotments from the government. During the reign of terror, the streets run red with tomato juice, or blood, or something. When the time comes for the grand finale, the public-spirited citizens of San Diego, the fair town victimized by this horror, manage to herd all of the slurping. gurgling killer tomatoes into the local football stadium. As the hit song, "Puberty Love," is blasted on the stadium's public-address system, the giant tomatoes miraculously shrink back to normal size, thereby allowing the San Diegans to squish them one by one and make a mess of the stadium's playing field. The title song adds color to the proceedings here, including such inspiring lyrics as "I know I'm going to miss her/A tomato ate my sister."

Attack of the Mushroom People (Alternate Title: *Matango the Fungus of Terror*—See WORST TITLE OF ALL TIME) [1963]

This horror classic was directed by the incomparable Inoshiro Honda, the same man who gave the world *King Kong Escapes, Monster Zero* and *Godzilla's Revenge*. This time his story concerns seven merry Japanese voyagers whose yacht is blown off-course to a mysterious fog-shrouded island. Fortunately, they find an abandoned ship that has all the comforts of home and decide to camp out there. Alas, this touching idyll is interrupted by the ravages of hunger and they begin to scour the enchanted isle in search of yummies. A strange type of fungus is quickly discovered, but the captain's log on the abandoned ship indicates that it is not kosher. Unfortunately, one of the voyagers can't help himself—he must have that mouth-watering fungus. Noticing no adverse side effects, some of the other folk recklessly dig in. Shortly thereafter, some of the women think they see giant mushrooms roaming around the forest, but they decide it is merely a Fig Newton of their imagination. As one crew member aptly comments, "Everything seems pretty weird." What these chumps don't realize is that there is a substance in the fungi which destroys nerve tissues and slowly but surely turns human beings into giant, ambulatory clusters of mushrooms. One of the crew members (Akira Kubo) is miraculously preserved from this transmogrification, and it becomes increasingly difficult for him to enjoy meaningful interaction with his friends. As every science-fiction fan knows, walking mushrooms can only chirp and giggle like demented chipmunks. Finally, the one "normal" survivor is rescued and taken back to civilization.

At the film's conclusion, we realize that he has been narrating the entire story from his padded cell in an insane asylum where he was committed for telling the story of a mushroom named Matango. The Japanese psychiatrists refused to believe that any self-respecting fungus would take such an insipid name. Our hero finally turns to the camera, as a close-up shows mushrooms sprouting from his face, and whispers the film's unforgettable climactic line, "I ate them!" Frankly, Akira, we don't give a damn.

Invasion of the Star Creatures [1965]

Bob Ball (funny man), and Frankie Ray (straight man), two American GIs, are kidnapped by aliens from an all-female planet. These creatures are superior beings in every way except for the fact that they cannot act, Needless to say, the delectable dainties have never been kissed, so Ball and Ray do their manly best to uphold the honor of the U.S. Army. In a cave where the spaceship is parked, they try to establish the right romantic mood by offering some particularly rotten impersonations of Jimmy Cagney. When the bosomy aliens can stand it no longer, they decide to summon the "Carrot Creatures" to deal with the upstart servicemen. These vegetable mutants are outfitted in leg stockings, potato sacks, flappy pitchfork hair and Ping-Pong ball eyes. *Boxoffice* magazine, one of the few publications to take notice of *Star Creatures* when it was released, gave the film the following rave review: "What a lot of baloney! Such a waste of time, film and effort. The title was good, but was it a spooky film? Nope! A comedy!! Closed the first night." In one memorable scene, Bob Ball, the poor man's Stan Laurel, is given a back flip by a veggie monster. He intelligently remarks. "Wow! That's the first time a salad's ever *tossed* me!"

"Comedian" Bob Ball experiences a close encounter of the carrot kind during an intimate scene in Invasion of the Star Creatures.

Please Don't Eat My Mother (Alternate Titles: *Glump* and *Hungry Pets*) [1973]

Released by Harry Novak's Boxoffice International Pictures, the same company that perpetrated *I Dismember Mama* (*See: The Worst Title of All Time*), this film was promoted with the sophisticated ad line: "A Laugh with Every Burp!" The unforgettable Buck Kartalian plays a 43-year-old virgin who feeds his mother, a policeman, and assorted young lovers from a nearby park to the voracious vegetable he is growing as a houseplant. When the public response proved less than sensational, Boxoffice International went back to the old drawing board and rereleased the same film under the title *Hungry Pets*. The ad showed three scantily clad centerfold girls and implied that they were the Hungry Pets described so eloquently on the marquee. Presumably, filmgoers would be more titillated by a porno flick than by a vegetable movie, which just goes to show that people are always more interested in tomatoes than they are in tomatoes.

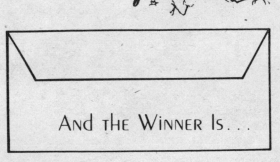

And the Winner Is...

... Attack of the Mushroom People

A very special Golden Turkey, stuffed with mixed green salad and basted in Green Goddess dressing, is presented to this Japanese tour-de-worst. *Mushroom People* takes itself so much more seriously than the other vegetarian fantasies nominated in this category that it wins the award, stems down. This saga proceeds in the solemn tone of a film with a message—in this case warning all shipwrecked travelers never to eat a mysterious fungus unless it has been approved by the Board of Health. If not for the wide distribution of this film, walking, talking clusters of mushrooms might be running around enchanted deserted islands in every corner of the globe.

Not surprisingly, *Mushroom People* has built up a loyal cult following among bad-film fanatics. In Los Angeles, one late-night TV movie host aired the film a half-dozen times in the same year. During the intermissions, the host entertained his fans by making phone calls to "Pizza Fella" who was in the process of being strangled by a mushroom who stubbornly resisted immersion in tomato sauce. He also introduced a sing-ing-dancing vaudeville act known as "The Mushroom Taber-nacle Choir." We'll take ours with anchovies and sausage—but be sure to hold the vegetables.

The Worst Performance by Sonny Tufts

No book on the worst film achievements of all time would be complete without a special section devoted to the immortal Sonny Tufts. Though his film career passed its zenith in the late 1940s, his memory has been kept alive and cherished by bad-film fanatics everywhere. This thriving cult of Sonny-worshipers includes no less a man than Johnny Carson who for years has used Tufts' name as a running gag on his TV show.

Born as Bowen Charleston Tufts III, the blond-haired, blue-eyed, 6' 4" superstar came from the most distinguished Back Bay Boston stock. One of his ancestors, Charles Tufts, had founded Tufts College. "Sonny," however, attended Yale where he starred on the football team and played a leading role in numerous dramatic productions. He also found time to write a column for the Yale Record, *displaying the same sort of scintillating humor that later sparkled in such unforgettable films as* Miss Susie Slagle's *and* Bring on the Girls. *Among his hilarious laugh-getters were such noteworthy lines as "My papa made his fortune in petroleum and sent me to college to get away from it oil," and "'Who was that hobo I seen you with?' 'That was no oboe, that was my fife!'" With ambitions as a full-fledged renaissance man, Sonny moved on from his triumphs as a comedy writer to a three-year stint as a voice student at the Metropolitan Opera. This rigorous training prepared him for a bit part in the Broadway musical* Sing for Your Supper *which led in turn to his first big break: a Hollywood screen test. According to all reports, his serious audition was taken as a comedy scene (a taste of things to come!) but the casting director was nonetheless impressed by Sonny's physical appearance and screen presence. As a result, Tufts won the part of Kansas, "The Shirtless GI," in Mark Sandrich's hit drama about World War II nurses,* So Proudly We Hail! *This role gave Sonny abundant opportunity to display his manly deltoids and pectorals, and so the frustrated opera singer was transformed overnight into a major beefcake star. Headlines proclaimed Tufts "The Male Sensation of 1944!" and Paramount anointed him as the studio's "Reigning*

Pin-Up King." That same year, a poll of film distributors across the United States picked Sonny Tufts as the Hollywood actor with the greatest promise as a star-of-tomorrow.

What happened? Unfortunately the industry and the public discovered that Sonny didn't know how to act. That's all very well, you may insist, but numerous Hollywood personalities have gone on to glorious stardom without any overt manifestations of acting talent. (See: the "Life Achievement Awards" in this book.) With Sonny, however, the problem went beyond mere ineptitude. There was a certain magic that took place whenever he walked onto a set that absolutely guaranteed low quality for the resulting film. During the 1940s, he made an astonishing series of bombs and clunkers and, not surprisingly, he found it hard to get work after 1952.

Though Sonny's acting career lay largely dormant, his off-screen image as a public personality began to blossom in new and unexpected directions. During the fifties he was arrested three times on charges of public drunkenness, including one particularly colorful incident in which he entered a brawl over a $4.65 dinner bill at a greasy spoon diner while in the company of a hula dancer named Luuki-ana Kaeoloa. In 1951, his wife, Barbara Lorayne Tufts, sued for divorce and complained publicly of his drinking and squandering of family funds. The year 1954 found Sonny in the news once more, when a stripper named "Melody Carol" sued him for $250,000. She charged that Tufts had taken a bite out of her upper left thigh, thereby leaving one of her key professional assets permanently disfigured. Tufts settled out of court for $600, but was arrested the next year for beating a Mrs. Adrienne Forman at another café.

In 1959, Tufts made a last, desperate attempt at a comeback. As he told the Los Angeles Mirror-News: *"I'm crusading for the role of Jim Bowie in* The Alamo *the way Frank Sinatra fought for Maggio in* From Here to Eternity." *Needless to say, Sonny lost the part—maybe he should've tried putting a severed horse's head in the bed of the studio boss. In 1969, our hero made headlines for the last time—he was hospitalized "after falling off a bar stool" at The Cock and Bull. He died of pneumonia in 1970 at the age of 54, but his cinematic legacy lives on.*

And the Nominees Are...

Cat Women on the Moon [1953]

Rocket-ship commander Sonny Tufts is sent to the dark side of the moon where, presumably, he will have a hard time buying a drink. He does, however, find a large number of bar girls dressed in low-cut, black leotards with velvet chokers around their necks. Because their Oriental eyeshadow gives them a vague resemblance to Siamese kittens, they are known as "The Cat Women of the Moon." (Hence the title ... pretty clever, huh?) Sonny reacts to their tasteless costumes by walking through his part with mouth agape and both eyebrows raised. Needless to say, the moonlings have never met a movie star before, so they use their feline wiles to score points with "The Male Sensation of 1944." Tufts, however, cannot be distracted from his wholesome romance with Marie Windsor, his ship's navigator. One of the Cat Women is so deeply touched by this devotion between the two has-been stars that she helps the rocket ship and its crew return to earth unharmed.

The male ultra-fantasy of visiting distant worlds populated exclusively by gorgeous, man-hungry females has served as the basis for several other terrible films, including *The Queen of Outer Space* (1958) with Zsa Zsa Gabor as one of the luscious denizens of Venus and *Fire Maidens from Outer Space* (1965) with the "lost girls of Atlantis" dancing to the strains of Bor-

Sonny Tufts displays the virile charm that made him "The Male Sensation of 1944."

The Cat-Women on the Moon *prepare to take on our hero.*

odin's *Polovetsian Dances*. *Cat Women of the Moon* is distinguished chiefly by three factors: 1.) the inimitable presence of Mr. Sonny Tufts, 2.) its initial presentation as a 3-D feature, and 3.) a fascinating lawsuit that followed its release. The film's producer, Al Zimbalist, initiated the legal action aimed at the radio program *My Little Margie*. In one of the show's episodes, the characters went to the movies to see a wretched sci-fi drama called "Cat Women from Outer Space." Zimbalist claimed that the radio program thereby "disparaged, ridiculed, parodied, mimicked and libeled" his important work of art. He asked for $1,200,000 in damages. Presumably, the two parties settled out of court.

Cottonpickin' Chickenpickers [1968]

This hillbilly musical concerns the adventures of two numb-skulled young men who want to make their way to Hollywood,

California, but instead end up in Hollywood, Florida, without knowing the difference. When food becomes scarce, they rob a chicken farm and then, over the next hour on the screen, are chased endlessly through the Florida swamps by characters named Bird-Dog Berrigan, Susie Zickafoose, and Liquid Louie Tailfeathers. Sonny Tufts portrays cousin Urie, an aging Everglades drunk with mangy chin-whiskers. He wanders around the swamps in a stupor, occasionally mumbling, grunting or burping—mostly at inappropriate moments. It is hard to tell whether his slurred speech is an attempt to render a Southern accent, or to show the mental impairment of his alcoholic character. As if the plot and dialogue weren't enough, this film also assaults the senses with a series of unbearable songs, including "Dirty Ole Egg Suckin' Dog" and "This Must Be the Bottom." The last title seems particularly appropriate since *Cottonpickin' Chickenpickers* marked Sonny Tufts' last appearance on the big screen.

Government Girl [1943]

Hailed by Bosley Crowther of *The New York Times* as "hopelessly dull," this film fails miserably in its attempt to follow in the footsteps of *Mr. Smith Goes to Washington*. Sonny plays the part of an aspiring young bureaucrat who is supposed to double the production of bombs at government-defense plants. (That's Air Force *bombs*, Sonny, not the cinematic variety.) His high-spirited secretary, the "Government Girl" of the title, helps him overcome some difficulties with a Senate committee; and to the surprise of absolutely no one, the two of them fall in love and get married. The part of the secretary is shamelessly overplayed by Olivia de Havilland who tries to be both "screamingly funny" and adorably cute. One might accuse her of scene-stealing, except that stealing scenes from Sonny Tufts is a good deal easier than taking candy from that proverbial baby. Tufts handles the role in his traditional grin-and-bear-it style, and looks as if Olivia de Havilland has been screaming into his left ear for an unendurable length of time. He is decidedly out of place in a cast in which nearly everyone else seems to be on the verge of comedic hysteria. We can just imagine Sonny protesting to the director, Dudley Nichols: "But I can't *over*act,

Mr. Nichols! I don't even know how to act." After the film's release, the New York *Herald Tribune* reviewed it with a classic understatement. "Let's face it," the paper declared. "*Government Girl* won't clutter up the race for the Academy Award honors . . ." Ah yes, but just think of its chances for the Golden Turkeys!

Sonny Tufts at the height of his popularity is besieged by a bevy of beauteous and youthful admirers.

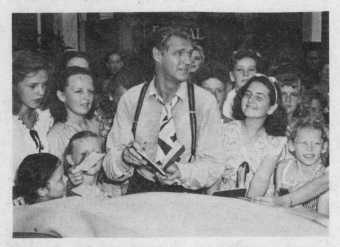

The Well-Groomed Bride [1946]

To describe this film as a romantic trifle would be taking it too seriously—it is actually more of a romantic hiccup. Remember *The Pride and the Passion*—the Stanley Kramer clunker of the 1950s in which the entire action revolves around an enormous cannon? Well, *The Well-Groomed Bride* concerns itself with a single bottle of champagne. Our man Tufts is once again teamed with Olivia de Havilland, who is so embarrassed by the script this time that she can't even get up the energy to overact. According to the plot's main premise, there is only one magnum of French champagne in the entire city of San Francisco, and two parties want it desperately. First, there's Margie (Olivia de Havilland) who will do anything to marry Army Lieutenant Torchy (Sonny Tufts). As it turns out, Sonny has promised to lead her to the altar if she meets him at the train with a magnum of champagne. (You see—here's a man who'll do anything for a drink.) Then, prepared to thwart Margie's plans, we have contestant number two in the champagne sweepstakes: Navy Lieutenant Briggs (Ray Milland, who was also hung-up on a bottle in *The Lost Weekend*). Briggs is under strict orders from his captain to procure the precious magnum for the christening of a newly built aircraft carrier. In what the studio modestly billed as "the merriest rivalry ever staged," the crafty Ray Milland eventually prevails. He lures the unsuspecting Sonny into reconsidering a former girlfriend, thereby breaking up the romance with Olivia, so that Milland ends up with both booze and babe. The finale shows Olivia standing at his side, happily smashing the precious champagne bottle against the bow of the aircraft carrier.

The character portrayed by Sonny Tufts is not conspicuously long on brains, and in this sense, our hero does the role justice. He spends a lot of his time grunting, gritting his teeth, and mugging with sophomoric Alley-Oop imitations. When he finds out that he is going to lose Olivia, his light-o'-love, he registers his pain by looking as if he is about to bite her. Judging from his bearish performance, it is difficult to know whether he is more interested in the girl or the champagne.

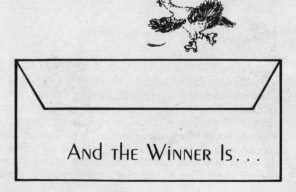

AND THE WINNER IS...

. . . Government Girl

In view of the particularly stiff competition in this category, we are fortunate that Sonny Tufts himself has made our selection for us. To let the star put it in his words: "After *So Proudly We Hail!* they thought they could put me in anything and make money. The material was just terrible. My second movie was something called *Government Girl* with Olivia de Havilland. One night, my wife and I were driving down Hollywood Boulevard past Grauman's Chinese. The line for the movie went around the block. I wanted to stop the car and tell all those people that the movie stunk, but my wife wouldn't let me. I felt awful about those poor people waiting in line to see the *worst movie ever made*. Olivia and the director thought that it was very funny; I thought it was as funny as three caskets. I was right."

He certainly was—and we'll bid a fond farewell to Sonny by observing that he may well have done better as a film critic than he did as an actor.

The Most Ludicrous Racial Impersonation in Hollywood History

IN THE BAD-OLD-DAYS of silent cinema, most Americans believed that nonwhites were simply incapable of serious acting and so accepted racial impersonation as a matter of course. When D. W. Griffith used white actors in black-face for the key slave roles in The Birth of a Nation, he followed one of the enshrined dramatic conventions of his time—much as a director on the Elizabethan stage would automatically cast young men in drag for all the women's roles. Very slowly, a sort of enlightenment reached Hollywood, but examples of absurd transracial casting persist to this day. Some of the most idiotic and unjustifiable instances are listed below.

And the Nominees Are . . .

Robby Benson sensitively portrays a Chicano gang leader in Walk Proud.

Robby Benson as a Chicano in *Walk Proud* [1979]

This tacky ripoff of *West Side Story* proved so offensive to Mexican-American sensibilities that it was never shown in many of the barrio neighborhoods for which it was originally intended. Mr. Robby Benson (né Segal) plays a Chicano gang-leader involved with an upper-class Anglo girl in a star-crossed romance. Needless to say, the Benson character—"Emilio Mendez"—owns a heart of gold beneath his macho-man exterior. After all, that sweet Robby Benson doesn't even look like one of those mean hombres from East L.A., now does he? No, he does not. As *Boxoffice* magazine points out, "he looks like a fraternity kid with a suntan." The contact lenses used to mask his baby-blue eyes and the swarthy makeup employed to darken his complexion are at best ineffectual; at worst, ridiculous. Nor does the light Spanish accent used in his speech or the greasy black treatment applied to his hair add to the persuasiveness of his characterization. At least the late Freddie Prinze was in reality half-Hispanic; Benson, on the other hand, walks though his film as if in imminent danger of biting into a tamale with the cornhusk unremoved. Although his earlier films such as *One on One* and *Ice Castles* have seldom been hailed as masterpieces, they look like pure genius when compared to *Walk Proud*. As *Playboy* magazine sadly but accurately reported, this film "measurably reduces the forward momentum of Robby Benson's career. Go back one step, gringo."

Marlon Brando as an Okinawan in *The Teahouse of the August Moon* [1956]

Ah-So! Honorable Marlon Brando-san in role of wily Oriental? Not possible, you say? Ah, but the ways of the mysterious East are inscrutable—as are the decisions of the casting director in this film. Brando applies his intense method-acting approach to his role as Sakini, an Okinawan operator who figures prominently in the lives of several GIs; and comes up with a characterization that suggests a cross between Charlie Chan and Don Vito Corleone. He uses the same breathy mumbling he

later made famous in *The Godfather*, but enriches it with what might pass for a sixth-grader's idea of an all-purpose Oriental accent. As Bosley Crowther in *The New York Times* reported: "Beneath a dark stain, bad eye makeup and a wig of shiny black hair, you see Mr. Brando enjoying a romp in his own little show." To register enthusiasm for his "colorful" part, Brando bobs habitually up and down like a comedic jack-in-the-box and succeeds in stealing virtually every scene in which he appears with his high-camp portrayal.

Charles Mack and George Moran as "The Two Black Crows" in *Hypnotized* [1933]

It is hard to believe that as late as the 1930s, well into the era of talking motion pictures, this minstrel show comedy team shuffled its way through a series of Hollywood "entertainments." Even by the standards of the time, their brand of ethnic humor seemed crude and primitive. Next to Mack and Moran, Stepin Fetchit is a comic of vast sophistication and irresistible charm, and Amos 'n Andy are witty and perceptive social commentators. Complete with shoe-polish makeup, incessantly rolling eyes, and raspy voices with accents of the "Yassuh, Boss!" variety, "The Two Black Crows" offer a pathetic caricature of American blacks. The film *Hypnotized* provided a perfect showcase for their distinctly limited talents. The "laughs" all take place on shipboard, as our fun-loving fellows travel across the Atlantic with a cargo of wild animals. Recognizing that Mack and Moran will provide little in the way of genuine amusement, the producers decided to enliven the proceedings with several scenes of animal abuse. A running gag shows our uncomprehending heroes twisting a lion's tail, while another sequence features the Two Crows trying to pour water down an elephant's trunk. The film career of this highly creative comedy team came to an abrupt halt in 1934 when Charles Mack died in an Arizona automobile accident. Moran carried on the act with several other partners (after all, who can distinguish individual features beneath all that burnt-cork makeup?) until his own death from a stroke in August, 1949.

Elvis Presley as an Indian in *Stay Away, Joe* [1968]

According to the stereotype, American Indians are stiff, proud and stoical, wearing the same grin expression in every situation and keeping their true emotions carefully concealed. By 1968, Elvis Presley had shown so little emotion in so many different roles, and worked out such a convincing on-screen impression of a cigar-store Indian, that casting him as a Native American seemed a natural and inevitable step. As might be expected,

The King is no ordinary-run-of-the-mill brave—this particular "injun" rides a motorcycle as well as a horse, and can he ever bust a bronc! Why, he's just about the best rodeo rider in these here parts. He also sings, delighting our senses with a host of inventive new songs, including the unforgettable title number, "Stay Away, Joe." The poster art for this film scraped the bottom of the Presley barrel. One placard showed our hero aboard a fierce Harley-Davidson chopper, pulled up alongside an elderly Indian wrapped in a traditional Navajo blanket. The caption, implicitly emerging from Presley's thick and sneering lips, declared: "89 Years Old and He Still Needs His Security Blanket!" Another poster featured Elvis's charismatic countenance staring off into space, while the headline announced: "He's Playing Indian, but He Doesn't Say 'How,' He says 'When'!" In responding to *Stay Away, Joe* we can only echo the terse but eloquent statement of countless Hollywood Indians over the years: "Ugh!"

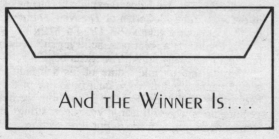

And the Winner Is . . .

... Marlon Brando
in *The Teahouse of the August Moon*

The award in this category must go to the best actor of the bunch. It would be foolish to entertain high expectations for the likes of Robby Benson, Mack and Moran, or Elvis Presley, but Marlon Brando is supposed to be a consummate professional. How could he allow his talent to be so obviously debased? He has no one to blame but himself. Brando became an enthusiastic admirer of John Patrick's Broadway stage play of *Teahouse* and went to see it four times. The role of Sakini intrigued him and developed into something of a personal obsession. Perhaps that helps to explain his shameless overacting in the film. John McCarten of *The New Yorker* states: "Made up to look like a relative of Dr. Fu Manchu, and babbling pidgin English at a great rate, he never succeeds in hiding the fact that he's really an All-American boy."

Despite the juvenile nature of his self-indulgence in this role, Brando was too old to qualify as one of the worst child performers of all time. For that distinction, we have a bevy of genuine brats who will tear at your heart-strings and turn your stomachs, as you will see in our next section...

The Most Obnoxious
Child Performer
of All Time

And the Nominees Are...

Sandy Henville ("Baby Sandy")

This blonde, blue-eyed charmer became known as "the World's Youngest Male Impersonator." At the tender age of one, Sandra Henville played a baby boy, starring opposite Bing Crosby in *East Side of Heaven* (1939). The credits to the film listed her as "Baby Sandy"—the unisex name deliberately designed to allow her to play both male and female roles. The tot continued her transexual ways through *Unexpected Fathers,* made later that same year. It was only with *Sandy Is a Lady* (1940), the first in her string of "B" epics, that Miss Henville at long last came out of the closet in all her resplendent femininity.

The combination of chubby pink cheeks, wide eyes and spit curls delighted millions of fans. Soon after the success of her first starring venture, Baby Sandy toddled through two other vehicles, *Sandy Gets Her Man* and *Sandy Steps Out*. Once again, the versatile star met both popular and critical success.

From that point, however, her story turns grim. Universal allowed Miss Henville's contract to expire, and made no attempt to renew it. Baby Sandy, once the toast of the pablum set, suddenly had a hard time finding work. During this lean period, the former star was reduced to working at Republic Studios in various bit parts. One still from 1941 shows her sitting on top of a hotel desk, while three men around her carry

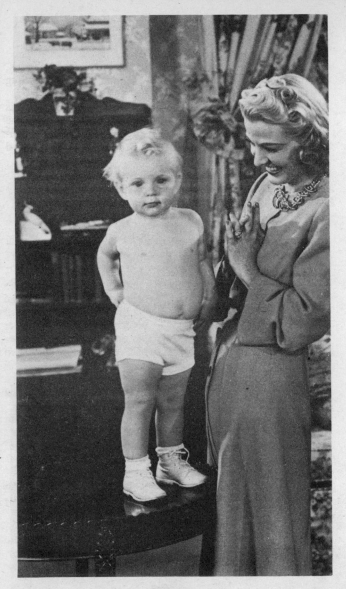

on a conversation, apparently oblivious to her faded charms. At this point, she was well over three-years-old and struggling to keep her figure.

In her last film (*Johnny Doughboy;* Republic, 1942) this unfortunate child, once on top of the movie world, suffered the ultimate indignity: her name appeared below that of Jane Withers on the credit line for this winner. Sandra Henville retired at the age of four.

Claude Jarman, Junior

According to a studio press release, director Clarence Brown "discovered" this adorable young man on Valentine's Day, 1945. Brown, who had been slated to direct the screen adaptation of Marjorie Kinnan Rawlings' best-seller *The Yearling*,

Claude Jarman, Jr., (with his movie father Gregory Peck) exudes the native intelligence and sophistication that made his performance in The Yearling *his greatest role.*

conducted a long, frustrating search of the Deep South in quest of an unknown, unspoiled countryboy to play the part of Jody Baxter in the film. Having nearly abandoned all hope, he walked dejectedly down the halls of a Nashville elementary school when he suddenly spotted our hero taking down Valentine decorations from the wall. In that fateful moment, as violins swelled to a crescendo in the background, movie history was made. Brown convinced the Jarmans to give Claude a screen test, and the eleven-year-old and his family were soon winging their way to a new life in Hollywood.

Jarman's role in *The Yearling*, as a boy who raises a pet fawn only to have it killed by his father, won him an award for "most outstanding child performance of the year 1946." In truth, his whiny voice and sing-song delivery carried no dramatic force whatsoever, but Jarman, after all, had been hired for looks rather than acting ability. In countless press releases, M-G-M tried to promote the wholesome image of their new child star. His activities in the Boy Scouts received careful scrutiny, as did his ambition to play halfback for the University of Tennessee football team. His participation in motion pictures went on for years, with numerous sugary performances that produced an uncomfortable reaction among diabetics and non-diabetics alike. Among his screen triumphs were films such as *High Barbaree, Roughshod,* and the highly acclaimed *Fair Wind to Java*.

In his later years, Mr. Jarman, Jr., became producer and president of his own film company, Tel-West Films. Recently he served as Director of Cultural Affairs for the city of San Francisco. He never did get the chance to play halfback for the University of Tennessee.

David "Dondi" Kory

Hollywood logic works its wonders in mysterious ways. One would think that the sentimental, crudely drawn comic strip *Dondi*, about a pathetic Italian war orphan who is adopted by American GIs and brought to the United States, offered little basis for cinematic entertainment. Director Albert Zugsmith, however, who previously crafted such wholesome family films as *High School Confidential* and *Sex Kittens Go to College,*

David Kory, with his co-star Mr. Dog Buddy, reads a headline concerning his own disappearance in Dondi.

reached a different conclusion. In collaboration with Gus Edson, creator of the comic strip, he set to work in 1961 on a movie version of *Dondi* and began a search for a little boy to play the title role. Advertisements in all newspapers that ran the comic strip brought more than 100,000 responses from mothers who thought their tiny tykes closely resembled the fictional orphan with the huge, staring eyes and drooling mouth. Eventually, Zugsmith and the other judges decided that one David Kory, the five-year-old son of a former Radio City Music Hall Rockette, looked most precisely like a cartoon. Young Kory won the coveted role, and with it a change of name. In all future publicity from the Allied Artists and his own agent, the boy became known as David "Dondi" Kory.

The resulting motion picture turned out to be so poor that there is plenty of blame to go around, but prime responsibility must lie squarely and clearly on Mr. Kory's fat little head. As *Variety* charitably reported: "The film introduces David Kory as Dondi. Lamentably, the child speaks as if he's got both a cold and a bagful of jelly beans in his mouth." Critic Steven H. Scheuer enthusiastically described Kory as "one of the most untalented child performers ever to appear on the screen." Instead of giving Dondi any sort of identifiable foreign accent—which clearly exceeded the child's acting abilities—the film-makers instruct Kory to speak in a bizarre dialect that can only be described as Mongoloid. When our pint-sized hero develops a crush on "Patti Page, the Singing Rage" (who plays a major role in the film) he declares to her: "Oh Goshers, Lady Buddy! Every time you're coming here you're looking more prettier!" This sort of polished, silver-tongued flattery immediately melts her heart (remember, it's Patti Page) and nearly steals the blonde songstress away from her boyfriend, David Janssen. At one point, Patti can control herself no longer and bursts out with a ballad describing Dondi's many virtues. One of the touching verses tells us:

> His smile can chase the clouds
> And brighten skies above
> And every empty heart
> Will fill up with love.

Whoever wrote these words had apparently been filled up with something else.

Following the modest financial success of *Dondi*, director Zugsmith planned a sequel with the intriguing title *Dondi Goes Native in Brooklyn* and even discussed the possibility of a *Dondi* TV show. Fortunately, these projects never materialized and David Kory returned to well-deserved obscurity—but not before leaving his chubby handprint on the silver screen.

Lee Harcourt Montgomery

This juvenile sensation of the 1970s specialized in making himself pathetic; in all his major screen roles he plays an unhappy young man with some debilitating physical or psychological affliction. As the son of Carol Burnet and Walter Matthau in *Pete n' Tillie* (1972) he portrayed a nine-year-old leukemia victim who dies before the comedy is over. A comedy about a couple trying to adjust to the death of their son may not be your idea of hilarity, but Lee H. Montgomery does his best to make the concept work. Before disappearing from the screen he succeeds in making himself so obnoxious that the audience breathes a sigh of relief when they know his role has ended.

In *Burnt Offerings* (1976) he is the son of another "fun couple"—this time Oliver Reed and Karen Black—who move into a spooky ol' house for the summer. The plucky lad has several close calls—he nearly drowns while playing in the swimming pool with his father, and shortly thereafter monster trees try to crush the car in which he is sitting. Finally, a chimney from the house falls directly on his head, doing him in for good and surprising no one who knows about Montgomery's fatality rate.

Despite these distinguished appearances (and a brief role in George C. Scott's incestuous ego-trip *The Savage Is Loose* in 1976), Lee H. Montgomery is still best remembered for his role in *Ben*. This sequal to the highly popular *Willard* tells the story of a touching romance between a frail, sickly boy and his pet killer rat. Montgomery's towering performance as the defender of a group of rats, numbering more than 3,000, led critic Judith Crist to refer to him as "a small repulsive fat-faced boy." At the conclusion of *Ben*, Lee H. outdoes himself. The

210

Lee H. Montgomery attempts to upstage a haunted house in Burnt Offerings.

rats have all been destroyed and the poor sickly boy sits alone in his room to mourn their demise. But lo, through some miracle Ben himself has survived and the faithful rodent makes it back to Lee's bedroom to visit with his friend. Witnessing the interaction between the two principals, it is hardly surprising that the rat who played Ben got considerably better reviews than did Lee H. Montgomery.

AND THE WINNER IS. . .

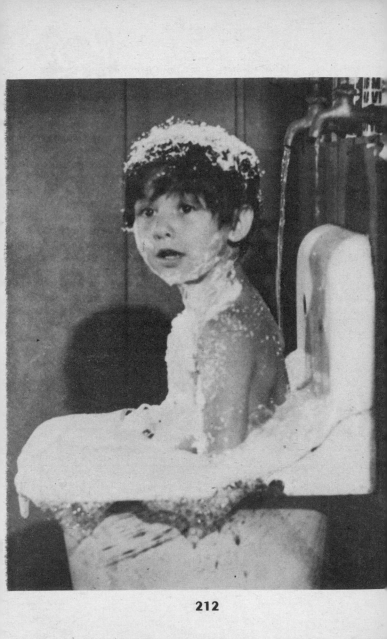

... David "Dondi" Kory

Thanks to his loud grating voice, idiotic staring eyes, perpetually open mouth and obvious pleasure in his own performance, this lovable war orphan sweeps the field. It should be noted that he receives a powerful assist from the inane script by producer-director Albert Zugsmith and cartoonist Gus Edson. With the words provided by these two, Dondi's handling of the English language is enough to send Henry Higgins into catatonia. The boy's insipid delivery works sheer magic on lines like these:

> "'Magination can get you places even faster than rocket ships!"

> *(To his pet mongrel)* "Quiet, Mr. Dog! They finding you here, they sending you back, then us both lonesome."

> *(An impassioned cry)* "Buddies! Where you are? Is me—Dondi!"

> *(A declaration of patriotic fervor)* "Goshers! America such wonderful place!"

> *(In a fit of religious ecstasy, the boy praises to The Lord)* "I wish you make them let me stay in America, Mr. Big-Buddy, please!"

We wish you preserve us from all future Dondi sequels, Mr. Big-Buddy, please!

David Kory is today twenty-five, his short-lived stardom a vaguely troubling memory from long ago. It is not known whether he continues to use "Dondi" as his middle name.

The Worst Film
You Never Saw

TURNING THE PAGES of this book, reviewing some of the wretched films which have been foisted onto an unsuspecting public, one might well conclude that Hollywood executives have no shame at all. This is not precisely true. In some rare instances, a finished film will turn out to be so irredeemably awful that its owners will perform a "mercy killing"—preventing its release to theaters across the country. This process not only prevents embarrassment—it saves money. Advertising and distributing a film can cost millions of dollars; and if the movie stands no chance of earning back this additional investment, it makes good sense to let it sink peacefully into oblivion. Each of the films nominated in this category disappeared before receiving national distribution, thereby saving innocent movie-goers from unnecessary evenings of agony. This is one type of timely abortion on which right-to-lifers and women's libbers can wholeheartedly agree.

And the Nominees Are...

Billy Jack Goes to Washington [1977]

In the aftermath of Watergate, a number of Hollywood figures developed an interest in filming a remake of Frank Capra's classic, *Mr. Smith Goes to Washington*. The time seemed just right for another version of the beguiling fable of an innocent man-of-the-people who comes to Babylon-on-the-Potomac and cleans up the cynicism and corruption of the Senate. Singer John Denver, for one, wanted badly to do the movie, but saw his hopes blown Rocky Mountain high by a superior bid for the rights to the old film from producer-director-writer-star-messiah Tom Laughlin.

Laughlin, as you may recall, is the Hollywood maverick who confounded the critics and experts by grossing more than $100 million with his two previous films, *Billy Jack* (1972) and *The Trial of Billy Jack* (1974). These melodramas chronicle the adventures of a black-hatted, soft-spoken Indian hero and former green beret who uses barefoot karate kicks to preach his hip cool gospel of peace and understanding. By beating the stuffing out of a number of overfed, middle-aged villains, Laughlin won a formidable cult following for his bizarre character. "It's a shame," he modestly confessed to *Time* magazine, "that the youth of this country have only two heroes—Ralph Nader and Billy Jack." Given this high estimation of his own popularity, is it any wonder that Laughlin-Billy Jack finds himself at the beginning of this new movie, appointed by the governor of his state, to fill an unexpired term in the U.S. Senate? It hardly matters that in his previous appearances Billy has been severely wounded by the National Guard, after standing trial for murder. We believe in rehabilitation, don't we?

From this auspicious opening premise, *Billy Jack Goes to Washington* staggers forward at the stately pace of a drugged brontosaurus. The film lasts for nearly three hours and in its numbskulled way tries to follow each of the twists and turns of the old Capra formula. Lucie Arnaz (daughter of famous parents and sister of that distinguished thespian, Desi Arnaz, Jr.) makes her movie debut in the Jean Arthur role as the new Senator's seasoned but soft-hearted secretary. Meanwhile, E. G. Marshall steps into Claude Rains' part as a corrupt older Senator. Unfortunately, Laughlin cannot resist the temptation of throwing his own paranoia and conspiracy theories into the stew, and so we enjoy plot "innovations" that bring the story up to date and take it "even beyond the Watergate experience." The secretary's husband, for instance, is murdered by government secret agents in the amphitheater behind the Tomb of the Unknown Soldier. This is not precisely the light, gentle touch one would expect in romantic comedy, but then nobody has ever accused Tom Laughlin of possessing a sense of humor. Billy Jack does manage to deliver several long, preachy speeches on the Senate floor but disappoints his fans by gesturing only with his hands and not with his bare feet.

215

Laughlin ran out of money in the middle of production, after having squandered $750,000 to build a precise replica of the Senate chamber on a Hollywood soundstage. With his creditors closing in around him, he bid for sympathy from the public by announcing that his family's personal living allowance had been "drastically cut" to a mere $50,000 a month. Finally, he secured the funds to finish his masterpiece. but when he tried to distribute the film, he ran into an elaborate barrage of suits and countersuits involving his creditors, business associates, the owners of the two previous Billy Jack films, and most of the rest of the world. The movie ultimately played a few local theaters around the country, and truns up occasionaly on TV. A generous production budget—in this case more than $7 million dollars—has seldom been wasted so lavishly and so completely.

The Day the Clown Cried [1972]

After playing an astronaut, a mad scientist, a man from Mars, and other challenging roles in his previous 40 films, what new worlds were left for Jerry Lewis to conquer in 1972? What about the nightmare world of Auschwitz? How about the premise of a lovable circus clown who entertains children about to be gassed by the Nazis? Sounds terrific, huh? Startlingly original, no? Tasteless and nauseating—definitely yes.

This was supposed to be Jerry's first serious film, and he directed and co-produced it as well as playing the starring role. When interviewed by a *New York Times* reporter at Caesar's Palace in Las Vegas, he sounded as dedicated and intense about this project as he is concerning his muscular dystrophy telethons. "The clown in the movie is a sort of Pied Piper who doesn't really get along with the other internees," he explained. "It is he who is assigned to try to keep the kids in the camp happy—and ignorant of the crimes being committed by Hitler. And it is he who, in the end, is expected to lead the children—and himself—to the ovens." Concerning his participation in this grim tale, Lewis observed, "I believe that I've grown enough to go ahead with what I feel is a very important film for me." To underscore his serious intentions, Lewis tried to sign French actress Jeanne Moreau for the meaty part of the clown's long-suffering wife. (Jeanne Moreau and Jerry Lewis??!!! Well, at first they thought Hepburn and Tracy were mismatched, didn't they?) Fortunately for her career, Moreau turned him down, and Lewis had to settle for Harriet Anderssen, Pierre Etaix and Sven Lindberg as his co-stars. Apparently, he never even approached Dean Martin.

Several factors helped to sink this project, including a ridiculous concept, wretched script, haphazard direction, and creative conflicts between Lewis and his co-producer Nat Wachsberger. At one point during the shooting on location in Sweden, Lewis walked off the set and became the object of a lawsuit from his one-time partner. Wachsberger managed to complete filming in spite of these difficulties, but the final version of the movie turned out to be so hopelessly bad that, to the best of our knowledge, it has never been shown in public. Perverted viewers who possess a taste for bizarre tales of clowns in concentration camps will have to content themselves with reruns of *Hogan's Heroes*.

The Extraordinary Seaman [1969]

Alan Alda may turn out to be one of the biggest stars of the 1980s, but his movie career got off to a dismal start with this certified stinker. M-G-M felt so embarrassed by the low quality of the finished film that they sat on it for two years before daring to expose it to public view. When the first trial runs produced the hostile response the studio had expected, the movie was quickly withdrawn and forgotten.

Alda plays the part of an accountant-turned-Navy-Lieutenant by World War II, who is rescued with his crew (Mickey Rooney, Jack Carter, Manu Tapou) by the British gunboat *H.M.S. Curmudgeon*. The commander of this craft is an alcoholic aristocrat played by David Niven. Halfway through the film, we learn that Niven is actually a ghost—which would explain why he always wears his dress whites. Some 40 years before, this "extraordinary seaman" drowned while in a drunken stupor, and he has now been allowed to return to earth to redeem the honor of his distinguished naval family by fighting in the new war. Faye Dunaway, as an American plantation owner trying to escape the Japanese invasion of the Philippines, also takes ship with this crew of unfunny losers. Niven tries to keep a straight face while snarlingly assuring her that "Women and ships don't mix," but finds himself overruled by Ms. Dunaway's quick work with a pistol. All of this is director John Frankenheimer's idea of sparkling war-time comedy. The climax of the film shows the Japanese bombing of the *Curmudgeon*, which sets off a crate of fireworks that Ms. Dunaway just happened to leave ondeck. A tremendous display of sparklers, shooting stars and other pyrotechnics is accompanied by a stirring rendition of *The Star Spangled Banner*. All in all, we haven't experienced such unbridled and uproarious "fun" since the last time we looked at a Tom and Jerry cartoon.

When director Frankenheimer turned in the finished version of his comedic clunker, the studio brass worried over its skimpy length. With a running time of only 75 minutes, it fell well below the average for a feature-length motion picture. To remedy the situation, the powers-that-be inserted several minutes of World War II newsreel footage. Needless to say, this sort of padding makes the film even more distasteful than before; we are treated, for instance, to more than six glimpses of Bess Truman trying unsuccessfully to break a champagne bottle while christening a ship. Nor do the high-flown titles, flashed on the screen to announce the subdivisions of this epic, add to our sense of cinematic adventure. These headings—"The Gathering Storm," "Their Finest Hour," "The Hinge of Fate"— are borrowed from Winston Churchill's multivolume history of World War II, and their use here implies that the entire struggle, like this film, could be dismissed as a bad joke. One of the few reviews received by *The Extraordinary Seaman* before it sank beneath the waves of well-deserved obscurity came from Kevin Thomas in the *Los Angeles Times*. "There is absolutely not one honest-to-goodness laugh to be found in it," he declares. *"The Extraordinary Seaman* is the most total fiasco since the Edsel."

Matilda [1978]

Producer-screenwriter Al Ruddy had high hopes indeed for this $5.2-million boxing epic. After all, the public had just taken to heart a dumb brute named Rocky Balboa, and Ruddy's film

Elliott Gould and Robert Mitchum flank the awesomely lifelike boxing kangaroo who plays the title role in Matilda.

offered a heavyweight contender even more unlikely and less intelligent than Sylvester Stallone. The title creature in *Matilda* is a 6′1″ boxing kangaroo who battles its way to a championship bout with the help of promoter Elliott Gould, sportswriter Robert Mitchum, and trainer Clive Revill. This may not appear to be a particularly promising premise for an emotionally gripping message picture, but producer Ruddy saw a deep significance in his saga of a marsupial mauler. "Most audiences will want to see how our characters operate and grow themselves, morally and spiritually," he told the press. "It is possibly the most sophisticated film ever to get a G rating . . . We are not treating it as a film for five year olds but it will be safe to take them."

This is only true if the five-year-olds are mentally defective—for surely any normal child could tell that the celebrated Matilda is nothing more than an actor walking around inside an outrageously bogus kangaroo suit. Concerning this hilarious costume—which would embarrass any self-respecting trick-ortreater—the talkative Ruddy enthused: "We debated about using both a real kangaroo and an actor in costume and opted for the latter as the cross-cutting proved too jarring to the viewer. However, the costume was a $30,000 investment that paid off as it not only provided freedom of movement, but we were able to program it with transistors to allow us to direct the actor's tiniest gesture." Despite the hoopla about the sophisticated equipment inside the stuffed kangaroo head, Tom Allen of *The Village Voice* wrote: "Matilda is worked by a person in a fur suit and fixed mask...The technicians do not even get the ears to wiggle and the mouth to pucker until the final minutes."

Despite these limitations, everyone connected with *Matilda* expected that the kangaroo impersonator would win a huge cult following. Reviewing the advertising and promotional campaign planned for the film, *Variety* predicted that "by the end of this summer, no living American should be unaware that 'Matilda' is a boxing kangaroo." Producer Ruddy arranged an unprecedented number of product tie-ins to coincide with the release of his movie, and several commercial plugs found their way into the story itself. The viewer might wonder, for instance, why Matilda makes such a fuss over a particular brand of tennis ball following one pugilistic triumph. The answer is that Penn Tennis Equipment, Inc., initiated a new line of "Kangaroo Court" tennis balls and committed nearly $200,000 to print ads promoting the film. In total, Ruddy and his associates managed to rope-in nearly $3 million in free advertising with similar gimmicks. It seemed a small concession to show Matilda twice stopping at "the sign of the golden arches" for cheeseburger snacks when these few minutes of film led to a major deal with McDonald's. The fast food chain planned to identify the boxing kangaroo with a new line of sundaes, and to use Matilda's photogenic face in TV spots, on print ads, posters and give-away glasses. The fact that you can't walk into a McDonald's today and order a "Matilda Sundae" says a good deal about the ultimate success of this film.

The public response during its brief trial runs proved so dismal that all plans for massive distribution and promotion had to be canceled. This outcome proves two points:

1. That Ruddy could not round up enough five-year-olds who cared about the "moral and spiritual" growth of his characters and

2. That some products are so poor that not even the most ingenious advertising can force them onto the public.

One veteran Hollywood producer, who has garnered several Academy Awards for his films in a distinguished career, told us "off the record" about some of the efforts by American International Pictures to get its big kangaroo-turkey off the ground. "I remember that people were going crazy then because the box-office situation was so hopeless," he recalls. "There was one city—I think it was San Francisco—where it just turned out unbelievably bad. I mean, the first night the film opened, after the lousy reviews in the local press, nobody came to see it. No, I'm not saying it was just a small crowd—I'm saying *nobody* showed up at that theater. They had to run the film for the ushers and the popcorn girls. Anyway, someone in that theater got a bright idea, since they'd at least get stuck with this loser for a couple of more days. They went out and changed the marquee—putting up in big letters a line from one of the reviews. It just said "Worst Movie of the Year" and then had the name of the critic. After that, believe it or not, they did pretty good business in that particular neighborhood. A lot of people were willing to pay, just to see what could make a picture so bad. It just goes to show that if a movie is really lousy enough, it could have a great commercial potential." That's a comforting thought. It suggests that Matilda—like its prototype, the diehard Rocky—may yet make a comeback.

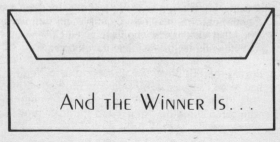

And the Winner Is . . .

... Billy Jack Goes to Washington

Tom Laughlin takes the Turkey as much for his offscreen bad sportsmanship as for his on-camera incompetence. In seeking to explain his monumental failure, he managed to blame everyone except himself—and in particular used the good old U.S. government as his scapegoat. Charging that he had been cruelly harassed, both during and after the shooting of his film, he hinted that the White House itself stood behind the entire plot. "It's unreal and it's frightening," he declared. "The public doesn't stand a chance. There is a concerted effort in Washington to keep information from flowing out." In Laughlin's fantasy world, our top leaders live in mortal fear that the crusading Billy Jack, during his four-week shooting schedule in the capital, might discover damning truths that had escaped all the investigative journalists who have worked there over the years. While nursing the wounds to his pride and pocketbook caused by his cinematic disaster, Laughlin could at least console himself with the idea that he had been martyred because of the uncompromising purity of his art. "Anybody who really is good at tapping into the deeper level of the collective psyche is almost never appreciated in his lifetime, or ever," he observed. Certainly the ingenious Al Ruddy—with boxing kangaroo viewed as a sort of "primal archetype"—can gain comfort from the same thought. Let us shed a tear now for these poor prophets without honor in their own country, and turn our attention to those other visionaries who have given Hollywood some of its most stunning techno-magical developments . . .

The Most Inane and Unwelcome "Technical Advance" in Hollywood History

EVER SINCE, the beginning of the film industry, movie moguls have searched for dramatic technical innovations that would increase the audience appeal of their productions. Some of these advances—such as sound in 1927, or Technicolor in 1935—permanently enriched the potential of the medium. Others amounted to little more than one-shot gimmicks designed to obscure the shortcomings of Grade D movies with little or no intrinsic value. Many of these inane innovations appeared during the fifties and sixties, as it became increasingly difficult for moviemen to lure audiences away from their TV sets and into the theaters.

And the Nominees Are...

"Hallucinogenic Hypnovision" [1965]

This process was designed specifically for Ray Dennis Steckler's *The Incredibly Strange Creatures Who Stopped Living and Became Mixed-Up Zombies* (*see:* The Worst Title of All Time). Ads for the new technology suggested that it was a scientific advance roughly comparable in importance to the development of the polio vaccine. One such advertisement told the public: "Warning! Unlike Anything Before! You are Surrounded by Monsters! Not 3-D but real FLESH-and-BLOOD MONSTERS ALIVE! NOT FOR SISSIES! DON'T COME IF YOU'RE

CHICKEN!" This astonishing bit of technical wizardry is easily explained: at various points in the film, the action was interrupted by a "spiraling hypnotic wheel" that appeared suddenly on the screen. This served as a cue to the theater ushers to run up and down the aisles, wearing bloody, phosphorescent masks that made them resemble the film's star, while waving cardboard axes at the "terrified" audience. Just as the publicity promised, we are "surrounded by Monsters"—or at least by idiots.

"Duo-Vision" [1973]

Developed for a film called *Wicked, Wicked*, this process utilized a split screen throughout the movie. On one side, we watched our heroine (Tiffany Bolling) going through the course of her daily life, while on the other, we saw a crazed killer stalking her through the city. Concerning the concept of showing two films at the same time on a single screen, one critic remarked, "Pity there wasn't enough material for even one."

"Emergo" [1958]

This wonder of modern science, brainchild of producer-director William Castle, enlivened the heavily advertised chiller *The House on Haunted Hill*. At a key moment in the picture, as Vincent Price turned a handle on the screen, an illuminated plastic skeleton slid along two trolley wires from the proscenium of the theater back to the balcony. The original skeleton weighted 15 pounds, but at a screening for Allied Artists executives, it lost its bearings, slipped off the wires and dropped into the audience, slamming chief of studio operations, Eugene Arnstein, on his unsuspecting noggin. After this controversial debut, Castle decided to use a less cumbersome skeleton for the film's national distribution. He set up a small factory on the Allied Artists lot to manufacture 1,000 inflatable skeletons, with electric motors attached, at a cost of $150 each. Meanwhile, a crew of twelve electricians set up "Emergo" in the theaters which would play *The House on Haunted Hill*. As the

Saturday Evening Post reported: "Breakage has been high, for as the balloonlike skeletons wing overhead they present irresistibly attractive targets to small boys with slingshots."

The cast of The House on Haunted Hill *stands stunned at the miracle of Emergo as an inflated skeleton descends over the theater audience on a string.*

"Psychorama" [1960]

For years, psychologists have explored the possibilities of communicating subliminal information through film—flashing images on the screen so quickly that they cannot be perceived by the conscious mind, but nonetheless leave an unconscious imprint on the viewer. A film called *My World Dies Screaming* (retitled *Terror in the Haunted House*) marked Hollywood's first attempt to make use of this technique. At different points in this experimental turkey, a skull is flashed to inspire terror, a crawling snake to inspire hate, two fluttering hearts to generate love, and last, but not least, the huge letters "B-L-O-O-D" to create fear. Unfortunately, Psychorama—also known as "The Precon Process"—left most audiences with headaches and confused recollections about the action onscreen.

"Percepto" [1959]

William Castle strikes again! The same man who brought the world "Emergo" came up with yet another scientific breakthrough the very next year. This new and revolutionary technique, "Percepto," helped make Castle's film *The Tingler* an absolutely unforgettable experience for those few unfortunates who paid to see it. Thanks to low-voltage motors hooked up under the theater seats, Castle administered sharp, unpleasant electric shocks at the climax of the film. In the movie, "The Tingler" is a slithering centipede created by mad scientist Vincent Price. The sting of this beast supposedly "breeds a living organism in the victim's spine, which, if not nullified, will shatter the vertebrae. The only way to nullify it is to scream." As the action of the film moves along, the monster bug wriggles into a neighborhood movie theater. We see it entering the lobby (presumably without a ticket) and then the screen (in our theater, not theirs) goes suddenly blank. With the auditorium in total darkness, Vincent Price's voice comes onto the soundtrack and he informs us: "Ladies and Gentlemen, please do not panic, but scream. Scream for your lives! The Tingler is loose in *this* theater, and if you don't scream, it may kill you!" While planted candy girls in the audience scream their heads off and faint, the soundtrack goes up to full volume with voices of assorted individuals shrieking, "It's on me!" "Help!" and "Look out, it's under your seat!" As if all this weren't enough to disgust even the most hardened veteran of Grade Z cinema, the audience simultaneously receives its electric shocks through the wonders of "Percepto." As the ads promised, "You actually feel real physical sensations as you shiver to its flesh-crawling action!" This is certainly true, if nausea is considered a "real physical sensation."

"Glorious Smell-O-Vision!" [1960]

Mike Todd, Jr. (Liz Taylor's step son), developed this miracle for his film *Scent of Mystery*, starring Denholm Elliott and Peter Lorre. The project had been on the mind of Mike Todd, Sr., before his untimely death and the son resolved to press forward with his father's revolutionary concept. The plot of this breakthrough film revolved around clues provided by two specific aromas—the scent of Chiappelli perfume from a "mystery woman," and a specific pipe tobacco from the villain.

When first offered to the public, Glorious Smell-O-Vision! ran into heavy competition from another "smellie" (trade word for these scent-oriented films) called *Behind the Great Wall*. This documentary tour of China features "AromaRama," in which smells were released through the theater's air-conditioning system. Smell-O-Vision, on the other hand, was pumped from a master-control system to plastic-tube outlets attached to each seat. Every scent could be neutralized by an odorless chemical four seconds later. The master-control system contained more than 50 essences which were concentrated in small metal vials and kept under great pressure. Among the scents used in the film were roses, peaches, wood shavings, bread, bananas, boot polish, salty ocean breeze, oil paint, wine, sugar cane, garlic, gun smoke, clover, coffee, brandy, lavender, incense, peppermint, and lemon. These fragrances were released according to signals from the film's "smell track," but occasionally poor synchronization led to confusion and embarrassment. Even when the system worked perfectly, audience response was decidedly mixed. *Time* magazine reported that "most customers will probably agree that the smell they liked best was the one they got during intermission: fresh air."

Scent of Mystery with Glorious Smell-O-Vision! played only in Chicago, New York and Los Angeles. The film threatened to become a major financial disaster, until it was released without the odors under the new title, *Holiday in Spain*. It eventually made a modest profit for its investors, though, as *Films and Filming* observed: "Denuded of its aromas, it still stinks." To this day, no one has attempted to revive either Smell-O-Vision! or its rival process, AromaRama. Perhaps some enterprising pornographer will take up the challenge in the future, giving a ripe new meaning to the title phrase "The Scent of a Woman."

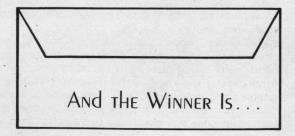

And the Winner Is . . .

... "Percepto"

All of the technological wonders described above had their unpleasant aspects, but only "Percepto," as administered by *The Tingler*, was a full-fledged pain in the.... William Castle, originator of the process and the film, announced in a press release during its production: "Today, the stages at Columbia Studios, where *The Tingler* has been loose for two days, will be open. We reluctantly had to close the set for your own protection as *The Tingler* is the most gory, ghastly, grisly gimmick that ever satellited to the screen from a launching pad of screams. *The Tingler* is still on-stage, but safely locked up. However, this unpredictable mass of pent-up fury that soars beyond the wildest flights of your nightmare fantasies, may somehow escape from bondage. For this reason, every visitor to the *The Tingler* set will be insured for $100,000."

In his personal behavior, the inventive Mr. Castle might well be qualified as an eccentric genius. He would frequently greet reporters with a joy buzzer in his hand, and he once wired a chair in his office for Percepto. With a mischievous smile, he used to administer unexpected shocks to his guests. "Do that again," growled one angry visitor, "and I'll slug you."

Audiences thrilled to the movie magic of Percepto as they viewed William Castle's inspiring saga **The Tingler**.

The Worst Lines of Romantic Dialogue in Movie History

And the Nominees Are...

Airport 1979: The Concorde [1979]

(Stewardess Sylvia Kristel approaches pilot George Kennedy while he sits at the controls of the supersonic plane.)

SYLVIA KRISTEL (seductively): You pilots are such—*men*!

GEORGE KENNEDY: They don't call it a *cock*pit for nothing!

The Assassination of Trotsky [1972]

(Assassin-to-be Alain Delon endures a nasty spat with his lover, Gita [Romy Schneider].)

ROMY SCHNEIDER: If you go I'll kill myself—Frank! I don't know who I am! I don't know who you are!

ALAIN DELON: You're Gita.

ROMY SCHNEIDER: Leave me alone!

Sylvia Kristel and George Kennedy.

John Wayne and Susan Hayward.

The Conqueror [1956]

(Genghis Khan—John Wayne—attempts to embrace the Princess Bortai—Susan Hayward—who responds by throwing a spear at his head and kicking him savagely in the groin.)

SUSAN HAYWARD: For me, there is no peace while you live, Mongrel!

JOHN WAYNE: Say . . . You're beautiful in your wrath!

Imitation of Life [1959]

(Photographer John Gavin conducts an intense conversation with aspiring actress Lana Turner. Overcome by her beauty, he touches her face with his fingertips.)

LANA TURNER: What's the matter?

JOHN GAVIN: Your bones.

LANA TURNER: What about my bones?

JOHN GAVIN: They're perfect. I could easily imagine my camera having a love affair with you.

Lost Horizon [1973]

(Michael York, a headstrong visitor to Shangri-La, falls for Olivia Hussey, one of the comely native girls.)

MICHAEL YORK: You are more beautiful than the women of Thailand. More feminine than the women of France. More pliable than the women of Japan. More . . .

OLIVIA HUSSEY: Stop, stop. I don't want to hear about all those other women. What I want to hear is that you won't leave me.

MICHAEL YORK: Oh, I adore you!!

Northwest Mounted Police [1940]

(Mountie Robert Preston develops an uncontrollable lust for Paulette Goddard, a passionate half-breed girl.)

ROBERT PRESTON: You're the sweetest poison that ever got into a man's blood! I love you! I WANT you!... Listen, you little wildcat, you're the only real thing that's ever happened to me. And nobody—nothing— could ever make me let you go!

PAULETTE GODDARD: Oh, I love you so terrible bad I feel good!—My heart sings like a bird!

The Oscar [1966]

(On the eve of the Academy Awards, actor Frankie Fane— Stephen Boyd—watches his marriage to Elke Sommer collapse.)

ELKE SOMMER: Whatever there was between us, Frankie, you could never call it love! Because "to love" means "to commit yourself" and "to belong." And you never belonged to anybody but yourself, Frankie! You don't belong—nothing belongs to you. So you may have your Oscar—and you may have everything—but you'll have nothing! Bye, Frankie! And I do hope the Oscar keeps you warm on cold nights!

STEPHEN BOYD: Go on and run! Yeah, you're too stupid to understand!

Plan Nine from Outer Space [1959]

(Jet pilot Gregory Walcott bids farewell to his wife Mona McKinnon before going off to do battle with invaders from outer space.)

MONA McKINNON: Be careful. Don't worry about me.

GREGORY WALCOTT: Aw, you're the only thing I *do* worry

Mona McKinnon and Gregory Walcott.

about! Forget about the flying saucers. They're up *there!* But there's something in that cemetery—and that's too close for comfort.

MONA McKINNON: The saucers are up *there*—and the cemetery's out *there*. But I'll be locked up in *there* (she points toward her bedroom). Now. Off to your wild blue yonders.

GREGORY WALCOTT: You promise you'll lock the doors immediately?

MONA McKINNON: I promise. Besides—I'll be in bed before half an hour's gone. With your pillow beside me.

GREGORY WALCOTT: My pillow?

MONA McKINNON: Well, I have to have *something* to keep me company while you're away!

Solomon and Sheba [1959]

(King Solomon [Yul Brynner] and the Queen of Sheba [Gina Lollobrigida] find their budding romance complicated by political factors.)

YUL BRYNNER: From the first. I knew that behind those lovely eyes is the brain of a very clever woman, who would never have traveled eight hundred leagues without a purpose.

GINA LOLLOBRIGIDA: You have found me out! How could I hope to deceive you? I have been trying to entrap you with these . . . (she shakes her arms) . . . to bind you in soft chains, so that I may do with you as I will.

YUL BRYNNER: Every woman demands a price from a man.

238

The Swarm [1978]

(After years of hesitation, druggist Fred MacMurray is finally ready to propose marriage to his aging lady friend, Maureen [Olivia de Havilland].)

> FRED MACMURRAY: Maureen, how long have we known each other? About thirty years? All that time, have you ever heard me beg? Maureen, I'm willing to beg now. I want you to marry me. I know people look at me and think that I'm just the man behind the aspirin counter, but inside I love you.

> OLIVIA DE HAVILLAND: How lucky I am!

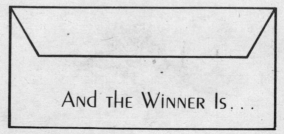

AND THE WINNER IS...

... Northwest Mounted Police

This Cecil B. De Mille atrocity featured not just one, but *two* couples spouting hilarious dialogue; the Paulette Goddard–Robert Preston romance was supplemented by an equally absurd interaction between Madeleine Carroll and Gary Cooper.

And now as an encore and a special treat for our loyal readers, we offer some of those additional Golden Words:

(Gary Cooper as Texas Ranger "Dusty Rivers" entrances nurse April Logan—Madeleine Carroll—with his simple eloquence.)

GARY COOPER: You know, I ... I kinda gotta feelin' that I could make things easier for ya. ... If you'd let me.

MADELEINE CARROLL: You're a grand person, Dusty. But there isn't anything anyone can do for me.

GARY COOPER: Sure there is. Come to Texas with me. ... You're the loveliest and gentlest lady I've ever known ...

MADELEINE CARROLL: Oh, Dusty!! You're an angel in leather!

GARY COOPER: Heh, heh—I'd look funny with leather wings.

Gary Cooper and Madeleine Carroll.

William ("One Shot") Beaudine, the gifted director of Black Market Babies, Billy the Kid Versus Dracula and more than one hundred other films, explains a difficult setup to some of his actors.

LIFE ACHIEVEMENT AWARD:

The Worst Director of All Time

And the Nominees Are...

William ("One Shot") Beaudine
[1890–1970]

While rushing onto the set of one of his "B" Westerns, Mr. Beaudine, facing a deadline imposed on him by Monogram Studios, exclaimed in frustrated disbelief, "You mean someone out there is actually waiting to see *this?*"

His brief statement beautifully expresses the love and devotion William Beaudine lavished on every one of his carefully polished works of art. He earned his enduring nickname, "One Shot," by filming virtually all scenes in his more than 150 movies in a single take. Never mind if the bat is dangling visibly on a string. So what if the cowboy villain dies with a huge grin on his face and only one of his eyes closed. "One Shot" Beaudine will print it anyway.

He got his start in the 1920s directing a number of silent films for the kiddies. He proved so adept at handling the challenges of this medium that even into the 1960s he continued to instruct his actors in the classic techniques of the silent cinema. The characters in Beaudine films invariably roll their eyes, gesticulate wildly, sneer, gasp, clasp hands in joy, and clutch their hearts in moments of passion. For many of these movies, the soundtrack only interferes with an otherwise entertaining show.

As might be expected, cinematic subtlety cannot be counted among Beaudine's virtues. In his second to last film, *Billy The Kid Versus Dracula* (1966), the master craftsman tries to show that a young gypsy girl is startled to discover Count Dracula looming over her sleeping bag. In depicting this emotion, Beaudine will not settle for a single close-up of the girl's gaping mouth and dangling tongue. Instead, he offers *three* separate shots of that same gaping mouth and dangling tongue. Later in the film, when Dracula (John Carradine) walks through a mine shaft with a torch, an off-screen stagehand is supposed to shine light in front of the actor's face to simulate the light of the flame. Unfortunately, the uncredited assistant misses the mark terribly—we see light shining in back of the vampire, to the side of him, directly in his face—but never precisely where the "torch" should be. Most directors would have viewed this disastrous result and either cut the scene from the final film or shot it a second time. Not Beaudine—after all, he felt obliged to live up to his nickname.

Among many golden moments from a long and distinguished career is the story of Beaudine's inspired ending to his masterpiece, *Mom and Dad* (1944). Released by a company called Hygienic Productions (that's the real name, honest-to-goodness!) the movie told the story of a sweet, innocent girl who fell in with the wrong crowd and managed to get herself pregnant. Though the entire film had been shot in black-and-white, for his conclusion Beaudine spliced on a live childbirth in full color. "I think he bought it from some educational film company," recalls producer Joe Solomon. "They just spliced it onto the end of our story, and nobody could tell the difference."

This is the sort of daring and innovative approach that contributed to Mr. Beaudine's greatest screen triumphs, including *Get off My Foot* (1935); *Mr. Cohen Takes a Walk* (1936); *Windbag the Sailor* (1936); *Torchy Blaine in Chinatown* (1939); *The Blonde Comet* (1941); *Blonde Ransom* (1945); *Blonde Dynamite* (1950); *The Ape Man* (1943); *Voodoo Man* (1944); *What a Man!* (1944); *Black Market Babies* (1945); *Spook Busters* (1946); *Hard-Boiled Mahoney* (1947); *Gas House Kids Go West* (1947); *Cuban Fireball* (1951); *Bela Lugosi Meets a Brooklyn Gorilla* (1952); *Billy The Kid Versus Dracula* (1966); and *Jesse James Meets Frankenstein's Daughter* (1966).

Since Mr. Beaudine's death in 1970, his son William Beaudine, Jr., has continued the family's traditional association with bad movies, serving as production manager for Tom Laughlin's disastrous *The Trial of Billy Jack* (1974).

Herschell Gordon Lewis [born 1926]

"We still have the old-fashioned Victorian morality in our films," says Herschell Gordon Lewis. "In *The Gore-Gore Girls* the maniac pulls the eyeball out of a girl's head and *squeezes*. And you see the knuckles tighten, and you see this eyeball all of the time. And finally it bursts, and this inky black glop squirts out all over the place. I have seen people faint, vomit, turn green, leave the auditorium and go to the washroom be-cause of that scene."

It is positively heartwarming in this age of cynical detach-ment to find a man who takes such obvious pride in his work. As you may have guessed, Mr. Lewis is Hollywood's undis-puted King of Gore. His films feature enough mayhem and dismemberment to make Sam Peckinpah look like Walt Disney. *Blood Feast* (1963), the crowning achievement of his career, cost a mere $60,000 to produce but earned back millions for its creator and his associates. Apparently, the "old fashioned Victorian morality" Mr. Lewis claims to purvey in his blood-soaked entertainments still has plenty of followers among the movie-going public.

The aspiring director prepared for his life's work by earning a Master's degree in journalism and a Ph.D. in psychology. It is entirely possible that the long, frustrating years in graduate school helped to spawn the murderous fantasies that later made him famous. After a brief tour of duty as an English professor at the University of Mississippi, Lewis began making movies. His first efforts were ordinary low-budget adventures, without severed limbs or detached bodily organs, and they all lost money. He then tried his hand at soft-core porno flicks like *Nature's Playmates* (1962), *Goldilocks and the Three Bares* 1963), and the ever-popular *B-O-I-N-N-N-G!* (1962). He en-joyed himself during this period of experimentation, but he had yet to develop the unique artistic vision for which he is known today.

His breakthrough came with *Blood Feast*—the film that

helped Lewis find himself as a director and a human being. Shot on an expansive nine-day shooting schedule in Miami, Florida, the story concerns an innovative caterer who serves bits and pieces of various young ladies to his high-society patrons. The most famous scene in the film depicts the youthful hero reaching into the mouth of one of his love victims and ripping out her tongue. To shoot this sequence, Lewis used a sheep's tongue—not the kind that you serve for dinner, but a raw one with the veins and muscles still attached. This hunk of roughly butchered meat was inserted into the throat of an unfortunate young actress and the cameras rolled while her co-star ripped it from her mouth, along with a sizable quantity of stage blood, gelatin and cranberry juice. Mr. Lewis recalled that the tongue had been imperfectly refrigerated for several days before the scene could be filmed, so that a liberal dose of Pine-Sol had to be applied to the rotting flesh before it was serviceable. This is certainly movie magic of the most imaginative variety, but don't expect it to be re-created on the Universal Studios tour.

Mr. Lewis and his newly formed company, Box Office Spectaculars, followed up their triumph with *Blood Feast* by turning out a series of additional charmers, including *Two Thousand Maniacs!* (1964), the story of a small town populated entirely by homicidal nuts; and *Color Me Blood Red* (1965), about a struggling artist who slaughters his models in order to use their blood for red paint. After a brief and unsuccessful departure from form to make an animated children's movie (*The Magic Land of Mother Goose*, 1966), Lewis returned to the juicy mode he loved, merrily detaching various bodily organs and dousing the screen with buckets of blood. The output of this highly productive stylist included *An Eye for an Eye, Suburban Roulette, The Pill, A Taste of Blood, How to Make a Doll* (all 1967); *Something Weird* and *She-Devil on Wheels* (1968); *The Ecstasies of Women*, and *Miss Nymphet's Zap-In* (1969). In 1970 came a tender, introspective work with the autobiographical title *The Wizard of Gore*, and then in 1972 his infamous triptych: *Gore-Gore Girls* (also known as *Blood Orgy*), *Year of the Yahoo* and *Stick It in Your Ear*. Lewis's skills as a director, which had been crude from the beginning, actually seemed to deteriorate as his career progressed. Plot, characterization, timing, emotion and credible acting all seemed increasingly irrelevant to the horribly violent images

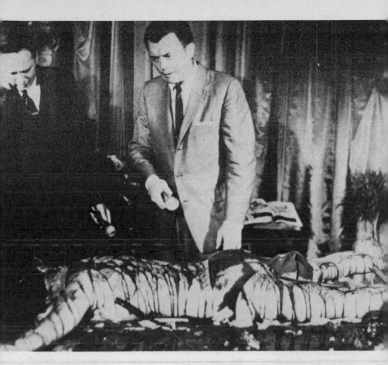

The police department disapproves of the unconventional catering methods developed in Blood Feast, the magnum opus of Hershel ("The King of Gore") Lewis.

he offered his loyal audience. Advertisements for *A Taste of Blood*, for instance, promised the public: "A GHASTLY HORROR DRENCHED IN GOUTS OF BLOOD SPURTING FROM THE VICTIMS OF A CRAZED MADMAN'S LUST!" Those lured to the theater by this memorable line of prose would show little interest in character development.

The 1970s brought some painful setbacks for our nominee. With the establishment of the MPAA rating code, his product *The Gore-Gore Girls* won the dubious distinction of being among the first films to receive an "X" designation. Mr. Lewis appealed the decision, but the board turned him down and thereby prevented all those under seventeen from enjoying his wholesome family entertainment. Nevertheless, the films of Herschell Gordon Lewis continued to make enough money to allow the director to branch out into a variety of other business enterprises. He set up his own advertising agency in Chicago, operated a series of auto-rental franchises, and purchased several theaters. To demonstrate his refreshing sense of humor, the King of Gore also took charge of a popular abortion referral service. In 1974, however, this entire mini-empire came crashing down around his head. Over 300 investors filed suit against Lewis, seeking to recover more than $500,000. His companies declared bankruptcy, while federal investigators looked into charges that his various business schemes had deliberately swindled the public. Arrested at his home in Highland Park, Illinois, Lewis faced trial on specific allegations that he had bilked a Michigan couple out of $4,000 by promising (falsely) to help them secure an abortion. The negatives to many of his popular movies, including his beloved *Blood Feast*, were sold along with his office furniture in order to defray his legal expenses and pay off his many creditors.

While these embarrassing circumstances may have temporarily derailed the inspired film career of this Master of Mayhem, we do not believe that we have seen the last of Herschell Gordon Lewis. He has many more gougings and dismemberments left to offer, and we expect an impressive comeback any day. As history has shown time and again, it's hard to keep a good man down.

Phil Tucker [born 1927]

When compared to the life's work of prolific geniuses like "One Shot" Beaudine and Herschell Gordon Lewis, the output of Phil Tucker is slender indeed. His reputation as a director rests squarely on a handful of major films, but the outstandingly low quality of each of them makes him a solid contender for this award.

A lanky, likable Westerner, Tucker looks back on his career with ironic humor and a touch of resignation. He is capable of passionate intensity, however, when it comes to defending his artistic achievements from the belittling sneers of the rest of humanity.

Before his arrival in Hollywood, Tucker served a tour of duty in the United States Marine Corps. He also worked as a dishwasher and wrote pulp stories for little-known science-fiction magazines. The turning point in his career came in Fairbanks, Alaska, where he won a job showing "low-budget strip pictures" at a local theater. This exposure convinced him that he could make cheapie-quickie sexploitation films as well as anyone else, and a few of his fun-loving buddies set him up in the motion-picture business. "I did what they called the 'After Midnight' series," he recalls. These early works included *Paris After Midnight, Hollywood After Midnight, New York After Midnight,* and *London After Midnight*. Then Tucker decided to risk everything in a startling creative departure, moving his art in a surprising new direction, and acting as producer-director for an ambitious new film entitled *Tijuana After Midnight*. He crafted at least twelve more films in a similar vein before realizing that he had exhausted the dramatic possibilities of this particular genre.

With this journeyman work behind him, Tucker felt ready to take on the magnum opus that will forever be associated with his name. In 1953, Tucker created *Robot Monster* (alternate title: *Monsters from the Moon* or *Monster from Mars*), the cult classic about robots who invade the earth in gorilla suits and deep-sea diving helmets. (*See:* The Most Ridiculous Monster in Screen History.) As a twenty-six-year-old *wunderkind* at the time of the film's release, Tucker helped to prepare some of the extravagant hype unleashed on the public by the hopeful distributors. The pressbook for the film announced that it had been "hailed as the most sensational screen offering of the decade" and urged viewers to "SEE Robots from Space in All Their Glory!!!" The *Los Angeles Times*, on the other hand, more accurately described the film as "one of the top turkeys of the year."

What made *Robot Monster* ineffably worse than any other low-budget sci-fi epic was its bizarre artistic pretension. The robot-gorilla, for instance, delivers a long, introspective soliloquy while speaking directly into the camera. "To be like the hu-man!" he passionately declares. "To laugh! Feel! Want! Why are these things not in the plan? . . . I cannot, yet I must.

249

George Nader and Claudia Barret battle in vain against the superhuman strength of Phil Tucker's Robot Monster.

250

How do you calculate that? At what point on the graph do 'must' and 'cannot' meet? Yet I must—but I cannot!" This sort of strained seriousness characterizes nearly all of Tucker's film work—in fact, it is very much part of his personality. To this day, he continues to defend *Robot Monster* from its detractors. "I still do not believe there is a soul alive who could have done as well for as little money as I was able to do," he says. Then, after a moment of silence, he adds, "For the budget, and for the time, I felt I had achieved greatness."

With critics, the public and his own business partners hooting derisively at his exalted opinion of his own work, Tucker plunged into a period of bitter depression. According to Los Angeles newspapers, he became so upset at the response to his film that he attempted suicide and wound up in the psychopathic ward of the Veterans Administration Hospital. Before long, he managed to bounce back and returned to the Hollywood scene, where he enjoyed intimate friendship with another easy-going, well-balanced artist of note—the late Lenny Bruce. The two pals worked together on a screenplay, which Tucker later directed with comedian Bruce as his star. The resulting film—*Dance Hall Racket* (1954)—tells the story of a young gangster-type (Lenny Bruce) who works behind the scenes at a strip joint. The audience enjoys endless and frequently repeated sequences of Mr. Bruce helping the strippers apply their pasties before they go on-stage. Shot in glorious, grainy black-and-white, horrendously edited, and surprisingly humorless throughout, *Dance Hall Racket* boasts even lower production values than *Robot Monster*. The organizers of the Los Angeles Film Exposition (FILMEX) in 1976, showed their appreciation for this film's finer points by showing it as part of a "high camp" double bill along with *Marijuana: Weed with Roots in Hell* (1933).

Tucker's third major film was his self-proclaimed "Masterpiece" and "greatest achievement," the drag-strip saga, *Pachuco* (1956). This violent, incoherent effort told the story of two Mexican-American toughguys making their way in their adopted homeland. It received its world premiere at a drive-in theater in west Texas, where the audience found itself so deeply stirred by Tucker's film that a major riot ensued. The spectators robbed the candy counter and box office, as well as literally tearing down the screen, before *Pachuco* had even run its course. Not surprisingly, the film failed to achieve a broad national distribution after this controversial debut.

In 1960, as America "stood on the edge of a New Frontier," Phil Tucker returned to the space monster format he had used with such memorable results some seven years earlier. This time, he produced and directed *Cape Canaveral Monsters*, with a plot concerning starfish-zombies who do battle with a pack of ferocious dogs.

Though Tucker never directed another film, his career richly deserves further investigation by critics and scholars. There is, for example, the question of his great "lost" film *Space Jockey*. Tucker says that he made the film shortly before *Robot Monster*, but that all prints of the memorable movie have since disappeared; the director himself does not know where to find one. Since no one seems to have ever seen the film, we must accept Tucker's own description of his handiwork. "My other films are okay," he modestly declares, "but this *Space Jockey*—now that was a real piece of shit. In fact, I'd say it's probably the worst film ever made." Considering Tucker's amazing track record in the films that *have* survived, we have every reason to respect his opinion. If our readers know of any means to track down this vanished classic, we hope that they will contact the authors as soon as possible.

After abandoning his career as a director of feature films, Phil Tucker worked as associate producer on several TV shows and documentaries. Most recently, he held a key post production job on that celebrated stinker *King Kong* (1976). (*See:* The Biggest Ripoff in Hollywood History.) It is satisfying to learn that the indomitable Mr. Tucker has found a practical and appropriate use for his gorilla-suit experience with *Robot Monster*. We eagerly await his future endeavors.

Edward D. Wood, Jr. [1922–1978]

Every great director has evolved a highly personal style—a unique approach that makes a film exclusively and unmistakably his own. Ingmar Bergman broods with dark intensity over questions of life, death and eternity. Alfred Hitchcock keeps us on the edge of our seats with balletic, beautifully choreographed tales of suspense. John Ford composes cinematic

Space invaders (Dudley Manlove, Joanna Lee, John C. "Bunny" Breck-inridge) review the script with narrator "Criswell," for Edward D. Wood's science fiction masterpiece, Plan Nine from Outer Space.

paeans to sturdy heroism and the simple virtues. Frank Capra shows the essential decency and humor of the common man. Woody Allen confronts human frailty and mortality with nervous neurotic laughter.

And what are the distinctive characteristics of the directorial style of Edward D. Wood, Jr.? How can we adequately summarize his enormous contribution to the development of American cinema in the last half of the twentieth century?

His six major films—*Glen or Glenda* (1952), *Bride of the Monster* (1953), *Jail Bait* (1954), *Plan Nine from Outer Space* (1959), *Night of the Ghouls* (1960) and *Necromancer* (1972)—form a most impressive canon that is bound together by strong unifying themes. Taken together, these elements comprise an intricate and iconoclastic style that gives to each of Wood's films the indelible signature of genius. Among his special attributes as an artist are:

A POET'S EAR FOR LANGUAGE AND DIALOGUE

With our minds numbed by the humdrum lines in most ordinary films, we are hardly prepared for the soaring flights of verbal fancy with which Wood decorates his enduring entertainments. In *Glen or Glenda*, for instance, writer-director

Wood has "The Psychiatrist" (Timothy Farrell) comment on the action with a moving monologue about the terms of earthly existence:

> PSYCHIATRIST: The world is a strange place to live in. All those cars! All going someplace! All carrying humans which are carrying out their lives!... But life—even though its changes are slow—moves on.

In creating his special brand of poetry for the screen, Wood refuses to be bound by the crippling conventions of grammar and clarity. A classic exchange between two police officers in *Plan Nine from Outer Space* illustrates this daring approach:

> FIRST COP: Did you get anything out of her?
>
> SECOND COP: True, she was frightened, and in a state of shock. But don't forget, she tore her nightgown and had scratched feet.
>
> FIRST COP: Yeah, I hadn't thought of that.

The meaning remains elusive and obscure, while the audience is overwhelmed by the rich sonorities of Wood's language.

A HARD-EDGED, DOCUMENTARY NARRATIVE STYLE

To keep his complex and unusual plots together, Wood frequently uses a narrator who will introduce, explain and comment upon the confusing action onscreen. Wood freely admitted that the inspiration for this technique came from repeated viewings of Orson Wells' immortal *Citizen Kane* (1941). *Plan Nine* is narrated by the famed television psychic "Criswell," seated at an office desk, speaking grimly of the horrors that will befall the actors as the story unfolds before our eyes. "My friends, can your hearts stand the shocking facts about grave robbers from outer space?"

In *Glen or Glenda*, Mr. Wood's most obviously autobiographical film, the narrative technique is even more subtle and inventive: he employs two different narrators with different points of view. First, we see Bela Lugosi in an easy chair in his study, hysterically spouting such memorable lines as, "Pull the String! Pull the String! Life has begun! A story must be told!" Next, we hear from psychiatrist Timothy Farrell who tells the story of the pathetic transvestite Glen/Glenda while a police detective listens in rapt attention. This device might have proven tedious after a while, but suddenly, when we least expect it, Wood cuts to shots of buffalo herds running uphill and the sounds of atom bombs dropping, with Lugosi's face superimposed over the buffalo stampede. "Bevare! Bevare! Bevare, of the big green dragon that sits on your doorstep!" Lugosi lucidly intones. "He eats little boys! Puppy dog tails! Big fat snails! Bevare! Take Care! Bevare!"

A DELIBERATE ATTEMPT TO BLUR THE LINE BETWEEN ART AND ARTIFICE

One of the major premises in Wood's aesthetic is his stub born conviction that the director should always show his hand, and subtly reveal to the audience that the action onscreen is merely illusion. His *mise-en-scène* is particularly intriguing in *Plan Nine* when he shows studio floodlights above his haunted cemetery set. It is also pure genius to instruct an actor to trip over a tombstone, causing the cardboard replica to bend notably.

Such touches abound in Mr. Wood's films. In *Bride of the Monster*, a secretary picks up a phone to answer it, even though it has never rung. She says, "Hello?" to herself and begins a conversation while the audience assumes she is hallucinating. According to one of Wood's production assistants, the ring of the phone was supposed to be dubbed in after the scene had been shot, but the veteran director simply forgot about it. Later in the same film, crazed scientist Bela Lugosi tries to reassure the suspicious heroine that she has nothing to fear in his laboratory. The girl is particularly worried about Bela's hulking, fat assistant, Lobo (Tor Johnson), who leers at her silently. "Don't be afraid of Lobo," says Lugosi. "He's as harmless as kitchen." *Harmless as kitchen?* It's true that Tor Johnson's huge, bloated torso may seem as large as an entire kitchen, but "*harmless* as kitchen"? The line in the script had originally read: "Don't be afraid of Lobo—he's as harmless as *a kitten*."

Unfortunately, Lugosi suffered from a severe drug-addiction at the time of the production and after blowing his line, refused to do a retake.

A TRAGIC, UNSENTIMENTAL VIEW
OF MAN'S DOOMED STRUGGLE
AGAINST ELEMENTAL FORCES

Perhaps the clearest expression of this grim but heroic *Weltanschauung* occurs at the conclusion of *Bride of the Monster*. Wood's script calls for Bela Lugosi to be squeezed to death in the tentacles of a giant octopus. Originally, he planned to create this "special effect" by splicing together footage of a large octopus in an aquarium with horrified reaction shots of Lugosi's face. Unfortunately, the film of his sea-monster-behind-glass turned out to be blurred and unconvincing, so the resourceful Wood came up with a masterful alternative. He would dazzle his audience with a "spectacular" mechanical octopus he had "copped" from Columbia Studios. Only one problem remained: no one in Wood's crew could find the motor that was supposed to cause the beast to wiggle its fearsome tentacles. Stuck with a model octopus that did absolutely nothing, Wood instructed an off-screen stage hand to throw Bela Lugosi on top of the rubber creature and to hope for the best. The film's unfortunate star struggles valiantly to convince us that a life-and-death battle is taking place between a terrified human and an insatiable beast. Lugosi sits on the passive octopus while flailing his own arms and trying to pull the tentacles around his body.

According to Wood's script, this triumphal sequence would mark the last scene of the film, but the director ran into problems with his "executive producer." This gentleman, owner of a meat-packing plant in Arizona, had agreed to finance Wood's work of art under two conditions: one, that his son, Tony McCoy, play the romantic lead and, two, that the film end with a nuclear explosion as a powerful statement against the arms race. Wood argued that the killer octopus made for a far more persuasive and meaningful finale, but the meat-packing magnate remained adamant. Therefore, in the finished version of the film, the scene of Lugosi tangling with an octopus in what appears to be a duckpond is quickly followed by stock footage of a mushroom cloud. Apparently, Lugosi, his lab assistant, the various monsters and the rest of the human race are all destroyed, with the handsome, charismatic Tony McCoy and his movie girlfriend as the world's only survivors.

Unfortunately, the stylistic elements described above that made Edward D. Wood, Jr., such a unique personality, also served to deny him the public recognition he so richly deserved.

Like all artists who are obviously ahead of their time, he suffered for his originality and his refusal to accept cinematic convention. After *Plan Nine from Outer Space* (1959), he enjoyed few opportunities to use his incomparable skills as a director. He earned his living by writing pornographic books and articles, mostly for "Pendulum Publications" and "The Eros Press." His literary titles include *TV Lust* (a moving story about the sexual adjustment problems of young transvestites), *Diary of a Transvestite Hooker*, and a gemlike short story entitled "The Fall of the Balcony of Usher." He knew that his writing could never approach the high standards he had set for himself in his film work, but he preferred all the frustrations of a literary career rather than compromising his artistic standards in order to direct. In 1972, after 12 years away from the world of films, he had the chance to make his last feature: a hard-core porno movie called *Necromancer* in which Wood himself appears as a lustful wizard. Two years later, he worked once more with celluloid, this time producing and directing a 20-minute "home study" film, shot in glorious 8 mm., as part of Pendulum Publications' "Encyclopedia of Sex" series.

Even under these difficult circumstances, he maintained a strong sense of himself and of his value as an artist. "He enjoyed playing the role of The Director," recalls one of his friends who worked with Wood on his last two projects. "This meant that The Director sat there on his chair like De Mille, shouting out orders with this megaphone, and he would have this person doing that, and everybody running all over the place. Even right up to the end, he still had this notion in his head that he had this entourage, but the poor people that he did have around him couldn't be relied on to cross the street."

Edward D. Wood, Jr., died of heart failure while watching a televised football game in December of 1978.

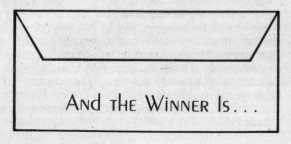

And the Winner Is . . .

... Edward D. Wood, Jr.

Alone among the nominees in this category, Mr. Wood has inspired a genuine cult following. The votes from fans across the country have made *Plan Nine from Outer Space* one of the leading contenders for the title "The Worst Film of All Time." One particularly ardent admirer wrote to us of his plans to organize an Edward D. Wood film festival in Minnesota. To promote this worthy project, the Minneapolis *Tribune* ran a lengthy column comparing Wood with Federico Fellini. In the short time since Wood's death, pressure has mounted from bad-film fanatics all over the world for a timely reappraisal of Wood's life and work.

In order to place this extraordinary figure in better perspective, we interviewed several individuals who had worked with him on his classic films. The details of Wood's early life remain sketchy, though apparently he hailed from the area of Niagara Falls and fought with distinction in the U.S. Marine Corps during World War II. Shortly after the war, he arrived in Hollywood, though no one knows how he first found his way into motion pictures. He certainly cut an unusual figure in the movie colony, and all those who met him vividly recall his outlandish female clothing. "He wore pantsuits. Women's pantsuits," remembers one close friend from Pendulum Publications who asked not to be identified by name. "He wore high heels, too, or medium heels at least. Panty hose. And angora sweaters. I never saw him in a dress or a skirt, but he loved those pantsuits. He used to sit in his office with a cigarette, striking a very masculine pose. But he had on a pantsuit with panty hose—heavy beard—he was a very typical ex-marine, to some degree. He had a very deep voice, physical mannerisms like a man, and he was totally ludicrous. Yet he was completely at ease. He was a very self-confident man. He said that he was already into being a transvestite by the time he enlisted in the Marines. And when he was making a landing in the Pacific, he was wearing bra and panties underneath his uniform."

Charles Anderson, one of Wood's closest friends and his assistant on several of his films, enjoyed reminiscing about the legendary director. "He was just about the most colorful film-maker who ever lived," Anderson recalls. "Many times, I toyed with the idea of doing a book inspired by Ed Wood—a novel. But I'm not even sure that a novel could do him justice. Ed Wood's world was really something which is out of a movie. You may have either read, or seen the movie, *The Day of the Locust*. It's the Nathanael West story which has to do with the Hollywood "fringies." Well, the man who wrote that book didn't know what he was talking about. Because if he wanted to deal with Hollywood fringies, he only had to meet Ed Wood, and get involved in his circle.

"They used to all get together once a week, every Friday afternoon, at the Brown Derby. We pushed together two or three tables to make this long table. Seated at the top of the table was that psychic, Criswell, holding court. Try to picture this at the Brown Derby. At Criswell's side is some young boy—his protégé, I guess you could call him. Then descending down the table you have this collection of people who Ringling Brothers would have given their eyeteeth to hire. There was Tor Johnson, that fat monster who used to act in all of Ed's movies. Ed once told me that whenever Tor Johnson used to come over for a visit, he always ended up breaking Ed's toilet seat. Then going on down the table there was also a wealthy woman—a little, withered-up prune of a woman, named Violet. She was always invited to these Friday afternoon gatherings of the Fringies, because everyone thought that maybe one of these days they could convince her to back their latest project.

"In a certain respect, you would say that Ed was almost equivalent to Andy Warhol when it came to making movies.

The legendary director Ed Wood (right) prepares a publicity campaign for one of his films with three unidentified starlets and his perennial star, Bela Lugosi.

Andy Warhol, back in his early days, had his own little stock company. And that's what Ed worked with—the same concept.

"When a picture was going to start, Ed would just have a general casting call. It would be almost in the same way that you've heard Fellini doing it. You know—he'd just say, 'Everybody Come!' All his friends, and friends who they knew, and anybody else who they could recommend. It was just a major event. It would go on for days. Mostly, it was just socializing. As I recall, it would take maybe two or three weeks, if all was going well.

"Bela Lugosi was always a big part of things. He made *Bride of the Monster* and *Glen or Glenda* with Ed, and then of course he died right after they started *Plan Nine*. Ed was the last director Lugosi worked with. Ed used to drive him around to this place on La Brea Avenue to get paraldehyde. Lugosi was in bad shape by this time. He had gotten past the point of being affected by liquor, so he had to drink paraldehyde. Lugosi and Ed were very interesting to work with as a pair.

"Ed was substantially on alcohol too. And this was one of his biggest problems, although right up till the end he was always getting some kind of contract from people. But it was always a pattern of exploitation. They knew that Ed was down and out, financially—maybe even psychologically—although he always thought highly of himself. And his wife, Kathy, certainly felt very highly toward him. As she said when he died, 'The world has lost a great writer.' And there were some who snickered at that.

"When it came to his movies, you had to be polite to him. If you were his friend, you just had no choice about it. When his films used to appear on television, at three in the morning or something like that, I would get a call in the middle of the night. Once you knew Ed Wood, you might as well get used to the phone ringing at anytime. And so Ed would call up, high as a kite, and announce that in five minutes, *Bride of the Monster* or such and such was going to be on. So naturally, one was expected to get out of bed and drop everything and watch it.

"Ed was, without a doubt, the most generous person I have ever met. He would virtually give you the shirt off his back. Generosity without any kind of limit. One time, when it was getting close to Christmas, I was in a bad way. And he had thousands of Raleigh cigarette coupons—it was a treasure chest of Raleigh coupons. And he said, 'Here, take these. Get your daughter a toy or something.'

"He was constantly being put out of one place after another. Half the time it was because he didn't have the money for the rent; the other half, it was because of his dogs or something like that. He had four or five of them, at different times. And he loved those darn things. One of them was called, 'Monster.'

"The worst thing was at the last place they lived at—Ed, and Kathy, and the animals. It was an apartment on Yucca Street. This place was, my God, the pits! It was the hellhole to end all hellholes! They would be crammed into just one room. And with those animals and everything, it was just horrendous.

"The people who ran the place refused to accept his rent anymore. They just wanted Ed to clear out of there. So finally they called the sheriff and had him evicted. Ed, meanwhile, had been saving all this cash. When the sheriff came, Ed went to the drawer and pulled his money out and said, 'Look, here's the money.' Well, the sheriff wouldn't take it. Nobody would take the money. So they just hauled all of his stuff out of the apartment, dropped it in this cavernous hall. By that time, half of the dogs were out in the street and gone forever. And all of the belongings were just left there. They called a friend—whose name I don't recall—and asked if he would pick them up. Their belongings were never seen again.

"So they were taken in by these people and that was around midweek—Tuesday or Wednesday. That next weekend, Ed was watching television. He was watching a football game with these people, and he suddenly closed his eyes. They thought he had gone to sleep. But he hadn't. They called the emergency paramedics and all, but they couldn't revive him. He just had heart failure. He was fifty-six—still a young man. Nobody knew what happened to the body. To this day, nobody seems sure where it's buried. There is some belief that it's cremated. But nobody knows for sure.

"When you look back over the way he was living, somehow it seemed like all the pieces fit into place. I mean, after you go through his films, who else could you possibly put in the same group? He and I were always good friends. You know, I loved the man."

Candice Bergen reaching for immortality in The Day the Fish Came
Out.

LIFE ACHIEVEMENT AWARD:

The Worst Actress of All Time

And the Nominees Are...

Candice Bergen [born 1946]

No critic has been quite so scathing in denouncing Ms. Bergen's lackluster performances as the actress herself. A brief chronology of her statements to the press is revealing:

1967: "I don't think acting is for me, and I'm not committed to it...I'm faking it all the way. I've never really been happy being an actress although motion pictures are a wonderful medium. I'm not quite sure what I want to do yet."

1970: "I'm great at the physical stuff: running, jumping, riding. Acting—that's another story."

1971: "At least I know my limitations—which are legion. I'm really not very good at anything except portraying a natural situation."

1974: "For so many years now I've said I don't want to be an actress while sitting on the set; it seems to me time now to try to do it well...I'm always an Anglo-Saxon princess who gets kidnapped by someone swarthy."

1977: "For ten years I've begged not to be taken seriously as an actress, and it's not going to be easy to overturn that impression. But I'm not going to make movies like those I've made in the past...I had no idea what I was doing!"

1979: "I just can't make any more films for the wrong reasons . . . I will no longer work for money. People say you can't stop making films. But I will. Or I'll go to class, but I won't make bad movies any more . . . Some of them embarrass me so much I wish I could burn them and start all over . . . I would like to kill myself for all that, for all the growing up I did publicly and on the screen."

While Candice Bergen feels suicidal about her film career, the critics have been positively murderous. To quote Rex Reed's critique of her performance in *The Magus* (1968), she has "stunning hair, stunning teeth, a stunning tan, a stunning smile and a stunningly emotionless inability to display a single emotion in the simplest scene that has anything to do with even the most rudimentary knowledge of what acting is all about." A decade later, she hadn't learned much, as Gary Arnold of *The Washington Post* noted in his review of *The Domino Principle:* "Evidently carried away by the challenge of impersonating An Average Housewife, Bergen affects a country twang and appears in a frumpy brunette wig. She has, indeed, succeeded in making herself plain, but couldn't anyone tell her that a plain Candy Bergen has no reason for being on the screen at all?"

Apparently not, for she continues to churn out wretched films with astonishing regularity and to speak intently of her artistic ambitions as an actress. Her great natural beauty and frank talk to interviewers have helped to still whispers about her obvious lack of talent, but a quick glance over her list of screen credits shows her to be a solid contender for Worst Actress honors. Since making her debut as Lakey the Lesbian in the film version of Mary McCarthy's *The Group*, Ms. Bergen has displayed the same emotional range and dramatic intensity as her father's dummy, Charlie McCarthy. Concerning some of her specific cinematic triumphs, she has proven as eloquent as anyone else:

The Day the Fish Came Out [1967]
   "Should have been good . . . Instead, the Cacoyannis film was a consummate disaster . . . And I was terrible. Terrible!"

The Magus [1968]
   ". . . Awful. I didn't know what to do and no one told me. I couldn't even scrape together the semblance of a performance."

The Adventurers [1970]

"I did *The Adventurers* for the money . . . Selling out wasn't as hard as I thought it would be."

The Hunting Party [1971]

"All I do in this movie is get raped and have orgasms. But I've really mastered orgasms. You need a soulful, El Greco look plus an asthma attack. . . . I think when this is all over I'll enter a convent."

Perhaps that *would* be a good idea; at least it might have prevented those other screen gems (which Candy forgot to mention), such as *The Sand Pebbles* (1966); *Live for Life* (1967); *Getting Straight* (1970); and *Soldier Blue* (1970).

Then came 1972: an extraordinary year for Candice Bergen. During that one twelve-month period, her two best films reached the public: *T. R. Baskin* (where she turns in a touching and reasonably convincing performance) and *Carnal Knowledge* (which features Ms. Bergen in a first-class supporting role). Whether the stars were in the right places that year, or Jupiter aligned with Mars, or whatever, we don't know, but soon thereafter Candice sank back to her normal level of cinematic achievement: *11 Harrowhouse* (1974); *Bite the Bullet* (1975); *The Wind and the Lion* (1976); *The Domino Principle* (1977); Lina Wertmuller's *The End of the World in Our Usual Bed on a Night Full of Rain* (1978), and the execrable *Oliver's Story* (1978) all showcased the truly extraordinary acting skills of this versatile leading lady.

In recent years, Ms. Bergen has devoted much of her time to photojournalism, to political activism, and to promoting Cie perfume on television. She has also signed a book contract to write her autobiography with Random House. These pursuits should by all means be encouraged; they may even keep her away from the silver screen.

Vera Hruba Ralston [born 1921]

In 1942 a dazzling new star appeared on the Hollywood horizon. Vera Hruba Ralston, a figure skater from Czechoslovakia, stole the show in a complex drama called *Ice Capades Review*. Republic Pictures saw her phenomenal potential and signed her to a long-term contract. Over the next sixteen years, she made twenty-six pictures for the small studio and became Republic's number one star. From *The Lady and the Monster* (1943) to *The Notorious Mr. Monks* (1958) she had the chance to play against such luminaries as Twinkle Watts, Fortunio Bonanova, and Vera Vague. Her films invariably produced a hostile reaction from the critics and a lukewarm public response, but the executives at Republic believed in her talent and continued to star her in film after film. In 1958, fatally weakened by its string of Vera Ralston financial disasters, the studio itself went belly up and had to close its doors for good. Even in this moment of despair, the kind-hearted head of Republic Studios stood firmly behind his embattled star. "*I* think she's terrific!" declared Herbert J. Yates, in defiance of the critical brickbats that rained in from every direction.

Coincidentally, Vera Hruba Ralston and Herbert J. Yates lived as husband and wife during her glory years at Republic. A few cynics have gone so far as to suggest that this relationship had something to do with Miss Ralston's blossoming career. Joseph Kane, who directed the one-time skater in nine of her starring roles, recalled of Mr. Yates, in an interview with Todd McCarthy and Charles Flynn:

"The man was a very good financier. Then, of course, he got interested . . . You've heard of Vera Ralston, I presume . . . well, she was a skater. This was at the time Sonja Henie was such a big success, so he decided if Sonja could do it, this girl could. She was a very pretty girl at the time, she was a blonde. Very pretty blonde. Looked a little like Marilyn Monroe, that type of girl. But, of course, she couldn't talk English. That was a problem, but he was going to star her anyway.

"So this poor gal goes in and stars in her first picture. And she did it phonetically, not knowing what she was saying. If you can believe it, that's how she did her first picture. It was called *The Lady and the Monster*. Von Stroheim was in it, he was the mad scientist . . .

"She got so that she understood English. She could talk all right, but she never was a very good actress. They seemed to think she could play anything from giants to children, as we used to say. Movies get so close to you, you have to be a certain type . . . He [Yates] was more or less deciding what she would do. And she went along and did whatever

Vera Hruba Ralston, "The Queen of Republic Studios."

he suggested . . . She was always very cooperative, worked very hard, tried very hard."

Trying hard could not save her from humiliation in classic turkeys such as *Lake Placid Serenade* (1944), *Hoodlum Empire* (1952), and *Fair Wind to Java* (1953) in which she co-starred with the immortal Claude Jarman, Jr. (*See:* The Most Obnoxious Child Performer of All Time). For someone who could be so graceful on skates, the tall, husky Vera proved incredibly clumsy on solid ground. Her raspy voice and heavy accent bewildered audiences everywhere—many of her films would have benefited from subtitles.

This idea seems to have been the one device Yates failed to try in his ceaseless attempts to secure success for his sweetheart. The two lovebirds lived together for a full ten years before they were legally married, though Vera, a decent girl, insisted that her mother live with them to prevent hanky-panky. The wedding finally took place in 1952 following the death of Mr. Yates' first wife; the bride was thirty-one, the groom seventy-two. When Republic closed down in 1958, Yates and Ralston were forced to look for work—along with Yates' four children, all of whom had been Republic executives. Though the demise of the old studio freed Miss Ralston from her obligations as an exclusive Republic star, no one made a move to snap up her contract. Herb and Vera eventually decided to retire in Santa Barbara, California. They lived there in *almost*-perfect bliss (one brief separation) until 1966, when Herbert J. Yates died at the age of eighty-six. After recovering from a near-fatal illness herself, Vera Hruba Ralston married again to a show-biz man, Charles D. Alva. Today, the one-time "Queen of Republic Studios" continues to live quietly in Santa Barbara. At latest report, Vera Hruba Ralston Yates Alva has made no plans for a comeback.

Mamie Van Doren [born 1933]

"Some people say it's bad to copy other girls, but I think you can learn a lot that way," says Mamie Van Doren. "Most girls instinctively choose someone like themselves to copy anyway, and this helps them develop their own personalities."

In Tinseltown, as everyone recognized, Mamie "developed" her own personality in precisely the manner described above—by "copying other girls." The blonde bombshell has frequently been described as a third-rate imitation of Jayne Mansfield (who was in turn a second-rate imitation of Marilyn Monroe). Her formidable natural assets helped her to win starring roles in several of the more notorious stinkers of the 1950s.

These were dizzying heights for a humble farm girl born as Joan Lucille Olander in Rowena, South Dakota. But Miss Van Doren's career got off to an auspicious beginning: for a young woman aspiring to the title Worst Lady of the American Cinema, what better place to start than a co-starring role with Tony Curtis? (*See:* Life Achievement Award: The Worst Actor of All Time.) Mamie made her first two films with Curtis: *Forbidden* and *The All American* (both 1953). Apparently the old master taught her Everything She Always Wanted to Know About Bad Acting but Had Been Afraid to Ask. From the beginning, she received notice for her "imposing" screen presence (the phrase "it's what's up front that counts" might have been invented for this versatile performer), and she naturally moved on to biggers and betters. These included starring roles in *Yankee Pasha* (1954), *Francis Joins the WACs* (1954), *The Second Greatest Sex* (1955), and *The Girl in Black Stockings* (1957). Then came 1958, and a moment of destiny for Miss Van Doren. Two years earlier, she had appeared briefly in a minor feature, *Star in the Dust*, under director Albert Zugsmith. This recognized *schlockmeister* was now making his camp classic *High School Confidential!* and he assigned Miss Van Doren the starring role. So began her long and fruitful association with the producer-director who shaped the rest of her career. Lovers of great films rave about the interaction between Marlene Dietrich and Josef von Sternberg; connoisseurs of cinematic turkeys are equally adamant in their praise of the Zugsmith—Van Doren collaboration. This dynamic duo went on to create such masterpieces as *The Beat Generation* (1959); *The Private Lives of Adam and Eve* (1960); *College Confidential!* (1960); and everyone's favorite, *Sex Kittens Go to College* (1960). In this last-named film, Miss Van Doren plays a stripper with a genius IQ who is appointed chairperson of the science department at an elite university.

In her personal life, Mamie proved no less colorful than her characterizations onscreen. Having heard that Marilyn Monroe

Mamie Van Doren in her most celebrated role, High
School Confidential.

married baseball great Joe DiMaggio, Mamie, a third-rate actress, became engaged to a third-rate ballplayer: sore-arm pitcher Bo ("Bad Boy") Belinsky. (See: Worst Left-Handed Pitcher of All Time—but that's another book.) Mamie and Bo were frequently caught together "performing some wild antics" along the Sunset Strip and other star spots, but this fun couple never tied the knot. Instead, Mamie went through tempestuous marriages with bandleader Ray Anthony (at least he threw a better screwball than Belinsky) and another professional ballplayer, pitcher Lee Meyers. This celebrated "whiz kid" who never made it in the big leagues was only nineteen at the time of their marriage, while his blushing bride was twenty-eight.

After a few more disastrous film ventures (The Navy vs. the Night Monsters [1966] and Three Nuts in Search of a Bolt [1966]), Mamie went into seclusion for a few years. The 1970s saw her regain national prominence, as she toured Vietnam entertaining U.S. troops (doing what, we're not exactly sure). Perhaps she harkened back to some of the triumphal moments in her film career, such as her tone-deaf rendition of "She'll be Comin' Round the Mountain" with Donald O'Connor and Francis the Talking Mule in Francis Joins the WACs. Her selfless devotion to the public welfare led Mamie to become fast friends with Henry Kissinger and Richard Nixon (described by Van Doren as "a very sexy man") during the President's reelection campaign. An active member of The Committee to ReElect the President (CREEP), she received a personal tour of the White House from Dr. Kissinger. When asked what happened at the conclusion of this jolly evening with Henry the K., Mamie told columnist Earl Wilson: "No comment! He took me back to my hotel—with a couple of security men. He was a complete gentleman . . . He's calling me when he comes back from Moscow. He has a lot of girlfriends. But I have a lot of boyfriends." It is intriguing to imagine the conversation between these two glamorous figures. Just think of Dr. Kissinger purring to his comely date: "Ah, Mamie! I'll never forget your performance in High School Confidential!"

Miss Van Doren herself said of her career in 1956: "I think Universal-International just didn't know what to do with a personality like me. I'm an individual and they'd probably have had to write a script just for me . . . If I'm not a grown lady now, I never will be!" Her adult performance in Sex Kittens Go to College just four years later must have pleased her, as she wore an outrageously tight sweater and walked as if she were guided by her breasts in the way some people are guided by their noses. When an intense emotional reaction is demanded in a scene, she performs the dramatic gesture of folding her hands over her stomach. If she delivers a line with a negative tone, the canny Van Doren will shake her head from side to side; if she is speaking positively, this master actress nods her head up and down.

In 1978, Mamie Van Doren opened a shop called Mamie Van Doren's Private Collection and Antiques. It is located on 428 31st Street in Cannery Village, Newport Beach, California. Phone: (714) 675-2820. Reportedly, her former fans drop in to see her from time to time.

Raquel Welch [born 1942]

In 1968, Raquel Welch starred in a detective film with Frank Sinatra called *Lady in Cement*. This title might stand as an adequate summary of her entire approach to acting. Directors who have tried to work with Raquel have appropriately dubbed her "The Great Stone Face." The only reaction she is capable of registering on-camera is one of fright; she depicts this emotion by suddenly opening her mouth as wide as she can.

Not only has she proven herself all but incapable of reading her lines on-camera, she also seems to have a difficult time reading scripts in the privacy of her home. How else can one explain her consistent choice of absolutely awful material? Raquel's presence in a film is a virtual guarantee of its low quality—she has been highly selective over the years and carefully confined herself to embarrassing and idiotic roles. The one film considered by most critics to contain her best performance—*Kansas City Bomber* (1972)—tells the story of an aggressive roller derby queen. While she is seen skating around the rink, shoving, clawing and punching at her opponents, Raquel is thoroughly convincing. When she removes her skates, however, she returns to the icy immobility her fans have come to expect.

A roll call of her cinematic achievements tells the story more eloquently than any description of her specific performances. Since her debut in Elvis Presley's *Roustabout* (1964), she has offered the human race:

A House is Not a Home (1964)
A Swinging Summer (1965)
Fantastic Voyage (1966)
One Million Years, BC (1966)
The Biggest Bundle of Them All (1966)
Shoot Loud . . . Louder, I Don't Understand
 (1966)
The Queens (1967)
Fathom (1967)
Bandolero (1968)
The Oldest Profession (1968)
The Beloved (1968)
Lady in Cement (1968)
100 Rifles (1968)
Flareup (1969)
Myra Breckinridge (1970)
Hannie Caulder (1971)
Kansas City Bomber (1972)
Fuzz (1972)
Bluebeard (1972)
The Wild Party (1975)
Mother, Jugs and Speed (1976)
Crossed Swords (1977)
The Animal (1978)
The Legend of Walks Far Woman (1980)

In addition to her distinguished starring roles, Raquel has played bit parts in a number of other films, including *Bedazzled* (1967), *The Magic Christian* (1970), *The Last of Sheila* (1973), *The Three Musketeers* (1973) and *The Four Musketeers* (1974). These are for the most part stylish and entertaining films and Raquel's appearances on-camera are too brief to cause serious damage.

Born Raquel Tejada in Chicago, she moved with her family to La Jolla, California, at the age of two. Her father boasted Bolivian descent, which helped to explain Raquel's dark coloring and mildly exotic beauty. Producers have frequently cast her as a Native American—as in *100 Rifles, Bandolero* and *The Legend of Walks Far Woman*. When Raquel plays an Indian, however, she invariably impersonates a member of the well-known "Cigar Store" tribe. After marriage at age eighteen, she studied acting at San Diego State College and various little theater groups in La Jolla. Her big break came in *One Million Years, B.C.* which was advertised with the line: "RAQUEL

Raquel Welch in Fathom *displaying the dramatic versatility on which she has built her career.*

WELCH WEARS MANKIND'S FIRST BIKINI!" Her difficult role as a cave girl required her to say precisely two words in the film: *"akita"* (help!) and *"sera"* (big bird!). The public hardly remembered the film, but took to heart (or at least to wall) the best-selling personality poster of the shapely star in her brief prehistoric costume.

Raquel enjoys a unique ability to make herself seem more attractive and vital in still photographs than in her movie performances. If even once in her long career she managed to project that aura of intense and smoldering sexiness that media hype has associated with her name, she would not deserve this nomination. But, as *Time* magazine pointed out in 1967: "Raquel tries to come on as the movies' newest sex queen. For that role, her credentials are ample, but Raquel welches on herself every time she speaks. Wide-eyed, open-mouthed, understanding things 'perfeckly,' going after stolen 'objecks,' she seems less a living breathing doll than an antiseptic Barbie doll who got lost on her way to the nursery."

Miss Welch defends herself against such attacks by saying: "I don't even try to be sexy. What I aim for is that kind of sensuality that foreign women have, that something that comes from inside."

With these noble goals, why does she fail so miserably?

Perhaps it's the fault of those thick camera lenses that prevent us from perceiving her *inner* goodness.

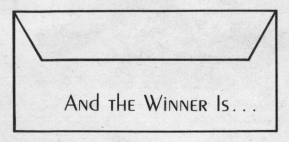

AND tHE WINNER Is...

... Raquel Welch

"I consider all the roles that I have done as camp," Raquel explained in 1970 to the New York *Daily News*. "So I guess the best way to survive is to play them to the hilt. If writers are going to put some cliché characters in their scripts, you might as well give it all you've got."

If Raquel has really given us "all she's got," then her famous body is a totally empty vessel; as Gertrude Stein once said about the city of Oakland: "There's no *there* there." In a few roles, at least, Miss Welch might have amused her audience with self-parody—*Myra Breckinridge* offered one such opportunity. Michael Sarne, the director on that film, warmly expressed his attitude toward his star by announcing to the press, "Raquel is only useful because she's a joke." Unfortunately, her thoroughly humorless approach to the part helped produce a film that *Time* called "about as funny as a child molester."

In recent years, our prize winner has begun to cut back on movie work to concentrate on her personal life and other pursuits. We are pleased to hear that her singing and dancing show in Las Vegas has produced warm audience response and surprisingly positive reviews.

John Agar during his halcyon days as "Mr. Shirley Temple."

The Worst Actor
of All Time

And the Nominees Are . . .

John Agar [born 1921]

According to an ancient aphorism: "Some men are born great. Some men achieve greatness. And some men have greatness thrust upon them."

John Agar definitely belongs to the last-named category. He never studied acting as a boy, nor could his childhood friends detect any sign of deep-seated dramatic ambitions on his part. Had he not fallen in love with Shirley Temple, "America's Little Sweetheart," he probably would have pursued a constructive career in business or the professions and spared us his fifty-two wretched screen appearances.

Fate would have it otherwise, however, and the former Sergeant in the Army Air Corps married Miss Temple in 1945. The press went absolutely wild with stories of the romance and marriage of the seventeen-year-old one-time child star, and Agar became a national celebrity overnight. The handsome veteran, known for years as "Mr. Shirley Temple," signed a movie contract with David O. Selznick just 60 days after leaving the service.

It took the studio bosses several years of intensive work with Agar before their "discovery" seemed ready to handle an important part. His big break finally came in 1948, and the circumstances could hardly have been more auspicious. The fledgling actor had the chance to work under John Ford, perhaps the greatest of all American directors, in the cavalry classic

Fort Apache. His co-stars included John Wayne and Henry Fonda, and his part featured a touching romance with (you guessed it) Shirley Temple. Most critics felt that Agar acquitted himself honorably as a stubbornly romantic, somewhat bone-headed young cavalry officer. Even more important, his work on the film marked the beginning of a long-term friendship with "Duke" Wayne that led them to make a total of five more films together, including *She Wore a Yellow Ribbon* (1949), *The Sands of Iwo Jima* (1949), *The Undefeated* (1969), *Chisum* (1970) and *Big Jake* (1971). These roles stand as Agar's greatest achievements in Hollywood. In none of them does he display conspicuous acting ability, but he does manage to look comfortable working with Wayne. In the later films in particular, his presence is about as reassuring and familiar as the company of a battered, dull old shoe.

If his work with Wayne represented his only contributions to the American cinema, Agar would be remembered as just another mediocre supporting actor—hardly a worthy candidate for the coveted Golden Turkey. But fortunately for bad-film buffs, the collapse of his marriage to Shirley Temple pushed him down that Glory Road toward the roles in low-grade Westerns and horrendous science-fiction films for which he is best known. His many achievements in this vein include *Revenge of the Creature* (1955), *Star in the Dust* (1956), *The Mole People* (1956—See: The Worst Rodent Movie of All Time), *Daughter of Doctor Jekyll* (1957), *Attack of the Puppet People* (1958), *The Brain from Planet Arous* (1958—See: The Most Brainless Brain Movie of All Time), *Journey to the Seventh Planet* (1962), *Women of the Prehistoric Planet* (1965), *Waco* (1966), *Curse of the Swamp Creature* (1966) and *Zontar: The Thing from Venus* (1967).

Despite the wide range of this material, Mr. Agar maintains a consistent approach to acting—namely, he refuses to act. In *Curse of the Swamp Creature*, for instance, he smokes several packs of cigarettes onscreen but seldom emerges from a comfortable easy chair. No matter what the specific form of the zipper-backed monster he must confront, Agar's reaction is always the same: he furrows his noble brow, forces his eyeballs to bulge slightly and, in moments of extreme tension, will even drop his lower lip. At least once in each of his films, Agar displays the single bit of thespian virtuosity he has learned over the years, by performing the astonishing feat of raising his left cheekbone and his right eyebrow at the same time. In his Westerns, Agar attempts to imitate his hero Duke Wayne by affecting a loose-stepping, smooth and easy stride. Unfortunately his legs are much too short to carry it off, and he only succeeds in presenting an uncertain waddle, with his hands extended far to his sides for balance.

One of Agar's truly characteristic roles came in Albert Zugsmith's production of *Star in the Dust*, co-starring Mamie Van Doren (*See:* Life Achievement Awards: The Worst Actress of All Time) as his intended. In the course of this project, the director wisely decided that the back of Agar's head offered as much expressive range as his face, so many of the actor's big moments in the film are shot from behind. We receive a spectacular view of Mr. Agar's slick, greasy black hair and manly neck, along with close camera shots of the even more entertaining features of Miss Van Doren's astounding anatomy.

In his personal life, Mr. Agar has scrupulously avoided the boredom and predictability so typical of his appearances on-screen. His scandalous divorce from Shirley Temple, including public charges of wife-beating, made headlines around the world. He also endured four drunk-driving arrests, and two brief jail terms. During one of these run-ins with the law, the actor told an unsympathetic courtroom that his drinking problems stemmed from his unhappy first marriage. Rushing to the defense of a sacred American institution, the judge indignantly declared, "Don't try to blame this on Shirley Temple!" and sentenced Agar to 60 days.

Membership in Alcoholics Anonymous helped Agar to solve his personal problems and to develop a strong religious commitment. Today he is active in several evangelical Christian groups at the fringes of the Hollywood community. He has also prospered as the owner of a chain of cotton-candy machines throughout Southern California.

Despite this idyllic existence, he will come out of retirement now and again whenever a film comes along that meets his traditional standards of excremence. So it was that he accepted a part in Dino de Laurentiis' multi-megaton bomb, *King Kong* (1976), as a worried official of the City of New York. Apparently John Lindsay, another terrible actor (*See:* Worst Performance by a Politician) had no interest in playing the role.

Richard Burton [born 1925]

Yes, it's true Burton has a reputation as a "Great Actor," and it's also true that his work on the Broadway stage (*Hamlet, Camelot*) has been genuinely distinguished. He has also turned in a number of magnificent movie performances, including *Look Back in Anger* (1959), *Who's Afraid of Virginia Woolf?* (1966), *The Taming of the Shrew* (1967), *The Spy Who Came in from the Cold* (1965) and *Equus* (1977). Unfortunately, these occasional triumphs only serve to highlight the pathetic waste of talent in most of his films; for every *Equus* in which he appears, there are at least a half-dozen *Cleopatra*'s or *Boom!*'s.

His list of film dis-credits is long and impressive, and includes *The Rains of Ranchipur* (1955), *Seawife* (1957), *The Bramble Bush* (1959), *Ice Palace* (1960), *Cleopatra* (1963), *The Sandpiper* (1965), *The Comedians* (1967), *Doctor Faustus* (1967), *Boom!* (1968), *Candy* (1968), *Staircase* (1969), *Raid on Rommel* (1971), *Villain* (1971), *Hammersmith is Out!* (1972), *The Assassination of Trotsky* (1972), *Bluebeard* (1972), *Massacre in Rome* (1974), *The Voyage* (1974), *The Klansman* (1974), *Exorcist II: The Heretic* (1977), and *The Medusa Touch* (1978).

It would be easy to blame this incredible string of losers on bad choice of scripts, a bad agent, bad luck, or whatever, but to do so would slight Burton's conscientious hard work to ruin nearly every film in which he appears. His personal contribution to the wretched quality of these productions cannot be over-estimated. This grand "Prince of Players" is capable of over-acting more outrageously and shamelessly than any Hollywood talent since Barrymore, yet he lacks The Great Profile's sense of humor. With his lips pursed, nostrils flaring, muscles standing out in his neck like stalks of celery, and his rich voice disgorging even the most trivial lines as if they were ripped painfully from his interior regions, Burton can make even mildly promising material look thoroughly ridiculous. Given this rare talent, he simply outdoes himself with scripts that are foolish to begin with.

An example of his extraordinary technique is provided by a famous interchange in *Exorcist II: The Heretic*—perhaps the very worst of many, many dismal performances. Psychiatrist Louise Fletcher asks Burton, who plays a haunted priest, "What am I up against, Father?"

Richard Burton emoting for the ages in The Assassination of Trotsky.

In response he is supposed to say a single word: "Evil." But what actually emerges from his mouth is a long, canine howl that makes the word nearly unintelligible. "Eee-ville!!!" he shrieks, with enough extra breath to blow out all the candles on his fifty-fifth birthday cake.

Burton's apologists cite his stormy marriage to Elizabeth Taylor as the reason for their hero's artistic deterioration; like Doctor Faustus in his film, he sold his soul for the love of Helen of Troy. In cinematic terms, the Taylor-Burton collaboration proved disastrous during even the happiest days of their romance. In addition to the celebrated big-budget turkeys that they lovingly stuffed together (*Cleopatra, The V.I.P.s, The Sandpiper* and *Boom!*—a top contender in our Worst Films Poll), Mr. and Mrs. Burton turned out some lesser known but equally worthy gems. Among them is *Hammersmith Is Out!* (1972) a cockeyed retelling of the Faust legend with Burton as a homicidal maniac and straitjacket Mephistopheles who is intent on taking over the world. One of the major characters in this so-called black comedy is Jimmie Jean Jackson, a gum-chewing, hash-slinging waitress who receives the rare opportunity to become Beau Bridge's mistress. The charming Jimmie Jean is played by none other than—that's right—Liz Taylor. Despite her juicy role, hubby Richard nonetheless contrives to upstage her with his sparkling nonperformance. As *Variety* graciously remarked: "Burton, as the lunatic Hammersmith, goes through the film with a single (the director told him never to close his eyes) bored expression."

In his two other screen triumphs of 1972 (a big year for bad-movie buffs), Burton conclusively demonstrated his independence—he could make terrible films with or without Elizabeth Taylor. First came the abysmal *Bluebeard*, which led Gary Arnold of *The Washington Post* to comment: "Richard Burton seems to be announcing his availability for Vincent Price roles . . . Unless he's comtemplating a permanent career in exploitation movies, it would be difficult to sink below this credit." William Wolf expressed similar sentiments in *Cue* magazine: "As for Burton's acting," he wrote, "I sincerely hope this remains the worst picture of his career."

Imagine the delight of these sorely pained critics when, just a few months later, Burton startled the world with a brand-new stinker: *The Assassination of Trotsky.* Hollis Alpert of the *Saturday Review* reported: "Richard Burton plays Trotsky with a glacial loftiness (not to mention a variety of accents) that makes the sequences themselves seem contrived." Arnold of the *Post* hailed the film as yet "another miserable Richard Burton performance—his Trotsky resembles nothing so much as Lionel Barrymore playing Dr. Gillespie. How about Burton and Desi Arnaz, Jr., in a revival of the Kildare series?"

The proposed TV show never materialized, but Burton moved forward in his seemingly endless quest for the ultimate loser; a lonely Captain Ahab in pursuit of the Great White Turkey. By 1978, he had built up a formidable following among connoisseurs of cinematic ineptitude, not to mention the members of Overactors Anonymous. In promoting his new film *The Medusa Touch*, the ads showed a huge head shot of Burton with the single word "TELEKINESIS" printed next to it. The producers knew that all they had to do was to show his face in the papers and all the bad-film freaks in town would come *swarming* to the theater. Unfortunately, that elite and unusual segment of the population did not prove large enough to make the film a success.

It is entirely possible that Burton, even at this late date, could startle the skeptics and redeem the talent the world once believed he had. Against all logic, he maintains a reputation as a serious dramatic artist and finds it relatively easy to win parts in major films. Nevertheless, as the years go by it becomes increasingly likely that he will continue to shuffle along the dreary road he seems to have chosen for himself. Producers are beginning to realize that Burton is a major liability for most film projects, and the public has begun to suspect that this strutting Emperor of the boards actually wears no clothes. As Roger Ebert comments in the Chicago *Sun-Times*, "There is no longer any novelty in watching the sad disintegration of Richard Burton's acting career." Jay Cocks of *Time* magazine writes with even greater cruelty and candor: "Richard Burton, once an actor, now performs mainly as a buffoon."

Tony Curtis [born 1925]

"I was playing stickball in the street when my mother screamed out the window, 'Bernie—they want you in Hollywood!'"

So began the improbable odyssey of Bernie Schwartz—

a.k.a. Anthony Curtis—a.k.a. Tony Curtis—certainly one of the most prolific bad actors in the business. Over the course of a long and varied career, his intense, cerebral performances have enriched 70 feature films, from the uplifting *I Was a Shoplifter* (1949) to the powerful *Bad News Bears Go to Japan* (1978).

In his interviews and statements to the press, Mr. Curtis attributes his extraordinary technique to years of hard work and self-discipline, but surely inheritance also had something to do with it. His father, Manuel Schwartz, had been a successful stage actor in Budapest before coming to New York and pursuing a new career as a tailor. Apparently, Mr. Schwartz could not speak English fluently enough to act professionally in America, but this same impediment never deterred his ambitious son, Bernie.

Tony Curtis, the dynamic star of Black Shield of Falworth.

Growing up in a tough Bronx neighborhood, Bernie joined the Boy Scouts when he was twelve to correct his "near delinquency." A truant officer took the spirited lad to the Jones Memorial Settlement House where, in the words of the star-to-be, he "learned honesty and self-respect" and also began his acting career. His first role—that of a beautiful fairy princess in a play about King Arthur—served as preparation for both one of his best (*Some Like It Hot*) and one of his very worst (*The Black Shield of Falworth*) movie parts.

He joined the Navy in 1944, but injured himself with a winch chain aboard the submarine *U.S.S. Dragonette*. After his discharge he studied acting on the GI Bill at the Drama Workshop in New York and attracted the attention of a talent scout for Universal–International Pictures. Signing a less-than-lavish Hollywood contract, he began his film career at the princely salary of $75 a month.

His first performance on the big screen involved a bit part in a confusing clunker called *Criss Cross* (1949). He appeared in the film for only twenty seconds in a scene in which he dances with that Grande Dame of Grade B Movies, Yvonne de Carlo. That brief exposure generated hundreds of fan letters from adoring young ladies who demanded longer and better views of that "tall, dark and handsome *hunk*." U–I, not being a studio to pass up anybody or anything exploitable, quickly cashed in on their sudden stroke of luck. They deposited their befuddled property in more than a dozen quickie films over the next three years, including a starring role in *The Prince Who Was a Thief* (1951). In this Arabian Nights epic, Curtis utters the legendary line which will be forever associated with his name: "Yonder lies de palace of my fadda, de Caliph." Similar triumphs followed, including *Son of Ali Baba* (1952), *Flesh and Fury* (1952)—with Tony playing a deaf prizefighter with a heart of gold), and *The Black Shield of Falworth* (1954—where Curtis gets to wear sheer, baby-blue tights and wields a sword as if still playing stickball back in the Bronx). By this time, our rising star had amassed a huge following of panting, prepubescent bobby-soxers, who swooned every time he appeared onscreen. More discerning movie-goers also passed out—from indignation or laughter at his attempts at serious acting.

The essential ingredients in the Curtis style have remained consistent for the last 30 years. When he wants to convey deep emotion, Tony will simply begin speaking quickly, spitting out his words and garbling his sentences. He is also a master at snarling and gritting his teeth. For particularly demanding roles, he can wiggle his head expressively up and down like the face of a jack-in-the-box on a loose spring. Recognizing that his basic assets as a star had nothing to do with acting ability, Curtis approached Lloyds of London in 1951 to insure his profile for $100,000.

No one, however, could confuse him with John Barrymore—or even with Richard Burton. The closest Curtis ever came to great acting was a brief stint rooming with Marlon Brando shortly after they both arrived in Hollywood. Through the fifties and early sixties Tony flat-footed his way through a large number of dull and dismal films, including *So This Is Paris* (1954—his only singing [!] part); *Forty Pounds of Trouble; Kings Go Forth* (1958); and *The Vikings* (1958)—a film that did more damage to the Scandinavian public image than any Hollywood development since Muki the Wonder Hound. (*See:* Worst Performance by an Animal.)

Then in 1962 came his breakthrough film, and a role that helped him make the transition from merely bad to downright awful. In *Taras Bulba*, he played a fiery Cossack warrior; the hard-riding, lunkheaded son of barbaric chieftain Yul Brynner. Bernie Schwartz as a Cossack warrior? United Artists is an Equal Opportunity Employer. On the set of this film he met his second wife, Polish actress Christine Kaufman, but waited till her eighteenth birthday to marry her. The two lovebirds had much in common; she was beautiful and she couldn't act for beans.

Through the sixties and seventies, Tony's triumphs came fast and furious with *Captain Newman, M.D.* (1963), *Wild and Wonderful* (1963), *Goodbye Charlie* (1964), *Sex and the Single Girl* (1964), *Boeing, Boeing* (1965), *Not with My Wife You Don't* (1966), *The Chastity Belt* (1968), *Those Daring Young Men in Their Jaunty Jalopies* (1969), *Lepke* (1975) and *The Manitou* (1978). In this last film, Curtis proves that he can still deliver a famous bad line with the same panache he brought to *The Prince Who Was a Thief* almost three decades earlier. He plays the hip psychic boyfriend of Susan Strasberg, who begins growing a fetus in the back of her neck. When the doctor gives Tony the somewhat surprising news of this unusual pregnancy, the star wrinkles his brow and then explodes: "In hah NECK?!!!!"

In fairness to Curtis, it must be noted that he has contributed fine work to a few films in the course of his Hollywood adventures. He won an Oscar nomination for a convincing performance as a white bigot chained to escaped convict Sidney Poitier in *The Defiant Ones* (1958). In 1959, his normally grouchy and deadpan approach brought hilarious results with his role as a female impersonator in *Some Like It Hot*. *The Great Race* (1965) featured Curtis in a good-natured and winning self-parody.

These occasional successes have not been enough to erase Tony's lingering doubts about his own acting abilities. In 1953, he entered psychoanalysis, and later told an interviewer: "You know where the real trouble lies with a guy like me? You go too far too fast. So—you begin to think about it. You're on a quick ride and going great, but the question always is Are you really talented or just dumb lucky?" We presume that years of analysis have helped Mr. Curtis realize the value of dumb luck.

In 1977 Curtis tried his hand at a new career, earning nearly $300,000 for his first novel, *Kid Andrew Cody and Julie Sparrow*. "The book wasn't taken seriously by the critics," he complained. "They treated it as they would if someone like Jayne Mansfield had written it." Jayne Mansfield? What about his former co-star Mamie Van Doren? (*See:* Life Achievement Award: The Worst Actress of All Time.)

Shortly before his book's release, Curtis looked back on his film career and lamented the fact that he had never received an Oscar: "I've put thirty years into acting and it would be nice to have got back (*sic*) a little respect from the profession. But I never got it. Never.

"As far as I'm concerned, they can take their awards and shove them."

Oh really? And what do you suggest we do with the Golden Turkey?

Victor Mature [born 1915]

"If I'm not the most hated man in pictures, I don't know who would be a more deserving claimant of that honor," Victor Mature told a Hollywood fan magazine in the 1940s. "I am identified in print as a 'lush Lothario,' 'Technicolor Tarzan,' 'overripe Romeo,' etc., etc. Directors who make pictures with one eye cocked on the Academy Award, dismiss me as 'ham—uncured and incurable.' . . . Little guys are forever yearning to cut me down to their size. Even the scripters who get paid out of the same till as I do find it hard to resist the temptation to take a poke at me by writing in cute little scenes in which I am supposed to cavort as a strong boy of sorts. But don't get me wrong, whatever you do. I picked this racket. And I love it." This cheerful attitude helped him survive a seemingly endless series of high camp roles in which he flexed his muscles, knitted his heavy eyebrows, and paid little attention to his lines or fellow actors.

Vic Mature first came to Hollywood as a starstruck teenager from Louisville, Kentucky. He made his way to Gilmor Brown's Pasadena Playhouse and became a student there. During these early days, he lived like a caveman (a role that would later fetch him fame) on an empty lot adjoining the playhouse. He picked up a piece of tarpaulin and constructed a pup tent for himself with his bare hands, and sustained himself on chocolate bars, canned sardines and other non-perishable items that he stored in the back seat of his broken-down jalopy. Actually, the self-imposed Neanderthal life-style may have been nothing more than a brilliant publicity stunt. As a columnist John R. Franchey wrote, "Any number of Victor Mature's chums will take an oath that the tent business was one hundred percent hokum: he could have moved in with any one of them until things picked up." Nevertheless, the story of the struggling young actor who camped in the open outside the theater hit the newspapers and caught the attention of gagman-turned-producer, Hal Roach. Roach offered Mature the part of a gangster named Lefty in *The Housekeeper's Daughter* (1939) and then used him in the key role of Tumack the Caveman in *One Million B.C.* (1940). At the climax of this film, the dinosaur-fighting "Gorgeous Hunk of Man" dragged Carole Landis back up to his cave and thereby assured himself worldwide attention. It is no coincidence that both Victor Mature and Raquel Welch (*See:* The Life Achievement Award: The Worst Actress of All Time) started their careers in different versions of this prehistoric saga. Playing a caveman demands a minimum of verbal mastery and dramatic subtlety while affording a maximum opportunity for display of the male or female Body Beautiful in skimpy, cunningly designed fur costumes.

After his smashing success as Tumack, Mature starred in a few playboy roles in Betty Grable musicals or as a hard-boiled gangster in mysteries. As he commented to the press: "These roles are great for box-office buildup and popularity promotion, but it's also vital for an actor to establish the fact that he can handle a good, straight dramatic role." Many observers doubted that Mature's stereotyped new parts actually constituted "good, straight dramatic roles"; others questioned whether the beefcake star had in fact "handled" them. Mature's major problem onscreen involved his apparent inability to react to the world around him. His dull, bovine eyes projected a lifeless quality that suggested stoical indifference to snarling wild beasts, seductive sexpots, unexpected plot developments, or anything else the studios could throw at him. It seemed easy to confuse him with one of the huge cardboard boulders on which he perched and bared his chest in any number of his

Victor Mature protects Hedy Lamarr from a ravenous beast in his epic role in Samson and Delilah.

more famous roles. He showed traces of humor and self-awareness in John Ford's *My Darling Clementine* (1946) and Henry Hathaway's *Kiss of Death* (1947), but these more-than-adequate performances proved the exception rather than the rule.

His most characteristic part came in 1949, when he played the Biblical strongman in C. B. De Mille's hilarious spectacle *Samson and Delilah*. To prepare for this challenging characterization, Mr. Mature received a curled, greasy hair piece and a brand-new loincloth. Highlights of the film included several struggles between Hollywood's Hunk and hungry actor-eating animals with a special appetite for ham. In one particularly memorable scene, Mature cruises the desert in his brand-new '57 chariot with the lovely Delilah (Hedy Lamarr) riding shotgun. Suddenly, their path is blocked by a snarling lion. Mature hops down from the chariot, as if preparing to fix a flat tire, and proceeds to wrestle the creature to its death. All the while,

Miss Lamarr cringes in fear on a nearby pile of rocks. After finishing his job and wiping his hands on his tunic, Mature jumps back on the chariot to his lady love's horrified stare. "But you might have been hurt!" she declaims.

"It was nothing," Mature responds, without blinking an eye. "It was only a *young* lion."

At the end of the film, the muscles on Mature's meaty chest fairly explode as he grunts, sweats, and pushes down the Philistine temple with one mighty heave. When asked why he never went to see *Samson and Delilah*, Groucho Marx reportedly explained: "I never see movies where the man's tits are bigger than the woman's."

Apparently, Mature never heard that comment, for he never took kindly to contemptuous comments about his manly charms. According to *Silver Screen*, he once "thrashed the daylights out of a celebrated playwright rash enough to call him an 'adenoidal Adonis.'" Despite this sensitivity, he seemed to take a perverse pride in the outlandish nature of his onscreen character. "I'm braver than the lions I kill with my bare hands," he revealed. "I outglare man-eating sharks. I'm a Roman gladiator, a fearless hunter on the screen . . . Hollywood continues to think I am gullible, and keeps casting me with various wild animals who have one thing in common—they are totally uninterested in my well-being."

In *The Las Vegas Story* (1952), Vic plays a local policeman who falls in love with a married woman, Jane Russell. *Time* commented: "In their big confrontation scene, Jane delicately dilates her nostrils and Victor clenches his jaw so hard that his ears wiggle, thus making it clear to the dullest movie-goer that this is an incendiary passion." In *The Robe* (1953), Mature plays Demetrius, a liberated Greek slave who converts to Christianity. Inevitably, he is upstaged by the scenery-chewing of fellow Golden Turkey nominee Richard Burton, as a Roman tribune fascinated by Christ's robe. Mature returned for the sequel, *Demetrius and the Gladiators* (1954) in which he stabs three (count 'em, three!) ferocious tigers to death during a featured bout in a Roman amphitheater. "Victor Mature is a bulky fellow who helps in filling the huge Cinemascope screen," *Time* generously observed. *Chief Crazy Horse* (1955) features endless close-ups of The Hunk's face in an effort to show off his bright red Indian makeup. He looks pained as well as painted, as if planning revenge against the agent who placed him in this role. The film's final shot shows the dead Chief riding off into a purple cloud in the sky.

In his later career, Mature has occasionally accepted roles in which he laughs at himself onscreen. His obviously auto-biographical part as an aging Hollywood muscleman in Neil Simon's *After the Fox* (1966) proved genuinely amusing. His most recent outing, in *Won Ton Ton: The Dog Who Saved Hollywood* (1976) had less to offer, with Mature as a gangster in an unwanted cinematic mongrel that died at the box office.

Today, the former caveman and gladiator owns a busy television shop on West Pico Boulevard in Los Angeles. He reflects philosophically on his recent business success: "It's a gold mine, sure, but it's much more than that to me. I've met a lot of people in our industry that I probably would never meet otherwise . . . It seems that whenever anyone wants a television set, he says, 'Guess I'll call that jerk actor, Vic Mature.'"

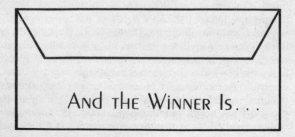

And the Winner Is. . .

... Richard Burton

Our prize winner resembles the proverbial Pretty Little Girl with the proverbial Pretty Little Curl: When he is good, he is very, very good; but when he is bad . . . well, he's just the pits.

A typical performance by the likes of Agar, Curtis or Mature can provide an audience with an evening of unintended jollies, but to watch Burton at his worst is positively painful. Please remember: his long list of stinkers is not comprised of quickie Westerns or Ali Baba movies, but of arty, ambitious, heavily financed productions involving some of the best talent in Hollywood. Anyone can make a bad film when working with hack directors and inane scripts, but it takes a true genius like Burton to come up with garbage when teamed with serious artists like Vincente Minnelli (*The Sandpiper*), Peter Ustinov (*Hammersmith Is Out!*), Vittorio de Sica (*The Voyage*), and Joseph Losey (*Boom!* and *The Assassination of Trotsky*.) King Richard has developed a sort of Midas syndrome in reverse: nearly everything he touches turns to trash. In terms of wasted opportunities, of promising projects soured through his personal efforts, no one in Hollywood can equal him. As Burton's character declares in one memorable line from his recent film *The Medusa Touch* (1978): "I have a talent for disaster."

It's too bad Edward D. Wood is no longer alive so that our three Life Achievement Award winners could be brought together in an epic-making exercise in cinematic excess. How about a remake of Wood's *Bride of the Monster* with Raquel as the unsuspecting victim, Burton in the Bela Lugosi role, and Wood himself updating and revising his original script? With a catchy disco soundtrack (is Peter Frampton available? Florence Henderson?) it could be unbeatable.

Though this tantalizing vision will never materalize, our readers, in selecting the Worst Films of All Time, have discovered actual movies that are nearly as bad. These stern judges hand down their verdicts in the chapter that follows . . .

Richard Burton as Mark Antony pleads with the audience to accept his celebrated shlock-buster, Cleopatra.

297

THE VOICE OF THE PEOPLE:

Our Readers Choose the Worst Films of All Time

At the conclusion of our first book on bad movies we asked our readers to send in ballots with their nominees for the worst films ever made.

We received an avalanche of mail in response—more than 3,000 ballots from 46 states and 18 foreign countries. The average voter listed ten bad films, but some diehard fanatics named as many as 200. More than 2,000 different films drew votes—proving the endless and dizzying variety in the wonderful world of the worst cinema.

Despite this wide divergence in opinion, our poll showed a strong national consensus concerning the very worst-of-the-worst. A few films were named again and again by readers from around the world, and piled up literally hundreds of votes.

In the heated competition for our Grand-Prize-Sweepstakes Award as the Worst Film of All Time, two movies finished in a virtual dead heat. We'll get to them later. But first, we present our list of Dishonorable Mention films; the leading vote-getters among the runners-up . . .

Dishonorable Mention

King Kong (1976)	283 votes
The Swarm (1978)	249 votes
Sgt. Pepper's Lonely Hearts Club Band (1978)	233 votes
Airport 1977 (1977)	219 votes
Orca (1977)	217 votes
Airport 1975 (1974)	209 votes
At Long Last Love (1975)	186 votes
Grease (1978)	167 votes
Boom! (1968)	152 votes
Lost Horizon (1973)	134 votes
Damien: Omen II (1978)	125 votes
The Oscar (1966)	119 votes
Godzilla's Revenge (1969)	110 votes
Gable and Lombard (1976)	106 votes
Moment by Moment (1978)	99 votes

If your favorite baddie failed to make the list we're sorry to disappoint you, but it wouldn't be the first time in American history the public has made a mistake in an election. Obviously, our readers felt particularly partial to films that have been released in the past few years. While it's undoubtedly true that the late seventies brought a bumper crop of cinematic garbage, the preponderance of recent films on this list probably reflects the short memory of the average film-goer rather than a well-considered survey of the full sweep of Hollywood history. We were shocked, for instance, at the glaring omission of Phil Tucker's *Robot Monster* (1953) from the roster of top contenders; this incomparable dog received only 53 votes in our national poll. Many other movies beloved by bad-film buffs failed to qualify for Dishonorable Mention, but rather than quibble with the popular will, let us move on to the two Hollywood classics that managed to dominate the balloting . . .

The Worst Film of All Time: First Runner-Up

Exorcist II; The Heretic [1977]

In a neck-and-neck for first place, this distinguished movie polled 384 votes—only nine ballots behind the ultimate winner. Under these circumstances, the First Runner-Up Award constitutes more than a consolation prize; it is a singular distinction which reflects on everyone associated with the production.

The critics enthusiastically agreed with our readers in judging this film. "There is a very strong possibility that *Exorcist II* is the stupidest major movie ever made," wrote John Simon in *New York* Magazine. "What motives beside greed could have led a director like John Boorman, who in some of his earlier films showed a certain intelligence as well as some craftsmanship, to concoct this foul-smelling witch's brew of meaningless turbulence, this storm not exactly in a teapot, but in a vessel of a somewhat similar sort."

"This may just well be the worst sequel in the history of films," wrote Steven Scheuer, "a stupefying, boring, vapid and non-scary follow-up to the box-office champ of 1973 that spawned a new cycle of Devil films. *Exorcist II* is a disaster on virtually every level—a sophomoric script, terrible editing, worst direction from John (*Deliverance*) Boorman, inevitably coupled with silly acting."

The silliest of the silly actors is of course, Richard Burton. (*See:* Life Achievement Award: The Worst Actor of All Time.) He is in fine form here, howling, growling, rolling his eyes and barking out delicious lines such as the classic: "Kokumo can help me find Pazuzu!" And who, pray tell, is *Pazuzu?* He is the evil demon (unnamed in the original film) who caused all the trouble for Linda Blair, Ellen Burstyn and Max Von Sydow before the action of this sequel ever began. Ms. Burstyn had the good sense not to get involved this time, but Von Sydow is back (as a ghostly vision, naturally, since he died at the conclusion of the first film), and so, unfortunately, is Linda Blair. Four years older and about forty pounds heavier than she was in the original, this chubby chickadee could attract only a very low-grade demon, which, in fact, Pazuzu proves himself to be.

The fun begins when Father Burton is ordered by his Cardinal to investigate the mysterious death of Father Max Von Sydow. With the help of Linda Blair's psychiatrist (Louise Fletcher, showing the same humanitarian concern that she did in her previous portrayal of mental-health professional, Nurse Ratchet), Burton manages to enter the troubled girl's subconscious. The key instrument of this invasion is a curious gadget called a "synch machine" complete with headbands, wires and electricity, that looks as if it might have been borrowed from Dr. Frankenstein's laboratory. While stumbling around inside Linda's head, Father Dick first encounters Pazuzu and soon hightails it to Africa to pursue the demon. Someone (was it the screenwriter, the director or Max Von Sydow?) has given him a hot tip that a young African healer named Kokumo has magic powers that will help Burton defeat the Evil One, and perhaps even help him win some decent movie roles in the future. Before finding the Man of His Dreams (Dr. Kokumo, I presume?), Burton stops at a strange village of mudhuts and tells the natives that he has been there before. "I flew with Pazuzu—in a trance. It's difficult to explain. I was under hypnosis." The natives have never heard such garbage in all their lives and, in an epic foreshadowing of the public response this film would receive, they throw stones at Burton.

At long last, our intrepid priest finds Kokumo (James Earl Jones) who is a specialist on grasshoppers, which appear to be Pazuzu's favorite animals. Unfortunately, the little buggers (er, bugs) follow Burton all the way back to Washington, D.C., where he is planning to settle his grudge-match with Pazuzu. There are now two Linda Blairs (one was entirely bad enough, thank you) representing the struggle of good and evil over her soul. The naughty child is dressed as a hooker and tries to seduce Father Richard into an alliance with the Devil but Burton, through a superhuman effort of the will, somehow resists her pudgy charms. While Linda's better half looks on approvingly, the perverted priest decides to use his bare hands to rip out the "evil heart" of Pazuzu-Blair in a bloody scene that appears to be John Boorman's homage to "Gore Master" Herschell Gordon Lewis. (*See:* Life Achievement Award: The Worst Director of All Time.) While Burton and the Bad Girl bounce up and down on a bed locked in a deadly struggle, the plot takes a sudden, unexpected turn as a plague of locusts invades Washington. The skies darken ominously as millions of the insects appear behind the Capitol building. All this would appear to be John Boorman's homage to Irwin Allen's *The Swarm*. (*See:* The Most Badly Bumbled Bee Movie of All Time.) We can only theorize on how this disconnected sequence came to play a part in the movie. Perhaps the producers, seeing early rushes for this film, commented that they were "disastrous," leading the screenwriter and director to try to pass it off as a disaster film. In any event, the deadly insects smash windows and car windshields and come zooming into the room where Burton and Blair are still doing jumping-jacks on the bed. At last, the filmmakers can think of no other way to conclude their masterpiece, and so the house itself collapses

"Kokumu can help me find Pazuzu."

in a pile of rubble, killing the grasshoppers but leaving Linda Blair (the wholesome version—you can tell from the halo) and Father Burton to wander off into the sunset together, trying to figure out what has happened to them.

After the film's release, Warner Brothers tried hard to figure out what had happened to *them*. The $11-million film did excellent business during its first week in theaters, despite horrendous reviews, but then rigor mortis set in. As *The Wall Street Journal* reported: "Word-of-mouth about the film was so derisive that in the second week its drawing power waned disastrously...Rarely, if ever, have box-office receipts declined so drastically."

Variety helped to explain these developments by reporting crowd reaction to early screenings of the film: "Pic was laughed at frequently during the first L.A. area screening last Thursday night at the Academy of Motion Picture Arts and Sciences, and on the opening day, Friday, patrons at the Hollywood Pacific

Theatre actually threw things at the screen. Much the same response, laughter and booing, has been reported from around the country, where the pic is playing in almost 800 theatres."

Director Boorman admitted: "Audiences were laughing at all the wrong things, and they created a kind of hostility. Theater managers didn't want to wear their tuxedos. They were afraid of getting lynched... There's this wild beast out there, which is the audience. I created this arena and I just didn't throw enough Christians into it."

So, what do you do when your work of art is being jeered off the screen wherever it's shown? You go back to the old moviola machine, that's what, and try once more to splice the thing together. "In what is possibly the most extensive surgery ever performed on a movie after it has gone into release," wrote Stephen Grover in *The Wall Street Journal*, "director and co-producer John Boorman is 'refashioning' his latest movie." Since everyone cracked up at the sight of Burton and Blair emerging unscathed from the collapsing Georgetown house at the film's conclusion, the new version buries Burton with the bugs and no doubt gives vent to some of the director's resentment toward his temperamental star. The revised movie—known to Hollywood cynics as *Exorcist III*—concluded by showing Linda Blair with locusts at her feet, beginning a magic dance (and apparently preparing for her next role in *Roller Boogie*) that makes the nasty insects disappear. We are led to believe that she learned this fetching two-step from the saintly healer Kokumo—after all, don't most American popular dancers have African origins? Before Blair or the audience can pause to ask questions, the credits are quickly shoved onto the screen. Warner Brothers shipped these new last reels to all the theaters that had rented the film; the cost of this last-minute switcheroo ran to more than $1 million.

It didn't help; audiences continued to hoot and belch, while votes for *Exorcist II* continued to pour in to our Worst Films Poll. In desperation, Director Boorman took one more stab at revising his film, preparing yet another recut version to placate the angry masses. This time Warner Brothers refused to indulge him with the American public, though they did use this latest edition (*Exorcist IV?*) for distribution overseas.

It has now been four years since this film's release, and the Hollywood community tries to pretend that it never existed. Devotees of bad films, on the other hand, cherish the memory

Richard Burton and Linda Blair withstand a plague of locusts and numerous other indignities in Exorcist II.

of *Exorcist II: The Heretic* and revel in some of the promotional nonsense that preceded its hilarious debut. In one revealing interview, for instance, Richard Burton spoke movingly of his personal relationship to Old Scratch. "That son-of-a-bitch is after us all the time," the great star explained. "I'm not doing this for the money. I'm an agnostic who doesn't believe in anything, but as one gets older the Devil invades your mind through all kinds of channels."

Perhaps this line of reasoning offers the best excuse for this bloated, big-budget bomberino; the entire cast and crew could line up before the public and declare in unison: "The Devil made me do it!"

The People's Choice
for the Worst Film of All Time

And now for that moment you've all been waiting for . . . the pres-
entation of the one film that conquered every rival and emerged
triumphant in the readers' poll. We could try to keep the suspense
going for a few more sentences and think of something else to say,
but if we did you'd go ahead and turn the page anyway and spoil
the whole thing . . . Therefore, without further ado . . .

And the Winner Is . . .

... Plan Nine from
Outer Space [1959]

The victory of this camp classic—with a whopping 393 votes—
is a magnificent and surprising achievement. Who could have
guessed that a Grade Z horror movie from the fifties would
outpoll all those well-publicized flops of recent years? *Plan
Nine* is the only film of the top ten vote-getters to have been
released before 1975—yet this oldie-but-baddie topped them
all.

It is easy to understand this movie's enduring hold on the
imagination of the public; once you have seen *Plan Nine* you
can surely never forget it. Though reviewed by few critics at
the time of its release, the film has left an indelible impression
on the handful of sci-fi writers and Hollywood historians who
have encountered it over the years. "By far one of the worst
films ever concocted," observed Vincent Beck in *Heroes of the
Horrors*.

"*Plan Nine* is so *very* bad that it exerts a strange fascination,"
reports John Brosnan, author of *The Horror People*. "It appears
to have been made in somebody's garage."

According to Donald F. Glut in *The Dracula Book*, the film
"is infamous among monster-film buffs as the worst horror film
ever made." Indeed.

Only one man in Hollywood history could have made such
a film: the late, great Edward D. Wood, Jr. (*See:* Life Achievement Award: The Worst Director of All Time.) He assembled
his regular crowd of fringies and weirdos to work on *Plan
Nine*, including Criswell, the celebrated TV psychic. This un-
impeachable source opens the film as narrator, telling the audience that they are about to witness a dramatization of a "true
incident" concerning "the fateful day" when Grave-Robbers
from outer space landed to destroy the earth.

Now hold on to your seats for a summary of the plot—
The two aliens, Eros and Tanna, have failed miserably in

their eight previous attempts at human annihilation. Now the time has arrived for the dreaded "Plan Nine: Resurrection of the Dead." What this means is that various recently deceased individuals are revived and controlled by the evil beings from the Great Beyond. After emerging from their graves, these tortured souls are forced to stumble around the cardboard sets like cartoon sleepwalkers with their arms outstretched. Among the ambulatory dead are "The Ghoul Man" (Bela Lugosi), his lovely wife, "The Ghoul Woman" (Vampira—popular hostess of the TV "Late Show" in L.A.), and last, but certainly not least, Police Inspector Clay (Tor Johnson—the poor man's Sydney Greenstreet). The police arrive on the scene at "the creepy cemetery" to try to quell the disturbances and proceed to employ all the latest criminological techniques. "One thing's sure," declares a ranking officer, "Inspector Clay's dead. Murdered." Then, with a burst of deductive brilliance worthy of Sherlock Holmes, he adds: "And somebody's responsible!"

With these quick-witted constables unable to contain the spreading horror, the U.S. Army takes charge of the situation. Through the magic of his brilliant sets, Director Wood whisks us to the Pentagon for a glimpse of the nation's top military brass at work in their natural habitat. We see General Roberts (Lyle Talbot) sitting in a small, bare "office" behind a golden oak stenographer's desk with one gooseneck lamp and two black telephones. We then enjoy five minutes of stirring stock footage showing tanks moving in, missiles preparing for launch, and battleships on the high seas, all intent on blasting the spacemen back to their planet of origin. Unfortunately, the aliens manage to escape the trap that has been so cleverly set for them, as three hubcap flying saucers sail merrily across the screen.

This humiliating and unprecedented defeat of American armed might (remember, Vietnam is still six years in the future) leaves only one man standing between the Grave-Robbers from outer space and their billions of intended human victims. This young crusader, an intrepid jet jockey named Jeff Trent (Gregory Walcott), sets out with his colleague, Colonel Edwards (Tom Keene), to destroy the invaders. Before he leaves home on this dangerous mission, he bids a tender goodbye to his wife (Mona McKinnon) in a poignantly romantic scene reminiscent of Hotspur's farewell to his lady on the eve of the Battle of Shrewsbury in *Henry IV*, Part I. Unfortunately, this devoted

Tor Johnson and Vampira arise from the dead in their best sleep-walker style as the dreaded "Plan 9" swings into operation.

but feeble-minded wife fails to follow the safety precautions recommended by her husband and leaves herself a sitting duck (or silly goose, anyway) for the bad guys. The zombified Tor Johnson, rising from his grave like a hippopotamus emerging from his waterhole, waddles toward the Trent house and grabs the screaming Miss McKinnon in his arms.

The battle lines are now clearly drawn: the aliens and their ghoulish cohorts are holding the hero's wife hostage onboard their spacecraft; Gregory Walcott must now overcome their incredible powers to rescue the woman he loves and to save the human race. To accomplish this noble purpose against impossible odds, our indomitable airman devises a complex and ingenious plan: he will enter the spacecraft and punch out the villains. He proceeds to do just that; though these aliens possess the technology to raise the dead, they apparently know no defense against a good right hook. As the titanic struggle subsides with Eros (Dudley Manlove) knocked out cold, a fire inexplicably breaks out inside the embattled flying saucer. Our romantic leads manage to escape in the nick of time, just as the saucer takes off and heads for the wild blue yonder. It doesn't get very far because this time the flying hubcap resembles a flaming sterno can. The police officers grimly inform us that all the aliens (both of them) have perished in the blazing wreck, thereby ending, at least temporarily, their insidious threat to the American Way of Life. Narrator Criswell then returns to the screen and assures us once again of the factual foundation for this diverting tale. "My friends, you have seen this incident based on *sworn testimony*," he insists, then adds persuasively, "Can you prove it didn't happen?... God help us in the future!" These last lines of the film, intended as both a warning and a poetic epilogue, inevitably leave us tingling with terror as we get up from the theater (or turn off the TV set at 4:30 in the morning).

As with any avant-garde work of art, an encounter with *Plan Nine* raises more questions than it answers. The sensitive viewer will immediately want to know, for instance, how Wood achieved the breathtaking special effects that play such an integral part in the appeal of his film. To learn some of the production secrets, we spoke with one of the director's assistants. "The flying saucers? I know they look like pie-tins, but they were actually paper plates," he recalls. "I mean, they were decorated and all, but basically they were paper plates. Anyway, when we wanted to show the saucer blowing up at the end of the film, we soaked one of the plates in gasoline, lit it with a cigarette lighter, and then told somebody to toss it toward the camera. It looked sensational." The scenes in outer space during the credits were created with a similarly sophisticated technique, using the same plates dangling around a large styrofoam ball. This crude mobile, with strings and wires plainly visible, was supposed to represent the flying saucers circling the surface of their home planet. When the strange crafts come to earth the illusion of flight is even more convincingly rendered: a stagehand sweeps a flashlight beam along the ground while the startled earthlings look up and point in different directions.

The elaborate and carefully constructed sets make their own unique contribution to the stunning realism of Wood's images. A single wall is ingeniously used over and over again, as part of an airplane cockpit, the flying saucer interior, and even the sky above the graveyard. Various pieces of fabric are draped over the wall at different times to help us understand that it has changed identity. A movie-goer can also divert himself by noting that the patio furniture shown outside the home of Gregory Walcott is actually identical to the furniture inside his bedroom. The graveyard set provides the film with many of its eerie moments, thanks to a number of dead tree branches and cardboard tombstones; in one scene a policeman accidentally kicks over one of the featherweight grave markers. The police car and uniforms are the only elements in the film that correspond to our normal notions of reality. They are, in fact, authentic, since Tor Johnson's son, Carl, happened to be a policeman and secured the use of the equipment from the local authorities.

Despite the resourcefulness of the director, there are slight technical shortcomings in the final version of *Plan Nine*. Even Wood's staunchest defenders will admit that the Old Master seemed to have a tough time with lighting. In one scene, as Mona McKinnon runs in horror from Bela Lugosi's double, she goes directly from a graveyard at midnight to a nearby highway at high noon. This same confusion between night and day occurs several times in the course of the film. Wood's friends blame the *auteur*'s inability to secure the services of an optical printer that would have processed what he had originally intended as "day-for-night" shots. As it is, the jumble between light and darkness helps give the movie a "timeless" quality that is highly unusual.

The frequent confusion in the use of Bela Lugosi and his double also intrigues those sensitive enough to perceive the higher artistic aims in Wood's apparent blunders. At the time he participated in *Plan Nine*, Lugosi entered a genuinely tragic period of his life. His career had slipped steadily since his starring role in Universal's *Dracula* (1931). Ten years after that triumph, he found himself working at low-budget studios like Monogram, playing embarrassing roles that frequently caricatured his previous success. He turned to drugs and alcohol to alleviate the physical and artistic pain that he suffered, and by the early fifties he had become a pitiful addict, unable to live without his daily "medicine." Nevertheless, he continued to work in films, not only because he needed the cash to support his habit, but because it was the one true joy left to him.

Around this time, he struck up an acquaintance with Ed

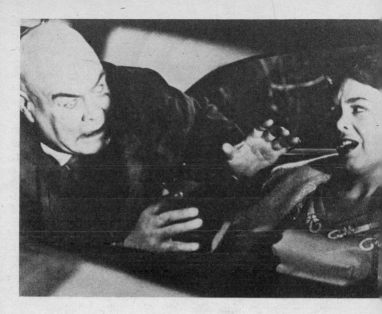

Walking corpse Tor Johnson intimidates the lovely Mona McKinnon in the film selected by our readers as The World's All-Time Worst.

Wood, an aspiring filmmaker who felt thrilled that an actor with the reputation and name-recognition of Lugosi would even consider working with him. Wood persuaded the one-time Dracula to appear as the narrator in his transvestite melodrama *Glen or Glenda* (1952). Though Lugosi's lines had little connection with the action of the film, the mere presence of The Great Man would lend Wood's work a much needed touch of class. In 1956 the two friends worked together once again in *Bride of the Monster*. By this time, Lugosi had undergone treatment for his narcotic addiction and had begun nursing hopes for a comeback. *Bride of the Monster*, however, proved something less than the ideal vehicle for that purpose. After watching the shrunken, withered star flailing his arms wildly at an inanimate rubber octopus, none of the executives at the major studios rushed to their phones.

Two years later, the unfortunate Lugosi reached the nadir

of his sad career. Wood contacted him once again with the exciting news that he had raised $800 "starter money" and planned to make another film. The title this time would be *Tomb of the Vampire* and Lugosi would dress up in his familiar Dracula suit for the starring role. Wood spent two days filming the veteran actor in and around his Hollywood home. His camera recorded Lugosi fumbling around the doorway of the residence, then strolling outside for a walk. There is even thirty seconds of Bela lurking ominously behind a tree.

After this promising beginning, Lugosi spoiled Wood's plans by suddenly dropping dead. *The Tomb of the Vampire* had to be abandoned, but an inventive genius like Wood could not allow the precious Lugosi footage to go to waste forever. After a few years, he wrote a new script that could combine the film already in the can with a totally different plot. He also hit upon the bright idea of using a "double" to finish Lugosi's role. It hardly mattered to Wood that the man he chose—an unemployed chiropractor—had notably lighter hair and stood nearly a foot taller than the recently deceased star. The director instructed the double to hold a black cape in front of his face at all times while on-camera so that the audience would never suspect the cunning replacement. When the resulting motion picture—*Plan Nine from Outer Space* (formerly titled *Grave-Robbers from Outer Space*)—received its national release in 1959, Wood advertised it as "The Great Bela Lugosi's last film." Discerning viewers will note that the actual Lugosi appears on-screen for less than two minutes.

With the top-billed star as a vague and shadowy presence at best, Wood's other actors had to carry the film. They were, by all accounts, an unusual lot. Dudley Manlove, who played Eros the Alien, had made a name for himself as a radio voice for Ivory Soap. Joanna Lee, his intergalactic consort, played in several other sci-fi stinkers, including *The Brain Eaters*. (*See:* The Most Brainless Brain Movie of All Time.) Today she is a successful writer of TV scripts. Mona McKinnon plays the hero's wife and is easily the worst actor in the epic. Her terrified screams emerge as half-hearted squeaks—as if she is too embarrassed by the whole business to let herself go. Her other big moment occurs when her hubby Gregory Walcott tells her that he has seen a flying saucer. "Saucer!" she gasps, as she points to the sky. "You mean—the kind from *up there?!*"

Walcott himself turns in the film's closest facsimile to a

professional performance, though at times he seems to have difficulty keeping a straight face. Alone among the galaxy of stars assembled for this film, he has gone on to a successful movie career, with minor roles in *Jet Attack, The Eiger Sanction, Norma Rae,* and *Every Which Way But Loose.*

Tor Johnson is no actor, but he *is* an intriguing screen presence, what with his huge sagging belly and heavy jowls. In an earlier era, he might have found a place in Mack Sennett comedies, except for the fact that he seems to have difficulty moving himself from place to place. The 400-pound former professional wrestler, known in Hollywood as "The Big Swede with the Heart of Gold," made more than half a dozen science-fiction movies in the early fifties.

Criswell, the prophet and TV personality whose visions of the future made the words *"Criswell Predicts"* a familiar phrase to most Americans, took his role in *Plan Nine* with the utmost seriousness. He insisted on writing his own lines and then delivered them in a florid, declamatory style—as if he were reading Mark Antony's speech at the forum in Act III of *Julius Caesar.* Despite this flamboyant attempt to become the next Richard Burton (*See:* Life Achievement Award: The Worst Actor of All Time), Criswell remains better known for his predictions than for this film appearances. A few years back, he promised that several completely homosexual cities would flourish as suburbs in major metropolitan areas by 1973; that in March of 1976 the U.S. government would give almost all of New Mexico back to the Indians; that Lake Michigan would be drained for land use by 1978; and that in 1979, Canada, the U.S. and Mexico would form a North American Common Market. These visions were certainly entertaining, if not accurate. For the future, Criswell anticipates serveral other fascinating developments, including an outbreak of cannibalism in Pennsylvania in 1982; a sudden plague of baldness among the women of St. Louis, Missouri, within three months of 1983, and, best of all an "Interplanetary Convention" to be held on March 10 sometime in the 1980s. This august conclave will be convened (where else?) on the Las Vegas strip and will include representatives from Mars, Venus, Neptune, the moon, and the United States. The famed psychic fails to mention whether "Eros and Tanna" of *Plan Nine from Outer Space* will be asked to attend.

Given this cast of characters, it is not surprising that the set for *Plan Nine* often resembled a three-ring circus. Ed Wood, the jovial ringmaster, tried his best to keep a tight rein on the proceedings. "After Lugosi died, Ed didn't have anybody working with him who had any kind of cinematic background," recalls one of the late director's intimate associates. "He was running the thing almost like a one-man show. He was writing the thing; he was directing it; he was in essence the producer, even though somebody else got credit for that role just because that person was putting up the money.

"Ed liked to sit there in his director's chair and give people orders. It was pretty strange, in his high heels and woman's clothing, you know, shouting out to everybody what to do. He had a megaphone—he liked to use a megaphone on the set. I think he knew that just in terms of weirdness alone, this would be a movie that people would remember. And I can tell you one thing for sure: he loved every minute of it."

The Worst Films Compendium from A *(The Adventurers)* to Z *(Zontar: the Thing from Venus)*—The 200 most Popular Nominees from the Worst Films Poll

As a special service to our readers we now present this alphabetized, annotated index to the worst movies ever made. Once again, the public made the choices. All titles receiving fifteen votes or more in the Worst Films Poll are listed below. These brief summaries provide a clear indication of the mind-numbing scope and variety of the film industry's worst achievements over the years.

THE ADVENTURERS [1970]
Harold Robbins' tacky book becomes a trashy movie with Ernest Borgnine, Candice Bergen, Olivia de Havilland, and that sensational discovery Bekim Fehmiu.

AIRPORT 1975 [1974]
The first sequel in the series somehow manages to cast Helen Reddy as a singing nun and Linda Blair as a kidney patient on a disaster-ridden airliner. Karen Black is the heroic stewardess who saves them all with the aid of airborne messiah Charlton Heston.

AIRPORT 1977 [1977]
The sequal-to-a-sequel combines the worst elements of its pre-
decessors with the irresistible appeal of *The Poseidon Adventure*,
as pilot Jack Lemmon takes a jet (complete with art smugglers)
underwater in the Bermuda Triangle. Jimmy Stewart and Olivia
de Havilland also appear.

AIRPORT 1979: THE CONCORDE [1979]
The Concorde, with kidney patient Martha Raye and the Russian
gymnastics team, is shot down with missiles, almost bombed, and
finally crash-lands in the Alps. Also starring Charo, John David-
son, and Jimmie Walker.

ANDY WARHOL'S FRANKENSTEIN [1974]
An amazing 3-D retelling of the classic story that has little to do
with the original. Gore abounds in the lab of the necrophiliac Dr.
F., as do terrible performances. Line: "To know life, you first
must f——k death through the gall bladder."

THE ASTRO-ZOMBIES [1969]
John Carradine at his extreme worst in this tale of extraterrestrial
corpses come to life. Resembles a cross between *The Night of the
Living Dead* and *Plan Nine from Outer Space*.

AT LONG LAST LOVE [1975]
Burt Reynolds and Cybill Shepherd, under the direction of Peter
Bogdanovich, destroy sixteen beautiful Cole Porter melodies. An
all-time fiasco. (*See:* The Worst Musical Extravaganza in Hollywood History.)

ATTACK OF THE CRAB MONSTERS [1957]
Despite the title, this is not a V.D. prevention film, but a Roger
Corman cheapie about giant crabs that menace the population of
a small island.

ATTACK OF THE FIFTY-FOOT WOMAN [1958]
The celebrated attack doesn't come until the last few minutes of
this wretched film, when Allison Hayes ravages a backlot village
while searching for her missing husband (*See:* The Most Ridiculous
Monster in Screen History.)

ATTACK OF THE GIANT LEECHES [1959]
Several Florida leeches, apparently having seen *The African Queen*
a few times, take over a swamp much to the dismay of Yvette

Vickers and Ken Clarke. An early effort from Bernard L. Kowalski, director of *Krakatoa, East of Java*.

ATTACK OF THE KILLER TOMATOES [1978]
A weak spoof on horror films about man-eating tomatoes that arise from a garbage disposal to menace San Diego. By the way, the tomatoes are finally killed, and dissolve into catsup. (*See:* The Worst Vegetable Movie of All Time.)

ATTACK OF THE MUSHROOM PEOPLE [1964]
Also known as *Matango—the Fungus of Terror*. A preposterous tale of Japanese tourists who are done in by a deadly fungus on a remote isle. (*See:* Worst Vegetable Movie of All Time and Worst Title of All Time.)

BARBARELLA [1967]
A preliberated Jane Fonda travels through space wearing little more than extraterrestrial Saran Wrap in this Roger Vadim production.

BATTLE FOR THE PLANET OF THE APES [1974]
Roddy McDowall is a simian humans-libber in this trite series entry. Paul Williams, John Huston, and Claude Akins aid in scraping the bottom of the monkey barrel.

BEACH BLANKET BINGO [1965]
More fun with Frankie and Annette in another plotless beach epic. Annette's Mouseka-ears are no longer the most prominent feature of her appearance.

BELA LUGOSI MEETS
A BROOKLYN GORILLA [1952]
Neither Lugosi nor the gorilla are major characters in this would-be comedy; instead, it showcases two fourth-rate Martin and Lewis imitators, Mitchell and Petrillo (remember them?).

BENEATH THE PLANET OF THE APES [1970]
Incredibly bad performances by infamous actors Charlton Heston, Victor Buono, and James Franciscus provide the only interest in this dull installment of the ongoing saga. Nuclear apocalypse at the end of the film would seem to preclude further sequels . . . but just wait.

THE BETSY [1978]
Another Harold Robbins book bites the dust as a wretched, mel-

odramatic film. Lord Laurence Olivier's attempt at a Texas twang is a hilarious flop, as is his incestuous relationship with his daughter-in-law, Katharine Ross.

BEWARE! THE BLOB [1972]
Larry Hagman directed and starred in the continuing saga of a carnivorous red mass that was frozen in the Arctic in 1958. It is accidentally thawed out at the beginning of the film but is chilled to death in a skating rink at the picture's end.

BEYOND THE DOOR [1974]
Italian *Exorcist* ripoff with Juliet Mills and Shakespearean actor Richard Johnson. Released in "Possessound," a device which hooked up theaters with four speakers for no apparent purpose.

BEYOND THE FOREST [1949]
King Vidor's production of murder and mayhem, as acted by Miss Bette Davis in her worst role ever. She is dismally assisted by Joseph Cotten and Ruth Roman.

BEYOND THE VALLEY OF THE DOLLS [1970]
This movie has little, if anything, to do with the original turkey. Three nubile young rock singers frolic in states of undress. Directed by Russ Meyer.

THE BIG NOISE [1944]
Laurel and Hardy in a wartime saga of two "lovable" oafs who manage to annihilate a Japanese submarine in their zany escapades. A pitiful exercise for the great duo.

BILLY JACK.[1972]
First of the celebrated Tom Laughlin ego trips, in which he creates the endearing character of a karate-kicking, bone-crunching, pacifist Indian.

BILLY THE KID VERSUS DRACULA [1966]
Cowboys and vampires make for strange bed fellows in William "One-Shot" Beaudine's bizarre film. (*See:* Life Achievement Award: Worst Director of All Time.) John Carradine (who else?) plays Dracula.

BLOOD FEAST [1963]
A landmark film by Herschell Gordon Lewis, the King of Gore, about a caterer who enjoys serving human limbs and organs at his

favorite affairs. (*See:* Life Achievement Award: Worst Director of All Time.)

BLOODY MAMA [1970]
Notorious criminal Ma Barker is portrayed by Shelley Winters as an eye-rolling, cackling Mommie Dearest. With Bruce Dern as a homicidal homosexual and Robert de Niro as a lovable heroin addict.

BLUEBEARD [1972]
Richard Burton scores again in the role of the perennial groom, with Raquel Welch and Joey Heatherton as his favorite wives. (*See:* Life Achievement Award: Worst Actor of All Time and Life Achievement Award: Worst Actress of All Time.)

THE BLUE BIRD [1976]
The U.S./Russian remake of the classic children's story suggests that détente may not be a good idea after all. Film conclusively proves Liz Taylor's need for a good girdle.

BOOM! [1968]
Tennessee Williams' play *The Milk Train Doesn't Stop Here Anymore*, destroyed as only Liz-'n-Dick can do it. Taylor's jewelry cost the producers $1 million. (*See:* Life Achievement Award: Worst Actor of All Time.)

THE BRAIN THAT WOULDN'T DIE [1963]
A surgeon keeps his decapitated financée's head alive through mechanical means, and tries to replace her mangled body by murdering a stripper. (*See:* The Most Brainless Brain Movie of All Time.)

BRIDE OF THE MONSTER [1956]
An Edward D. Wood, Jr., classic! Bela Lugosi, Tor Johnson, and a large rubber octopus star in the story of a mad scientist who tries to create a new race by electrically elongating normal human beings. (*See:* Life Achievement Award: Worst Director of All Time.)

BUG! [1975]
The world is threatened by versatile cockroaches who spit fire from their heinies and spell out words with their bodies. Filmed in beautiful downtown Riverside, California. (*See:* Worst Performance by a Politician.)

BURNT OFFERINGS [1976]
A charming house destroys Karen Black, Oliver Reed, Bette Davis, and Lee H. Montgomery (*See:* Most Obnoxious Child Performer of All Time) much to the delight of Eileen Heckart and Burgess Meredith.

CAMELOT [1967]
A popular Broadway musical with Richard Burton and Julie Andrews was ruined by casting Richard Harris and Vanessa Redgrave, not noted for their musical abilities. Full of artsy touches that make it one of the screen's most boring musicals.

*CAN HIERONYMUS MERKIN
EVER FORGET MERCY HUMMPE
AND FIND* TRUE HAPPINESS? [1969]
Nothing but a 106-minute ego trip for director-star Anthony Newley. The film is even more pointless and confusing than the title.

THE CAR [1977]
Universal strikes again with an automobile possessed by a demon that runs down people all by itself.

THE CARPETBAGGERS [1964]
Edward Dmytryk (of *Bluebeard* fame) directed this supposed sexathon about a manufacturing executive and his pseudocarnal exploits. Hilarious high camp cast includes Alan Ladd, Audrey Totter, Carroll Baker, and Bob Cummings.

CAT WOMEN OF THE MOON [1953]
A group of astronauts, led by the immortal Sonny Tufts, discover the title creatures on a sojourn into space. (*See:* The Worst Performance by Sonny Tufts.)

CHANGE OF HABIT [1969]
A singing doctor, Elvis Presley, falls in love with a nun (Mary Tyler Moore!) in one of the worst and most tasteless Elvis flicks. (*See:* Ecclesiastical Award for the Worst Performance by an Actor or Actress as a Clergyman or Nun.)

*CHILDREN SHOULDN'T PLAY
WITH DEAD THINGS* [1972]
Indescribable, improbable tale of a repertory theater group, two gay grave robbers, and several bargain-basement zombies on an

island cemetery. Starring the unforgettable husband-and-wife team of Alan and Anya Ormsby.

CHITTY CHITTY BANG BANG [1968]
High-budget disaster for the kiddies about a flying, swimming car that journeys to the fantasy kingdom of "Vulgaria." An automotive *Mary Poppins* with Dick Van Dyke and Sally Ann Howes (as "Truly Scrumptious").

THE CHOIRBOYS [1978]
A foul-mouthed comedy about fun-loving, whore-mongering, sado-masochistic, beer-drinking L.A. policemen. This Robert Aldrich classic of bad taste proved so offensive that Joseph Wambaugh (who wrote the book on which the film is based) asked that his name be removed from all the credits. Starring Charles Durning and Clyde Kusatsu.

CINDERFELLA [1960]
Jerry Lewis as Cinderfella (yuk yuk) enacts the classic fairy tale, assisted by Anna Maria Alberghetti, Ed Wynn, and Count Basie.

CLEOPATRA [1963]
Opulent, four-hour-long, $40-million bomb by Joseph L. Mankiewicz starring Elizabeth Taylor and Richard Burton (*See:* Life Achievement Award: Worst Actor of All Time). Rex Harrison is barely credible as Julius Caesar and Carroll (Archie Bunker) O'Connor is a less than ideal choice to play the Roman conspirator Casca.

A COUNTESS FROM HONG KONG [1967]
A very sad film from Charles Chaplin. Marlon Brando and Sophia Loren try to garner laughs by tripping over each other, holding their mouths, and acting seasick on an ocean liner.

THE CREEPING TERROR [1964]
An obscure little film featuring a carpet sample from outer space that devours the entire population of Lake Tahoe. The entire film is narrated; apparently the soundtrack was lost. If this ain't *the* worst, it's the next thing to it. (*See:* The Most Ridiculous Monster of All Time.)

CURUCU, BEAST OF THE AMAZON [1956]
Beverly Garland (the undisputed Queen of the B's) and John Brom-

field stalk the mysterious beast, which seems to be animal, vegetable, and mineral all at once. The photography doesn't help the film much.

DAMIEN: OMEN II [1978]
The lil' devil's back, and he's eight years older. Damien, who, incidentally, is the Antichrist, begins his evil doings aided by some unscrupulous business partners. Along the way there are the obligatory deaths with one man sliced in half by an elevator cable and a woman's head graphically squashed under the wheels of a Mack truck.

DAMNATION ALLEY [1978]
Jack Smight's film of man's struggle to survive in a cruel world after an apocalyptic nuclear war. George Peppard, Dominique Sanda, Paul Winfield, and Jan-Michael Vincent star as the survivors in an incredibly shoddy and pretentious production.

DANCE WITH ME, HENRY [1956]
Abbot and Costello muddle through their last film. The plot (such as it is) concerns their adoption of two little brats and their adventures in an amusement park.

THE DAY OF THE DOLPHIN [1973]
George C. Scott attempts to train an intelligent dolphin and becomes involved in international intrigue. The dolphin is certainly smarter than the producers, the same folks who brought you *Santa Claus Conquers the Martians*.

THE DAY THE FISH CAME OUT [1967]
Candice Bergen (*See:* Life Achievement Award: Worst Actress of All Time) in a floundering comedy of misplaced H-Bombs and lustful homosexuals.

DEATH RACE 2000 [1975]
According to this film, in the not-so-far-off future the national pastime will be violent "death races." An ideal picture for the family, starring Sly Stallone and David Carradine.

DEMON SEED [1977]
Julie Christie is raped by a lecherous computer, and the news that she is pregnant comes soon after. Director Donald Cammell's movie is more dumb than offensive.

DESTROY ALL MONSTERS [1968]
An all-star cast of Toho monsters (Godzilla, his offspring, Ghidrah, Mothra, Rodan, et al.) battle evil invaders from space. A sure-fire laugh riot.

DR. DOLITTLE [1967]
This tale of a man who can talk to animals is badly scored and acted. Director Richard Fleischer (of *Mandingo* and *Che!* fame) and the sadly miscast Rex Harrison are the main culprits.

DOCTORS' WIVES [1971]
A ridiculous soap opera concerning the hard-up wives of sexless surgeons. Starring Richard Crenna, Dyan Cannon, Carroll O'Connor, and Gene Hackman.

DOG OF NORWAY [1948]
Tiresome programmer starring Little Herschel Feldstad, and an untalented animal star named Muki. (*See:* Worst Performance by an Animal.)

THE DOMINO PRINCIPLE [1977]
Mazeltov! Candice Bergen (*See:* Life Achievement Award: Worst Actress of All Time) in yet another triumph! This time she wears a frump wig and sweeps Gene Hackman along in this tale of political espionage and intrigue. Also starring Mickey Rooney.

DON'T LOOK IN THE BASEMENT [1973]
Well, they warned you. Rosie Holotik (star of stage and screen) and a creepy sanitarium filled with mysterious patients are the big points in this American International cheapie.

DRACULA VERSUS FRANKENSTEIN [1971]
The evil Count and the mad doctor strike a pact in this film, to rid the world of hippies, Hells Angels and Las Vegas show girls. Lon Chaney, Jr., and J. Carrol Naish star.

DRUM [1976]
Dino de Laurentiis's slimy sequel to the ever-popular Richard Fleischer film *Mandingo*. The film shows love and sex between blacks and whites at the ol' plantation, with Warren Oates, Isela Vega (star of *Bring Me the Head of Alfredo Garcia*) and boxer Ken Norton as a muscle-bound slave who catches the eye of some of the South's wealthiest homosexuals.

EARTHQUAKE [1974]

The thrill of watching Los Angeles destroyed by a monster quake proved so satisfying to most audiences that they happily endured Godzilla-style special effects and an irritating gimmick called *Sensurround*. Cast includes fifty-eight-year-old Lorne Greene as the father of fifty-two-year-old Ava Gardner.

THE END [1977]

Burt Reynolds directed and starred in this black comedy about a terminally ill man who tries repeatedly to kill himself. Dom DeLuise is totally wasted.

EXORCIST II: THE HERETIC [1977]

The worst sequel ever. Linda Blair apparently neglected to pay her exorcist bills and so got repossessed. Richard Burton is the fearless priest who spends his time battling an African demon named "Pazuzu" (*See:* Voice of the People.)

FIRE MAIDENS FROM OUTER SPACE [1954]

Five astronauts meet scantily clad Amazons on the thirteenth moon of Jupiter and do their best to solve the local underpopulation problem.

FLESH GORDON [1973]

Porno spoof on *Flash Gordon* takes place on the planet Porno (where else?) where Flesh meets a Penisaurus and, with the aid of Dr. Felix Jerkoff, attempts to obtain the ultimate weapon, the Power Pasties. Humor seldom goes beyond that of a junior-high-school locker room.

THE FOOD OF THE GODS [1976]

Travelers Pamela Franklin and Jon Cypher are trapped on an island with Ida Lupino where all the animals have grown to tremendous sizes, and attack the actors because they are hungry for raw ham. (*See:* The Worst Rodent Movie of All Time.)

FOR PETE'S SAKE [1974]

Lame-brained comedy about a woman who gets her husband mixed-up in mob activity and low-grade slapstick. With Barbra Streisand imitating Lucille Ball and Michael Sarrazin in the Desi Arnaz role. La Streisand herself now wishes she had passed on this one.

FRANKENSTEIN'S BLOODY TERROR [1971]

Frankenstein's bloody terror is a film buff's bloody bore in the saga of a man who has to deal with werewolves, vampires, and their colleagues in his everyday life. Ads announced: "New Sickening Horror to Make Your Stomach Turn and Your Flesh Crawl."

FRANKENSTEIN CONQUERS THE WORLD [1966]
Well, he conquers several Japanese soundstages, at least. A hundred-foot-high Frankenstein-reincarnate battles a humongous dinosaur for the control of Mt. Fuji and Tokyo Bay.

FRANKENSTEIN'S DAUGHTER [1958]
A descendant of *the* Dr. Frank makes a female creature in his spare time. The girl, with a face only a mother could love, naturally escapes and causes considerable havoc.

FRANKENSTEIN MEETS
THE SPACE MONSTER [1965]
Two extraterrestrials, Princess Markcuzan and her appropriately-named aide-de-camp, "Dr. Nadir," arrive on earth to kidnap voluptuous bathing beauties from carefree Caribbean beaches. Despite the title, neither Dr. Frankenstein nor his beloved monster make even the slightest appearance in this hopelessly shoddy sci-fi epic. Filmed entirely on location in San Juan, Puerto Rico, by the makers of *The Horror of Party Beach*.

FROGS [1972]
Nasty Ray Milland angers the insect and reptile population of yet another small island. Oh-oh; the local creatures decide that he and his family have to pay this time, and led by the frogs, the creatures stage a massive attack.

GABLE AND LOMBARD [1976]
Another Universal junk movie that was advertised with the line, "They Had More Than Love—They had *FUN!*" Low point: Carole Lombard (Jill Clayburgh) licks Clark Gable (James Brolin) on the ear and presents the King with an extra-large, knitted "cock-sock" to keep him warm at nights.

THE GHOST OF DRAGSTRIP HOLLOW [1959]
Don't miss it! A bunch of swingin' teens and their nifty car club is threatened by a mean old ghost. Lots of horrible songs before the end title "THE ENDEST, MAN!" is flashed onscreen.

THE GIANT CLAW [1957]
Jeff Morrow and Morris Ankrum are very serious in this tale of

a huge, clumsy wooden bird that builds its nest on top of the Empire State Building.

THE GIANT GILA MONSTER [1959]
From the makers of *The Killer Shrews*. The Gila monster is actually a dime-store reptile that wanders around low-budget miniature sets, while talentless, nonprofessional teenagers are called upon to "react." Starring the unforgettable Shug Fisher as a lovable drunk who stumbles onscreen every ten minutes to comment on the proceedings and stare up in the sky.

GODZILLA'S REVENGE [1969]
Anything like Montezuma's Revenge? A young boy, neglected by his parents, lives for a dream world of famous monsters. Starring the Son of Godzilla in his first speaking role with lines like, "Come here! I won't hurt you!"

GODZILLA VERSUS THE SMOG MONSTER [1972]
"A Slithering Slimy Horror Spawned from the Poisons of Pollution" and our hero battle it out in this laughable film that has you cheering for the smog monster.

GOODBYE CHARLIE [1964]
Abhorrent film with Debbie Reynolds as the reincarnation of a male-chauvinist gangster. *Debbie Reynolds?* Tony Curtis (*See: Life Achievement Award: Worst Actor of All Time*) and Pat Boone also star.

GREASE [1978]
John Travolta and Olivia Newton-John star in a wonderful children's musical that demonstrates that it's better to be a slut than a wholesome girl. At the conclusion, director Randal Kleiser pays homage to *Chitty Chitty Bang Bang* by having his principals fly off into the sky in their customized hot rod.

THE GREAT GATSBY [1974]
The F. Scott Fitzgerald book that inspired this film is lost in the pointless opulence surrounding the two stars, Robert Redford and Mia Farrow.

THE GREEK TYCOON [1978]
A *National Enquirer* type ripoff story about a Greek shipping magnate who marries the widow of an assassinated U.S. President bears no resemblance to anyone living or dead, according to the credits. Anthony Quinn and Jacqueline Bisset try hard to look like

yesterday's newsreels. (*See:* The Biggest Ripoff in Hollywood History.)

THE GREEN BERETS [1968]
John Wayne stars in and co-directs this implausible yarn that makes the Vietnam War seem like wholesome, all-American fun.

THE GREEN SLIME [1969]
The true star of this film is an unidentified man in a slime suit (no kidding). A Japanese rocket bound for the outer regions is attacked by tiny creatures, which grow bigger as they dine on American and Italian astronauts. Starring Luciana Paluzzi and Richard Jaeckel.

GRIZZLY! [1976]
If a shark will scare them in the water, a bear can do it in a national park, right? Wrong. Christopher George runs around looking very upset in this slapdash effort. We prefer Yogi and Boo-Boo.

HAMMERSMITH IS OUT! [1972]
Taylor/Burton again, this time with Peter Ustinov as co-star and director, destroy yet another classic story. This time it's the Faust legend. Beau Bridges as the dim-witted protagonist shows his affection for Burton/Mephistopheles by picking his nose on-camera.

HARRY AND WALTER GO TO NEW YORK [1976]
An overproduced, overnostalgic, and overlong ripoff of *The Sting*, which manages to re-create vaudeville-type burlesque at its worst. Starring James Caan, Elliott Gould, Diane Keaton, and a cast of hundreds who were wasted shamelessly. A legendary financial disaster that nearly sank Columbia Studios.

HEAD [1968]
With such talent as Jack Nicholson, Bob Rafelson, and Frank Zappa, this film should have been much better. The small plot concerns the rock group The Monkees (remember them?) and their improbable adventures.

HELLO DOWN THERE [1969]
A family agrees to live in an experimental underwater home in this putrid comedy. Cast includes Richard Dreyfuss, Tony Randall, Janet Leigh, Ken Berry, Roddy McDowall, and Merv Griffin. Dreyfuss sings a love song, "Hey, Little Goldfish," to a porpoise.

THE HORROR OF PARTY BEACH [1964]
Del Tenney directed this horror about a section of beach infested by radioactive monsters, and worse yet, swingin' teenagers. It played on a double bill with *The Curse of the Living Corpse* when released, and featured hits like "The Zombie Stomp."

HOT RODS TO HELL [1967]
A band of hot rodders get their kicks by terrorizing Mimsy Farmer and her family as the group moves along a highway. In the finale, the father gets revenge, throwing in a few vicious licks in the name of the frustrated audience.

HOW TO STUFF A WILD BIKINI [1965]
Is beach bunny Annette really the Girl Next Door? In this formula beach-party opus she enters a contest for that title and loses. Co-star Frankie Avalon would use his talents more appropriately stuffing a Golden Turkey.

HURRICANE [1979]
Sleep-inducing remake of the 1937 John Ford film shows Daddy Jason Robards' incestual influence over his Little Girl, Mia Farrow. Daddy tries to stop her from mingling with the local body-beautiful native, Dayton Ka'ne.

HURRY SUNDOWN [1967]
Everybody's favorite director Otto Preminger is back with a delightful tale of race relations in the Deep South. The stereotypes here are worse than in *Spooks Run Wild* (1941). Watch Jane Fonda play Michael Caine's saxophone.

HUSTLE [1975]
Burt Reynolds and Catherine Deneuve give their worst performances in this tasteless film about a police detective and his black sidekick solving the murder of a young porno queen.

IF EVER I SEE YOU AGAIN [1978]
Joe E. Brooks apparently hoped to re-create his hit song and film *You Light Up My Life* with a sugary love story about a pair of long-lost loves. Jimmy Breslin is notable in his screen debut. (*See:* Worst Performance by a Novelist.)

THE INCREDIBLE MELTING MAN [1977]
An astronaut goes up in space, and upon his return, begins to melt into what appear to be puddles of candle wax. As the searchers look for the messy man, one observant individual spots a bush

with bits of melted wax on it, and exclaims, "Oh, my God—it's his EAR!!" At the end of the film, a janitor, seeing the mess, holds his nose, shakes his head, and shovels the goop into a garbage can.

THE INCREDIBLE
TWO-HEADED TRANSPLANT [1971]
This film attempts to explain what happens when the heads of a killer and a mentally retarded man occupy the same body. The diverse cast includes Bruce Dern and disc jockey Casey Kasem. (*See:* Worst Two-Headed Transplant Movie Ever Made.)

THE INCREDIBLY STRANGE CREATURES
WHO STOPPED LIVING
AND BECAME MIXED-UP ZOMBIES [1964]
A musical monster film shot in Glendale by the legendary Ray Dennis Steckler. He also plays a teenage pervert who checks out the local sideshows at a carnival, and meets a gypsy palmist who keeps the incredibly strange creatures in a cage.

INTERNATIONAL VELVET [1978]
Tatum O'Neal and Nanette Newman star in the remake-sequel of the famous story of a girl and her horse. If films like this are any indication, it's already time for Ms. O'Neal to retire.

INVASION OF THE STAR CREATURES [1965]
The misadventures of two bumbling soldiers, a few overweight women, dancing Indians, and extraterrestrial carrot-creatures add up to one of the least terrifying horror films ever made. (*See:* The Worst Vegetable Movie of All Time.)

IT'S ALIVE [1974]
"There's something wrong with the Davis baby," intoned the ads, "IT'S ALIVE!!" The nasty tot proceeds to kill a few people and create an hour-and-a-half of boredom for theater-goers along the way. High point: the man-eating baby attacks a milkman.

I WAS A TEENAGE WEREWOLF [1957]
Companion piece to *I Was a Teenage Frankenstein* finds Michael Landon as an unhappy teen who turns into a monster at the most inopportune moments.

JAWS II [1978]
Just when you thought it was safe to go back in your local theater,

comes this implausible fish story. From the director of *Bug!* (Jeannot Szwarc). One critic remarked that this sequel is one extended advertisement for the Universal Studios tour. Watch out for those plastic sharks!

JESSE JAMES MEETS FRANKENSTEIN'S DAUGHTER [1966]

William "One-Shot" Beaudine (*See:* Life Achievement Award: Worst Director of All Time) made this horrible Western horror about—that's right—outlaw Jesse James meeting the Doc's granddaughter. She, of course, is now in her grandpa's line of work, as an expert in dismemberment and transplantation. (*See:* Worst Title of All Time.)

JESUS CHRIST SUPERSTAR [1973]

This "opera" describing Jesus Christ as a First-Century Rock Star proved to be one of the most profitable movie musicals ever made. Featuring the world's first Disco-Crucifixion. (*See:* The Worst Performance by an Actor as Jesus Christ.)

THE KILLER SHREWS [1959]

What is a killer shrew when it's not a killer shrew? An Afghan hound in a shrew mask, of course! This laughable thriller actually used dogs for the title creatures, and the result is definitely flea-bitten.

KING KONG [1976]

Dino de Laurentiis's remake of the ape story was a fiasco from every point of view. A former (and future) high-fashion model named Jessica Lange co-stars with makeup artist Rick Baker who wears a baggy monkeysuit (*See:* The Biggest Ripoff in Hollywood History.)

THE KISSING BANDIT [1948]

Frank Sinatra, Kathryn Grayson, Cyd Charisse, Ann Miller, Ricardo Montalban, and J. Carrol Naish in a dreary vehicle which features Frankie taking up the title profession.

THE KLANSMAN [1974]

Ku Klux Klan versus liberal whites in the South, with Lee Marvin the man who has to settle disputes. Richard Burton's grotesque performance turns a merely mediocre film into a full-blown baddie. (*See:* Life Achievement Award: The Worst Actor of All Time.)

LADY IN A CAGE [1964]
Olivia de Havilland plays a courageous cripple who is trapped in her private elevator while a group of young people torment her and rob her house. Look for James Caan in a supporting role.

THE LAST HOUSE ON THE LEFT [1972]
Sick, sick, sick gore film about middle-aged parents out to avenge their daughter's death. The old couple must have seen *The Texas Chainsaw Massacre* a few times.

THE LEGEND OF LYLAH CLARE [1968]
Kim Novak in a sleep-walking performance as an actress who becomes obsessed with her part as "Lylah Clare," an old-time lesbian movie star. From Robert Aldrich, director of *Hustle* and *The Choirboys*.

LIPSTICK [1976]
This story of a piano teacher who rapes a top-fashion model and then goes after her thirteen-year-old sister introduced the Hemingway sisters, Margaux and Mariel, who have obviously studied acting with Sonny Tufts.

THE LITTLE SHOP OF HORRORS [1960]
What do you do when your prize plant develops a taste for human blood? This young man goes around town finding *apertifs* for his plant, which demands, "FEED ME! I WANT *FOOD!*"

LOOKING FOR MR. GOODBAR [1977]
Diane Keaton takes a break from Woody Allen films to do this sleazy story of a schoolteacher who seeks the perfect man in her friendly neighborhood bars. Choppily edited, full of artistic and sociological pretensions.

THE LORDS OF FLATBUSH [1974]
Henry Winkler and Sylvester Stallone made this B-effort before going on to respective TV and *Rocky* fame. Saga of youth gang of "greasers" in the 1950s.

LOST HORIZON [1973]
The WORST remake of all time, with the possible exception of *King Kong*. High-budget, highly ridiculous tale of Shangri-La and the various unhappy souls who discover it, including Peter Finch, Liv Ullmann, and George Kennedy.

THE LOVE MACHINE [1971]
Jacqueline Susann's tale of hot-blooded television executives is a bomb-of-all-bombs. Directed by Jack Haley, Jr. (of all people), and starring Shecky Greene, Jackie Cooper, Dyan Cannon and John Phillip Law as the man with the well-oiled apparatus celebrated in the title.

LOVE STORY [1970]
"Love means never having to say you're sorry" read the ad lines for this overly sentimentalized film starring Ryan O'Neal and Ali MacGraw. Concluding sequence, where MacGraw is dying, owes a lot to the Jeanette MacDonald school of bathos.

LUCKY LADY [1975]
Multimillion-dollar failure of the first degree. Liza Minnelli, Gene Hackman, and Burt Reynolds star as rum-runners during the 1920s. WITTY DIALOGUE: Liza: "It's so quiet you could hear a fish fart."

MADAME X [1965]
Lana Turner goes through oh-so-many hardships as a woman accused of murder who tries to defend herself. Her attorney is also her son, but he doesn't know that he is, and blah, blah, blah. From the director of *Airport 1979: The Concorde*, David Lowell Rich.

MAHOGANY [1975]
"Do you know where you're going to?" asked the theme song. The movie clearly didn't know where *it* was going to—Diana Ross plays a fashion designer who has struggled up from the ghetto, but still can't find happiness among the jet set.

MAME [1974]
Ludicrous screen adaptation of musical entertainment finds Lucille Ball in the role of Auntie Mame. Her deep-throated, tuneless singing qualifies her as the worst Elvis Presley imitator in world history.

MANDINGO [1975]
Richard Fleischer directed this celluloid bag of clichés and pat situations about a plantation in the South that bears little resemblance to what Scarlett O'Hara left behind. Prize fighter Ken Norton, as a rebellious stud, punches away at a script that could never last fifteen rounds.

MAN OF LA MANCHA [1972]
Peter O'Toole, James Coco, and Sophia Loren destroy the hit musical in one hundred and forty painful minutes. Critic Leonard Maltin said of it, "Beautiful source material has been raped, murdered, and buried."

MARS NEEDS WOMEN [1966]
Dop, a guy from *up there*, comes to Earth to kidnap some beautiful Earth chicks for the men of his planet. Complications occur when he falls in love with one of his kidnapees.

A MATTER OF TIME [1976]
Vincente Minnelli blamed the poor quality of *A Matter of Time* on his editors, American International Pictures. Liza Minnelli outdid *Lucky Lady* in this tale of a hotel maid who becomes a movie star, thanks to Countess Ingrid Bergman.

MESSAGE FROM SPACE [1978]
A Japanese sci-fi item that came to this country in an effort to capitalize on the *Star Wars* craze. Atrocious dubbing and shoddy special effects show the sure touch of master director Kinji Fukasaku. Where is Godzilla when we really need him?

THE MISSOURI BREAKS [1976]
Any film with Marlon Brando and Jack Nicholson can't be *too* bad, you think? Try this one on for size. Apparently director Arthur Penn hadn't seen *The Teahouse of the August Moon*, as he gave Brando another role with an accent: an Irishman in the Old West.

MOMENT BY MOMENT [1978]
A tedious May-December romance between a Beverly Hills housewife (Lily Tomlin) and a Hollywood street urchin named "Strip" (John Travolta).

MOTHER, JUGS, AND SPEED [1976]
Raquel Welch (*See:* Life Achievement Award: Worst Actress of All Time) plays one of the title characters (guess which one?) in this story of three ambulance drivers whose disregard for their patients is almost as strong as the critics' dislike for this film.

MUTINY ON THE BOUNTY [1962]
Marlon Brando dampens this remake of the 1935 M-G-M classic with his portrayal of Fletcher Christian. Trevor Howard, Hugh

Griffith, and Richard Haydn are all on hand to try to raise this Titanic.

MYRA BRECKINRIDGE [1970]
Perhaps the most repellent, disgusting film to be churned out of the bowels of Hollywood in the seventies, this spoof on sexual mores falls like a ton of bricks. Mae West, into her seventies, plays a sex-starved talent agent; Raquel Welch (*See:* Life Achievement Award: Worst Actress of All Time) is Rex Reed's transsexual twin.

THE NAVY VERSUS THE NIGHT MONSTERS [1966]
Mamie Van Doren (*See:* Life Achievement Award: Worst Actress of All Time), Bobby Van, and Billy Gray say words and move their faces in attempts to act in a melodrama about killer treestumps in the Antarctic.

NICKELODEON [1976]
Tatum and Ryan O'Neal team up with Burt Reynolds in this story of the early days of Tinsel Town. Tatum tries for worldliness/ cuteness in her role as a young scriptwriter, but comes across as totally artificial. Directed by Peter Bogdanovich as a follow-up to *At Long Last Love*.

THE NIGHT OF THE LIVING DEAD [1968]
The recently deceased of Pennsylvania come to life with an appetite for human flesh in this George A. Romero cult classic. A group of people barricade themselves in a farmhouse in an ingenious effort to keep the zombies out.

THE NORSEMEN [1978]
A laughably juvenile epic starring Lee Majors, who wears a drooping mustache as a heroic Viking. The anachronisms abound— including a shot of an oil tanker behind the Viking warship.

ODE TO BILLY JOE [1976]
The popular country song becomes a film and proves that "Ode to Billy Joe" should have stayed in the Top Ten where it belonged. The ubiquitous Robby Benson plays the title role. Directed by Max Baer, Jr., "Jethro" of *The Beverly Hillbillies*.

ONCE IS NOT ENOUGH [1975]
Another Jacqueline Susann novel provides the usual bilge about the "beautiful people" and their sexploits. Not worth wasting time

over; Melina Mercouri and Alexis Smith in supporting roles as a pair of lipsmacking lesbians.

ONE MILLION YEARS, B.C. [1966]
This prehistoric saga of Raquel Welch as a cavechick named Loana is supported by Raquel's most formidable Hollywood assets—both of them. (*See:* Life Achievement Award: Worst Actress of All Time.)

ORCA [1977]
The story of a macho whale who wants revenge on the man (Richard Harris) who killed his mate (wife, financée, or something like that). *Moby Dick* in reverse, from the people who brought you *The White Buffalo* and *King Kong*. (*See:* The Biggest Ripoff in Hollywood History.)

THE OSCAR [1966]
One man's climb to fame in Hollywood is chronicled on the evening of the Academy Awards ceremony. Stephen Boyd is the soulless heel, and Tony Bennett is his best pal, "Hymie Kelly." (*See:* The Worst Performance by a Popular Singer and Worst Lines of Romantic Dialogue in Movie History.)

THE OTHER SIDE OF MIDNIGHT [1977]
Heavy going, as a woman takes eight years (in two hours and forty-five minutes) to rise to film stardom. On the way to the top she aborts her own fetus in a bathtub. Stars Marie-France Pisier, Susan Sarandon and John Beck.

PINK FLAMINGOS [1972]
Cult movie starring Divine, the World-Famous Transvestite—no relation to Edward D. Wood, Jr. This movie has been running at 12:00 midnight on Saturdays for five consecutive years at many theaters across the U.S. Climax features the star eating doggy excrement he/she has lifted from the ground.

PIRANHA [1978]
Most of the action was shot in a swimming pool in Southern California. The plot: A demented scientist raises piranhas for use against the Vietcong in the Vietnamese War. Now that the war is over . . .

PLAN NINE FROM OUTER SPACE [1959]
The film classic! Aliens in flying garbage cans raise the dead in

their attempt at Earth conquest in this Edward D. Wood, Jr., film. (*See:* Life Achievement Award: Worst Director of All Time.) Stands the test of time to emerge as *the* bad film of the last fifty years. (*See:* Grand Prize—Sweepstakes Award.)

THE PRIDE AND THE PASSION [1957]

Frank Sinatra as a Spanish guerilla leader? That's one of the more plausible points in a story about Spain and France struggling for control of one large cannon.

THE PRIVATE NAVY OF SGT. O'FARRELL [1968]

Bob Hope and Phyllis Diller team up in this tedious comedy that combines World War II, Jeffrey Hunter (*King of Kings*) and Gina Lollobrigida (*Solomon and Sheba*).

QUEEN OF OUTER SPACE [1958]

Zsa Zsa Gabor is a Hungarian-accented slave girl on Venus who betrays her home planet for the love of a he-man astronaut. A landmark of feminist filmmaking.

RABBIT TEST [1978]

Joan Rivers' comedy about the first pregnant man raises all the obvious jokes, from delivery-room one liners to questions about breast-feeding. Joan should stick to her Las Vegas act.

REEFER MADNESS [1938]

This film reveals the dangers of the killer weed, marijuana, to concerned parents. Even the staunchest conservative on the subject will have to laugh as innocent, all-American teens try one puff of "the dope" and become insane, crazed addicts.

REFLECTIONS IN A GOLDEN EYE [1967]

Marlon Brando plays a frustrated army officer and homosexual peeping tom married to the insatiable Elizabeth Taylor. An "arty" soft-focus fiasco for distinguished director John Huston.

REPTILICUS [1962]

Reptilicus is the object of scientific study, a pre-historic monster perfectly preserved. But whoopsie—the beast thaws out, and proceeds to ravage Copenhagen. Denmark's answer to Godzilla will terrify no one. Starring Bent Mejding and Borge Moller Grimstrup.

THE RETURN OF DOCTOR X [1939]

Typical B-thriller of the late 1930s, but given special interest by the presence of Humphrey Bogart as one of the stars. Bogie plays a *zombie* in the time-honored sleep-walker tradition.

ROBOT MONSTER [1953]
The earth is destroyed by "The Calcinator Death Ray" wielded by gorillas from outer space who sport diving helmets. The public reaction to this film proved so negative that its director, Phil Tucker, attempted suicide shortly after it was released. (*See:* Life Achievement Award: Worst Director of All Time and The Most Ridiculous Monster in Screen History.)

THE ROCKY HORROR PICTURE SHOW [1975]
Two innocents stumble onto a haunted castle populated by Transylvanian transvestites, homosexuals, an incestuous brother/sister pair and other fun-loving types. Probably the definitive cult film, it has achieved vast and wholly inexplicable popularity.

THE SAILOR WHO FELL FROM GRACE
WITH THE SEA [1976]
The unfortunate seaman is Kris Kristofferson, who falls in love with Sarah Miles. Her little boy is understandably upset, and he and his friends decide to kill the sailor.

THE SANDPIPER [1965]
Elizabeth Taylor is a beatnik painter. Richard Burton is a minister. Eva Marie Saint is his wife. Naturally the painter and the clergyman fall in love, and we are subjected to yet another *tour de force* by Liz and Dick, uncrowned King and Queen of boredom.

SANTA CLAUS CONQUERS THE MARTIANS [1964]
The title adequately summarizes the plot: Santa goes to Mars to cheer up the Martian children, and comes home in time for Christmas. The performances in this film are as bad as any ever set before a camera.

SERGEANT PEPPER'S
LONELY HEARTS CLUB BAND [1978]
Peter Frampton, the Bee Gees, George Burns, Steve Martin, Aerosmith, Alice Cooper, Earth, Wind, and Fire all wasted in a film that resembles a two-hour long commercial for McDonald's. (*See:* Worst Musical Extravaganza in Hollywood History.)

THE SILVER CHALICE [1954]
Paul Newman is chosen to make the silver chalice to hold Jesus's

cup from the Last Supper, and it seems everyone is out to stop him from doing it, including the likes of Jack Palance and Virginia Mayo. Newman himself called it "the worst film of the fifties." (*See:* Most Embarrassing Movie Debut of All Time.)

SINCERELY YOURS [1955]
Liberace makes his movie debut as a perpetually smiling deaf pianist in a predictable tearjerker. Screenplay by a young, little-known writer named Irving Wallace.

SKIDOO [1969]
A horrid comedy about prison-bound gangsters "tripping-out" on L.S.D. One need only look at the diversity of the cast to appreciate its incoherence; Groucho Marx, George Raft, Mickey Rooney, Peter Lawford, Carol Channing, Burgess Meredith, John Phillip Law, Austin Pendleton, Frankie Avalon and Slim Pickens all do their very worst for director Otto Preminger.

SMOKEY AND THE BANDIT [1977]
Inexplicable box-office smash. Jackie Gleason is a redneck sheriff chasing Burt Reynolds and Sally Field, two bootleggers. They chase, talk on the CB, chase some more, fall in love, chase some more, chase some more . . .

SNOW WHITE AND THE THREE STOOGES [1961]
Dull retelling of the classic fairy tale, with the Three Stooges and a pie fight thrown in here and there. Snow White is played by Olympic skater Carol Heiss.

SOMEBODY KILLED HER HUSBAND [1977]
Notorious box-office flop that proved Farrah Fawcett-Majors' popularity did not carry to the screen. She plays an average housewife who falls in love with Jeff Bridges, a writer of children's books.

SONG OF NORWAY [1970]
The nerve-numbing musical from the husband-and-wife producing team of Andrew L. and Virginia Stone makes a mockery of the life of composer Edvard Grieg. (*See:* The Worst Musical Extravaganza in Hollywood History.)

SOYLENT GREEN [1973]
In the United States of the future, overpopulation is such a problem that food is rationed. By far the most popular entrée is "soylent green," a mysterious foodstuff. Charlton Heston sets out to find the secret ingredients. We hate to spoil the ending, but we will

say the delectable dish would have pleased the crazed caterer in *Blood Feast*.

S*P*Y*S [1973]
Ripoff attempt at M*A*S*H even stars Donald Sutherland and Elliott Gould. They play two spies (that's i*e*s!) from the CIA who try to remain intact in the line of duty.

SSSSSSS [1973]
A mad scientist finds a serum that turns men into king cobras. After flat-headed monsters, mindless zombies, and killer shrews, there wasn't much left for him to do. ZZZZZZ.

STARSHIP INVASIONS [1977]
Robert Vaughn's most embarrassing movie since *Teenage Caveman*. This Canadian flick about flying saucers is one of the funniest films to come out of that country since *Playgirl Killer*. Christopher Lee plays a conehead invader with Vaughn as an expert on U.F.O.'s.

THE STORY OF MANKIND [1957]
This historical gaffe casts Virginia Mayo as Cleopatra, Harpo Marx as Sir Isaac Newton, Hedy Lamarr as Joan of Arc, and Francis X. Bushman as Moses. (*See:* The Worst Casting of All Time.)

SUPERDAD [1974]
This Walt Disney film is a long way from *Fantasia* (or even *Bon Voyage*). Bob Crane is a man who wants to be part of his daughter's activities, whether she is going to the beach or water skiing. By the end of this touching saga there won't be a dry nose in the house.

THE SWARM [1978]
Irwin Allen's epic disaster about a swarm of bees that invade a town during a Flower Festival. The dialogue, special effects, and plot earn it a place in any list of the all-time bad films. (*See:* The Most Badly Bumbled Bee Movie of All Time.)

SWASHBUCKLER [1976]
Technically abominable; pirates in the early eighteenth century never looked this ridiculous. Fine cast including James Earl Jones, Genevieve Bujold, and Robert Shaw can't save it from inanity.

TEENAGERS FROM OUTER SPACE [1959]
A young man is sent as scout for a vanguard of outer-space creepies

set on taking over the Earth. Things get complicated when he falls in love with a "beautiful" Earth teen.

TEENAGE ZOMBIES [1960]
Evil, pernicious spies plan to brainwash the youth of America, but not if a group of plucky teenagers can help it. The teens are caged and zombified before finally defeating the baddies. With *nothing* left to do at the end of the film, the teenagers gleefully shout, "Let's go—HORSEBACK RIDING!!!"

TENTACLES [1977]
This Italian ripoff of *Jaws* stars a giant octopus. The spaghetti-squid invades a seaside community right before the annual regatta. Shelley Winters provides unintentional comic relief as mother of one of the young sailors involved.

THE TEXAS CHAINSAW MASSACRE [1974]
The story of a woman that came to dinner—and the family that torments her for a good hour-and-a-half before serving the main course. Plot is virtually nonexistent and bloody "special effects" are disgusting rather than frightening. Rib-tickling dialogue.

THE THING WITH TWO HEADS [1972]
Now that we know what you get when you put a murderer's head on a retardate's body *(See: The Incredible Two-Headed Transplant)*, what do you get when you put bigot Ray Milland's head on Rosey Grier's body? Whatever you call it, it makes for an extremely poor film. (*See:* The Worst Two-Headed Transplant Movie Ever Made.)

TIDAL WAVE [1975]
This was originally a Japanese disaster film, but Roger Corman brought it to America, dubbed it into English, shot some new footage with Lorne Greene, and spliced it more or less at random into the original. The result is unintentionally hilarious. Most special effects seem to have been created in a bathtub.

THE TOWERING INFERNO [1974]
Irwin Allen's version of the *Airport* series; only difference is the locale. With a fire raging on top of one of the world's tallest buildings, the audience finds itself wishing for all the stock characters to die.

THE TRIAL OF BILLY JACK [1974]
The half-breed/Vietnam vet/karate king is back, this time on trial

for murder while fighting various White House conspiracies with his "sizzling exposé's."

TROG [1971]
The great Joan Crawford's last film. She discovers what appears to be the missing link in Darwin's theory, but, wouldn't you know it, the creature (Trog) escapes, creating havoc.

TWO-MINUTE WARNING [1976]
A predictable suspense film featuring Charlton Heston as a hard-boiled cop. A sniper is loose somewhere in a football stadium crowded with people, and it is up to C.H. to find him. *Black Sunday* did the same sort of story better, and it even utilized the Goodyear Blimp.

VALLEY OF THE DOLLS [1967]
Three separate vignettes about stardom and the price it extracts, with Sharon Tate, Barbara Parkins, and Patty Duke as young women who make it big in Hollywood, only to start taking "dolls" (pills). Miraculously, the film succeeds in making the Jacqueline Susann novel (on which it is based) look classy and complex by comparison.

VILLAGE OF THE GIANTS [1965]
Nepotism in full swing, as Beau Bridges, Johnny Crawford, Ron Howard, and Tisha Serling star in a story of giant teens and their dictatorship in a small town. The special effects are horrendous, with "scale" sets suggesting a pro basketball team suddenly turned loose in a nursery-school classroom.

VIVA KNIEVEL! [1977]
Producer Irwin Allen glamorizes the motorcycle "daredevil" in a feature-length essay in boredom. The film (which stars Knievel as himself) was made before our hero served a jail sentence for flattening one of his critics with a baseball bat.

VOYAGE INTO SPACE [1969]
Absolutely hysterical! One of the worst of the Japanese monster movies, this one depicts the adventures of Johnny Sekko and his "Giant Robot." The production is so cheap that in one scene, when the bad guys are shot down, you can see one dead body moving around, inching off-camera.

WAY . . . WAY OUT [1966]
Astronauts Jerry Lewis and Connie Stevens head for the moon in

this juvenile production with an oh-so-naughty premise. To beat the Russians, they have to be the first couple in space to produce a baby. Loads of fun, right?

WELCOME TO L.A. [1977]
Frustrating, pretentious "art" film has little coherence as it tells of several residents of Los Angeles and their lives and loves. Producer Robert Altman has done, and can do, much better.

WHICH WAY TO THE FRONT? [1971]
Tasteless comedy about Jerry Lewis in World War II, organizing a group of millionaire playboy 4-Fs into battle. Their mission: Assassinate Hitler. The advertisements for this comedy (which also starred Paul Winchell) read, "YOU VILL LAUGH!" No vay.

THE WHITE BUFFALO [1978]
Another de Laurentiis epic about a giant buffalo that chews on Indians for bite-size snacks. Charles Bronson manfully does his bit to sink this infamous White Elephant.

YOU LIGHT UP MY LIFE [1977]
The story of a girl (Didi Conn) who grows up in show business, gets involved in a serious romance, and learns that you can depend on no one but yourself. The theme song is pleasant enough the first time you hear it, but by the seventeenth reprise it begins to wear thin.

ZARDOZ [1974]
A fatuous vision of the future in which the universe is ruled by domineering females who all lust for the macho magic that Sean Connery conceals under his skimpy loincloth.

ZONTAR: THE THING FROM VENUS [1964]
An alien is on his way from Venus. Will he bring peace and happiness, or death and destruction? Time will tell in this late-night perennial, starring the immortal John Agar. (*See:* Life Achievement Award: The Worst Actor of All Time.)

THE SUGGESTION BOX

The horizons for bad films are unlimited—as boundless as the reach of human imagination. Yes, we have studied the subject and we have paid the price, with bleary eyes and upset stomachs, but in a field so vast we cannot pretend to have the last word or any of the final answers. If you have additional information, ideas, second thoughts, suggestions or complaints, we would like to hear from you. We cannot promise to answer your letters, but your opinions will definitely be taken into account in any future volumes on the subject.

Mail will find us at the following address:
    Harry and Michael Medved
    610 South Venice Boulevard
    Number 4094
    Venice, California 90291

SPECIAL NOTE TO OUR READERS

Now that you've finished the book we will offer a very personal confession: one of the films described in the preceding pages is a total and shameless hoax. It never existed—except in the imagination of the authors. You may rest assured that all the other movies listed in this volume are the genuine article—real films with real stars, directors and production histories. We have included the single preposterous ringer as a challenge to our readers: try to spot the fraud among all the unbelievable baddies that have *actually* found their way to the screen. If you think you have the right answer, let us know—and feel proud that you have passed a crucial test as a serious student of bad films.

ABOUT THE AUTHORS

HARRY MEDVED, twenty, is a student at UCLA and the author of the pioneering movie book *The Fifty Worst Films of All Time*. In the last two years, he and his brother have co-hosted WORLD'S WORST FILM FESTIVALS in New York, Los Angeles, London, Sydney, Australia, Ottawa, Ontario, Whitewater, Wisconsin, and other centers of Western Civilization.

MICHAEL MEDVED, thirty-three, is a graduate of Yale and a well-known author and screenwriter. His books include *The Shadow Presidents* and the national best-seller *What Really Happened to the Class of '65?* He prepared for his work on *The Golden Turkey Awards* by spending his early childhood in Philadelphia, Pennsylvania, and developing a life-long devotion to the Philadelphia Phillies.

Glittering lives of famous people!
Bestsellers from Berkley